VAL ROSING:
MUSICAL GENIUS
An Intimate Biography

VAL ROSING: MUSICAL GENIUS
An Intimate Biography

by Ruth Glean Rosing

Sunflower University Press ®

1531 Yuma (Box 1009), Manhattan, Kansas 66502-4228

Cover: Decca album cover, *Fourteen Songs by Mussorgsky, Val Rosing, Tenor,* reproduced courtesy of MCA Entertainment Group. Album cover art by Eric Nitsche. Val Rosing photo, 1954, Amos Carr, Hollywood, California.

ISBN 0-89745-167-8

Layout by Lori L. Daniel

In memory of Val, who so enriched my life and contributed much to the world of music and drama.

Sculpture of Val Rosing by George Fife Waters, a protegé of French sculptor Auguste Rodin (1840-1917). Waters was born in San Francisco, California, in 1894 and specialized in portraits. He was a member of the American Artistic Association of Paris and Modern Society of Paris.

Contents

Acknowledgments

First and foremost I am indebted to that stroke of fate that brought me under the influence of Val Rosing. Repelled by ugly realism, frustrated in a materialistic world, he advised me, "You must invest in beauty." He passed through the operatic world kicking out its traditions, reforming its communication, and waking up audiences. It still has not caught up with him. His imagination was never bankrupt. Just to have known and worked with him would have changed my world. Marriage to him magnified and enriched my life.

Byron Belt, former assistant manager of the Chicago Lyric Opera, past president of Chicago's Cosmopolitan School of Music, and current music and arts critic, has my profound gratitude for his awareness and appreciation of the artistic and spiritual giant often concealed from others. Byron's friendship, confidence, and encouragement have been invaluable to me.

Some rich sources of friendship and assistance came from the early American Opera Company backed by George Eastman in Rochester, New York. Charles Hedley, tenor, was a source of much information, and there are no words to express my gratitude for his support of Val in those final days.

Margaret Stevenson ("Stevie"), Mata and Victor Roudin, and Roma and Jack Gurney also have resurrected those early days, and deep-rooted friendships have developed among us. I am indebted to author Quaintance Eaton for her assistance, and to Gary Provost for getting my "foot off the brake."

I would like to express gratitude to Maralin Niska who coached with Val during his final years and shared her surprised reactions and achievements.

And Chris Mahan! Chris was stage manager for the New York City Center, Metropolitan, and San Diego Operas. He was always there as stage manager for the centennial productions, and he is always there for me.

I am also indebted to Neil T. Bunker, bibliographer of the Eastman School of Music, and to the Music Center Archives of the Hollywood Bowl.

And to the reviewers — of the many reviews found among Val's papers, some carried neither date nor newspaper identification. I hope we will be forgiven for using rather than ignoring them.

Foreword

— From Meredith Willson's eulogy, November 27, 1963

You had to love Val Rosing the first time you met him. His only problem was that his heart was too big for the world he lived in. How many times did his genius insure glory for his colleagues, his actors, his singers, his musical directors? For stage pictures, and for bringing those pictures to life, his talent stood unapproached — Father Serra limping alone across a hundred-foot proscenium; an army of Spanish Cavalry and Indians pouring out of the Hollywood Hills; an ox-drawn train of prairie schooners attended by half a thousand pioneers spreading out onto the great Hollywood Bowl stage; and oftener than not, Val would be directing on stage himself in a hastily improvised costume. He made operatic history in the Hollywood Bowl staging *Faust* and in New York with Puccini's *Turandot* and Prokofiev's *Love for Three Oranges*. Val could teach a mummy to act. He could show a marble statue how to sing, demonstrating in that ear-shattering voice of his, shouting phrases and singing high Cs, roaring explanations and instructions, then proving them out with all the strutting, the posturing, the pleading, the weeping, and the laughing necessary to the perfect result he always saw and drove himself so relentlessly to achieve. But he was always a gentle man — a great, strong, vibrant bear — but a gentle man; a thoughtful, kind, articulate, overly generous, selfless, gentle man.

There are many people who flourish and prosper in our world, who then exit to leave a questionable influence on their compatriots and on their society, so to speak. Others manage to come and go without having had any effect on their fellow man whatsoever. Only a few leave the world and those of us whose lives they touched *better* for the goodness they ingenuously spread, more vitally and esthetically alive for the brilliance they eagerly shared, and spiritually comforted by those values surpassing human understanding that exist in a great and beautiful talent.

Val was one of these.

Meredith Willson

Introduction

The Glorious Past

"Please fill in the birth date for each child." It was a simple but devastating request. The WHO'S WHO blank before me shamed my deceitful little scheme. "Married," I had written, "to Ruth Grose Scates — 1959." And where the blank lines appeared for the enumerating of offspring: "Valerian, Diana, and Richard." One could not, after all, slight the offspring of an international figure, but if their dates were not listed, perhaps the world need not know that four marriage certificates had borne the name of Vladimir Rosing before it had finally been coupled with my own. But some statistical minded busybody from the office of London's WHO'S WHO was satisfied with nothing less than perfection — which meant the inclusion of the dates.

Val peered over his coffee which dripped generously over his tie each time the cup was lifted from its flooded saucer. "Problem?"

"Yes," I answered despairingly. "How can I avoid the embarrassment of four ex-wives and still give the birth dates of your three children? The figures will show at least one of them to be my elder and all of them to have been born before we were married."

With one impulsive St. Bernardian move, the cup was on the floor, and all of the loving warmth that had become my world was in the two arms that enfolded me. "But, my poor darling, you know that you are my only true love — my only, ever wife!"

"That's what I told myself and WHO'S WHO, but they aren't satisfied."

His face went into eclipse. "Does my past shame you?"

I laughed at the ridiculous suggestion, then was ashamed to realize I had provoked it.

And so it developed that in our few years of marriage and of working together, I was, to a degree, privileged to share *all* of his life.

I met Val in 1957 at Universal Studios in Los Angeles. After studying with Paul Althouse in New York and Lotte Lehman in Santa Barbara, I was learning operatic repertoire at the Los Angeles Conservatory of Music. Herbert Weiskopf, our Conductor and Musical Director, invited his friend Val Rosing to direct *Bohême* for us, and Universal Studios loaned rehearsal space. Llewellyn Roberts, my teacher at the time, advised, "Rub elbows with the greatness of this man." He was not so pleased when I took the advice literally and married a man so many years my senior.

The evening of the first rehearsal I was late. Herbert was at the piano, and Rosing was seated with the performers who had arranged their chairs in a semicircle. So this was the great Russian tenor. He appeared as unpretentious, whole-souled, and eager as a young pup alert for the next happening. His figure was sturdy and warmly relaxed, his face gentle. But he had antenna eyes, and his head angled sharply to focus on whatever caught his attention. He missed nothing.

I tried to enter inconspicuously, but might as well have tripped a burglar alarm. Rosing sprang from his chair (his simplest moves were triggered by a spring), pulled another chair into the circle beside him, and motioned to it. A smile spread generously over his face as he extended a handful of sweets from his pocket and turned his chair at an angle to study me. The group waited silently. Whatever was the object of his attention occupied 100 percent of it. Flushed, feeling like a taut-stringed violin, I waited out his appraisal. Herbert murmured an introduction and struck a chord. Val turned, ran a hand through his wispy gray hair, and the clock began to tick again.

He electrified us with his dynamic vitality. He shouted at us, "You are not pronouncing your 'consonances.'" And he pleaded with us, "Every motion must come out of the sound and rhythm. Don't make any unnecessary motions. Strive for minimum effort and maximum clarity!"

Maralin Niska, who worked with Val at that time and later sang with the Metropolitan National Company and Chicago Lyric, recently recalled that Val, coaching her in *Madame Butterfly*, was hilariously authentic as he became a geisha — bent knees pressed together, body modestly angled, head inclined, elbows out, and feet gliding gracefully across the floor.

Singing the role under Val's direction, with the Riverside Opera Association in California, Maralin drew this reaction from San Bernardino's *The Sun Telegram* music critic, Charles D. Perlee, after the November 18, 1960, performance: "Cho-Cho San was sung and acted in such a manner as to keep this reviewer on the edge of his chair whenever she was on the stage. . . . I must say that Miss Niska's *One Fine Day* was so realistic that it was not an aria."

Maralin said of Val, "He was so modest about his own vocal achievements that when I was told he was on a recording of the twenty all-time great Russian singers, I simply disbelieved it."

What we *did* believe, because we saw it with our own eyes, was that the man could make a puppet come to life.

Little did I know when, as Mimi, I made my timid knock at Rudolpho's door that first evening under Val's direction, it would open not only to the Bohemian poet's attic, but that it would also reset the mold of my existence.

I would come to know Val as a man who existed in the magic world of artistic beauty where he ignored many of the ordinary mechanics of everyday living. It was sheer coincidence if he wore socks that matched. Where his razor took shortcuts, there were triangles of unshaved whiskers on his face. He could not tolerate the conversation that accompanied haircuts, thus he avoided barbers as long as he could. One coat pocket always sagged with a paperback book from which he tore the pages as he read. His clothes were a necessary evil which adopted his body contours and frequently wore the day's menu.

He was also subject to strange sleeping habits. Margaret Stevenson, who was a member of Val's American Opera Company of the 1920s, remembered when a young baritone in Winnipeg once was given an appointment for the morning after Val had performed a concert. At the hotel, the baritone learned that Val was still in bed, but he was cordially invited to come on up to the room. Upon entering, the young man was quite astonished to see Val throw off the blankets and appear, completely dressed — even to his slippers. Brushing a bit of lint off of his velvet jacket, he was ready for the interview.

Val was a connoisseur of the finest culinary delicacies of which he partook generously. He relished the taste, smell, even the chewing sounds of exquisite food. He was a great admirer of Jepito, a Chihuahua we adopted in 1961. Jepito would lie at the entrance to the kitchen while I sautéed his meat and wait for me to leave, after which he would walk slowly to his plate, smell the food, take a bite, and raise his head to chew it with careful deliberation. Val would watch with fascination. "What an artist!" he would exclaim.

One day when he and Jepito returned from a walk, they sat looking at each other, and Val had tears in his eyes.

"What's wrong?" I asked.

His response: "I felt so bad when I walked Jepito today. I looked at that little body so full of courage, loyalty, and devotion. I think we should never give him less than the best cuts of meat."

For two years following the 1957 *Bohême* rehearsal, I worked in Val's productions, first as a soloist, then as a scriptwriter and assistant director. In the dress rehearsal for one of his state centennial spectaculars, hundreds of

Val, Ruth, and Jepito.

uniformed Air Force, Navy, and Marine Corp members were massing onto the main stage for the spine-tingling finale. A forty-foot flag rolled on and the band was blaring when Val, arms waving and voice thundering, stepped backward down the ramp to survey the final triumphant effect . . . and disappeared from sight, his voice trailing away to an echo.

Someone yelled for the standby ambulance, and a deathly silence descended upon the stage and arena. Six feet below the ramp, Val's body lay on the ground. I had almost reached his side, and the stretcher was arriving, when I heard a strange sound like a musical scale or a vocalise. Clinging to consciousness and wearing a bucket of black stage paint on his head, he assured me, "I had to see if my lungs were crushed; thank God, I still have my voice!"

If I didn't consent to a future with this man, I was obviously going to miss a great deal of excitement. When we were married in 1959, I assumed my role as caretaker of his gypsy disorder with false confidence. He fought my reforms at every step. He excused his careless appearance with an impatient, "No one will see me." When my ten-year-old daughter Dee convinced him he was not transparent, he shifted to a new defense: "My friends will forgive me." Someone once said, "He is really a handsome man when you get him all glued together." But the gluing, aye, there was the rub.

It was no ordinary experience to be caught up in the whirlwind of his love, laughter, innocence, and madness for half a dozen years.

When I spoke of writing a biography of Val, I harvested interesting comments: "It will be banned in Boston!" "Marvelous comic strip!" "Don't think you could ever get away with it!" "It would take twenty volumes!" One of his actors had once said, "A Rosing is a Rosing is a Rosing." But Val could never understand the implication.

Nicolas Slonimsky, prominent composer, conductor, and musicologist, who accompanied Val on some of his early concert tours, sized him up as "unique, erratic, unpredictable, but always sure of his artistic mission, which is ultimately what counts."

Val drew much of his inspiration from scenic beauty. He never tired of traveling, and preferred going by train or car in order to prolong the adventure. The blue and purple hues of distant mountain ranges, a white peak flung against the sky, or a shifting pattern of clouds — all were irreplaceable experiences in beauty. As we drove across vast stretches of desert or counted off complacent little towns, Val feared I might be bored, and he would entertain me with stories from his past.

The hours would melt away while he recounted with vivid color and animation his fascinating experiences: a childhood visit to Tolstoi, a stay in the Tsar's palace, a story about the time he was asked by David Lloyd George for an appraisal of the political developments of Revolutionary Russia, his formation in London of a committee for the repatriation of Russian exiles, or his friendship with Prince Yussoupov who had assassinated Rasputin. He relived experiences of his concert career, such as the time he had a command performance to sing for the Queen of Spain but was turned back by police guards at the border. After a night in the rain and cold, he received apologies and an entry permit, but by then one essential thing was missing: a voice.

As a result of my insistent persuasion to "Write it down, Val, write it down," there are numerous "stream of consciousness" notebooks with no punctuation, many words run together, and others implied with second or third syllables missing. The spelling is a combination of French, Russian, English, and "Val-ism," with grammatical construction patterned on the French (his *premiere langue*, since he started school in Switzerland at the age of four). But knowing Val, the key is there — or maybe he is an invisible prompter, in spite of his objection that a biography "forces one to walk naked down Main Street." If he is prompting me, it must be nerve-wracking for him when I sit and pray for illumination; for I remember that during my scriptwriting for his centennial productions he paced the floor in great distress whenever the typewriter keys were silent.

No help was needed, however, when I came to this treasure: ". . . and finally I find Ruth — forever — no more searching — I find my mate."

I hope in these pages he will return to those who knew him, and those who did not know him will think they did.

Chapter 1

On the Grand Scale

Carved into the serenely beautiful setting of the Hollywood Hills in California is a massive amphitheater where thousands of hot-house citizens cluster on summer nights to listen to symphonic music or pops concerts *à la* starlight.

The size of the Hollywood Bowl might intimidate some producer-directors, for it can cripple communication and dwarf perspective. But it was tailor-made for Val Rosing who was rehearsing a mammoth production of *Faust* in the summer of 1950.

A broad-brimmed straw hat protected him from the July sun and dwarfed his sturdy barrel-chested figure which dissected the Bowl at every angle, leaping over obstacles, taking risers two at a time, bellowing instructions with the ring of a blacksmith's anvil. The source of his atomic energy seemed to be his raisin-filled pockets from which he periodically supplied his mouth.

As he reached the stage, which had been transformed into the medieval city of Leipzig, he shouted with his Russian accent, "Nawtink like it — nawtink like it!" He shoved individuals into tighter groups and sculpted his own body into lightning-like poses which he expected them to emulate. He pushed heads together, shouting, "Don't let me see daylight between you!" As he moved backward among them, they learned to dodge quickly, for he seemed to accelerate in reverse gear to survey the result.

In a novel setting of sliding doors and transparencies, Faust could not only *hear* the voices of people outside in the street, but he could look out and view them as well. When he sang to Marguerite, all action among the villagers on the outside froze. With a few regroupings and final touches, Val brought to life a masterpiece in living flesh. He had signaled conductor Artur Rodzinski and had disappeared from sight, reappearing within seconds at the opposite rim of the Bowl where he could gain better perspective on his artistry.

The music of Gounod's *Faust* crashed though the Bowl, and a six-foot-five bass had begun to sing when the straw hat rose above a tier of box seats. Up came the arms, beating the air to an accompaniment of "No, no, no!" The conductor's baton rapped the music stand, and before the sound had died away, the hat was back on stage confronting, at a little more than waist level, the giant bass Jerome Hines. Some muffled instructions, a new pose, a booming "Okay, Pappy," from the bass, and the orchestra was allowed to begin again.

A committee of impressive businessmen had deposited themselves on one of the Bowl's wooden benches to discuss the presentation of a pageant in honor of California's Centennial of Statehood to take place in September of that year. As a Bowl official approached to join the group, the chairman asked, "Who is that maniac?"

The official laughed. "Don't you know? That is Val Rosing."

"He shoves those people around like they were cattle."

"They love him."

Then the entire company burst into laughter. Rosing, demonstrating a chaste maiden, had assumed a demure pose with downcast eyes and shyly clasped hands. Nadine Connor, singing Marguerite, imitated the pose, looking much less demure than Rosing himself. "Bend your right knee; you look like a telephone pole," he said. And then, "Angle your head and lower your eyes; bring the elbows out a bit from the body." Suddenly the image of a shy, God-fearing, Bible-bearing Marguerite was imposed upon the soprano, and her body became identified with the limpid tones issuing from her throat.

"He is a genius," said the Bowl official.

"He certainly obtains results," said the chairman. "It strikes me he is the kind of director we need for our pageant. What is his background?"

The official explained that Val was a Russian tenor who had escaped the Russian Revolution only to then "revolutionize" the rest of the world. He had given a record-breaking 100 concerts in London, and since then, he'd been trying to influence opera as well. Val thought opera singers should learn to act, streamline their figures, and sing in English.

George Bernard Shaw had agreed with him, and in 1921 they collaborated in a season of "Intimate Opera" in London. Less than two years later, he sold George Eastman on the idea of an American Opera Company. It was a tremendous success, but had to be abandoned during the Depression, and Val returned to England. Then during World War II he came back to become Entertainment Director at Camp Roberts, California.

And if that wasn't enough, Val had given New York City Opera its two greatest hits — in 1949, Prokofiev's *Love for Three Oranges*, and that spring, Puccini's *Turandot*. He was directing musical sequences for an MGM film, and would direct for the Chicago Lyric Opera that fall.

The committee was impressed. "Do you think we could talk with him?" the chairman asked.

"I have a meeting with him and Maestro Rodzinski immediately after their rehearsal," the official replied. "I would be glad to introduce you."

The committee was concerned that Val's financial demands would be too much for their shoestring budget, but the official assured them that if they could sell him on the artistic integrity of the project, their problem would be solved. Val had a tendency to sell himself short financially once his enthusiasm was captured.

On stage, Val was now standing with his arm about the conductor who protested, "How can we rehearse *Faust* without a tenor!"

Val laughed and made a grandiose gesture, "But Tucker is doing me a great favor by arriving two days before the performance. Metropolitan singers are not accustomed to rehearsal. Never mind, his singing will be excellent, and I am working out the dramatic action so that he will be covered on stage. I will tie his operatic hands behind him, and if he goes for the footlight, I will have him tripped. He is a charming fellow; he won't mind." Val referred to artist Richard Tucker.

Later Val met with the Centennial Committee. His answer came back quickly. "If you want a typical Hollywood pageant, I am not interested. But I could be greatly enthused over an authoritative script with beauty and dignity worthy of your state."

"Of course, of course . . . by all means," was the committee's response.

The *Los Angeles Times* on July 8, 1950, greeted *Faust* with the headline "10,000 CHEER INGENIOUS BOWL PRODUCTION AT GALA OPENING," and its critic Albert Goldberg said,

> Opera in the vast expanse of the Hollywood Bowl presents many problems and at first blush "Faust," of all operas, seemed least likely to respond to the necessary magnification. But that opinion was formed without reckoning on the imaginativeness of Vladimir Rosing's stage direction.

In the *Los Angeles Herald-Examiner*, Patterson Greene upbraided the city for its delinquent discovery of Rosing. He poked fun at Californians who had gone to New York to see *Three Oranges* "well acted . . . in English . . . and funny, lamenting the lack of such back home in Los Angeles" while all the time they had Val Rosing "back home" where he and Albert Coates had established the Southern California Opera Company in 1940, giving rise to such singers as Jerome Hines, Nadine Connor, Brian Sullivan, and Mona Paulee.

Val was itching for another production in the Bowl; he loved the place. While waiting for the Centennial script, he toyed with the idea of placing lighted crosses on the hillside above the Bowl, each representing an early California mission. What if real covered wagons could be used, somehow, to symbolize the Gold Rush? And what could he do for a finale that would produce a spine-tingling rush of patriotic fervor? He could visualize soldiers, marines, sailors — all in uniform — as a tremendous flag slowly moved to center stage where it would dominate the scene and portray California's story as one with that of the nation.

When the first draft of the script was delivered to his office at the American Operatic Laboratory (which he had cooperatively organized for GIs after the war), Val was having coffee with staff conductor Herbert Weiskopf. He quickly tore open the envelope and then drew a sharp breath. Herbert looked up inquiringly.

Val said, "Listen to this" as he read from the script:

> The head and neck of a great prop dinosaur (mounted on a truck) appears over the top of the trees that cover the footlights. The dinosaur moves across stage, behind the trees, dipping and waving its neck. There is a suggestion of a pleased smile on its reptilian features as the Narrator speaks: "Believe it or not, folks, you are looking at the first Californian . . . or maybe I should say, the first tourist!"

Herbert wore the shocked expression with which he was known to reward the perpetrator of a musical *faux pas* — similar to the expression of a hen which has just been adulterated. He got up as if to leave, but Val said, "Oh, no, sit down; you are going to hear this":

> The prehistoric dinosaurs came to Los Angeles millions of years ago, because it had something to offer. They stayed because they got stuck in the La Brea tar pits on Wilshire Boulevard and couldn't get away.

Herbert started to laugh, but then realized it was not appropriate, so he cleared his throat and shifted uncomfortably. Val's pitch rose, and his accent became more pronounced as he continued to mock the script:

> You can still get stuck on Wilshire Boulevard — but not unless you

stay too long in the night spots, and even then you're not stuck too bad, because in exchange for your money you get the best food and drink in the world. If you buy enough of the latter, you may still see dinosaurs. . . . At the Los Angeles County Museum they have succumbed to the Southern California habit of wearing as little as possible; they just stand around in their bones.

The words steamed from Val's lips:

And smog . . . smog is a kind of California hospitality. We keep it down by the railroad station, so that visitors from Pittsburgh won't get overcome by the fragrance of our orange blossoms all at once.

He threw the script across the room. "They can get themselves another director!"

Herbert coughed. "Yes . . . well . . . uh . . . I'd better be going, Val."

The committee tried to soothe his ruffled feelings with the promise of another script, but Val objected. "It's July and we're talking about a September 8th production! Impossible!"

"Give us a break; we'll tailor it to what you want," the committee pleaded.

The rewrite from Jack Moffitt and Ed Ainsworth came back. Val was tempted; maybe he could work with it. Or was he putting his neck on the block? Well, he was at heart a gambler, so with a big black pencil he went to work, and rehearsals began.

By the night of the dress rehearsal, he had reconstructed, improvised, and pulled together a first act. Those attending were astounded and conversation overflowed with superlatives. Val came on stage and motioned for attention. "You have just witnessed a triumphant first act; you will now see in the second act the greatest disaster you have ever observed." And it was.

Val and the big black pencil kept each other company throughout the night. Together they revised and restaged the second act after which Val crossed himself — Russian style, from right to left.

The following night, Meredith Willson's baton led the orchestra through his own music composed for the occasion. As the overture died away, Lionel Barrymore's voice drifted from a sound booth high in the Bowl. "Across the misty pages of time, the name of California is written large in letters of gold. California is more than a state; it is also a state of mind, born of the dreams of men. . . ." The Bowl was transformed into a vast panorama of California history brought to life by a cast of a thousand people, their action fixed under a battery of lights. One set of actors transmitted the dialogue from a sound booth while a second cast synchronized the action and silent words on various stage levels which emerged from darkness as floodlights discovered them. In one scene, a small party of soldiers and priests was etched against the sky atop a mountain ridge before descending to the valley. Twenty-one white crosses representing the California missions momentarily illuminated the hills above the Bowl. Shafts of gold pierced the sky, and against the gold-laced canopy, covered wagons moved down the mountainside.

As the second act began, committee members and administrative personnel were tense. Val had given instructions to the lighting director, stage managers, conductor, narrator, and speaking cast. He had briefed the general cast as best he could. Then he appeared in costume and said to them, "Watch me and listen to me, for I will be on stage with you. We are going to reconstruct the second act. Are you with me?"

They gave him a round of applause. The music began. He pushed and shoved them through the Civil War, silent films, talkies, and World War II. The next day the *Herald-Examiner* wrote:

> Perhaps the greatest ovations went to the finale in which the entire company gathered upon the enlarged stage, and to the gasp-evoking effect when a great semi-circle of fountains started spouting water upon the hillside and the jets of spray were caught in the glare of colored lights.

It called the production the "greatest spectacle ever offered in the Hollywood Bowl." The *Los Angeles Times* called it a "miracle of production," and said, "Val Rosing performed a feat of staging which is said never to have been approached in California before."

Added to that was Charles Laughton's declaration, "One of the greatest dramatic experiences of my life has been Val Rosing's 'California Story.'" And Arthur Godfrey agreed: "This is the greatest show that exists in America today."

Val had gambled and won.

Chapter 2

A Champagne Launching

In the middle of the Russian winter of 1890, a priest, dressed in heavy robes of gold and silver, plunged an unsuspecting infant, Vladimir Rosing, into the tepid water of the baptismal font and extracted a dripping, howling tenor. Looking on with profound admiration were his barrister father, Sergei; his brown-eyed, soft-spoken mother, Zinaida; his Aunt Matilda; his two sisters, eleven-year-old Vera and four-year-old Liuba; and his godparents, the widowed Governor of the Kremlin, General Arkady Stolypin, and his niece, Natalia.

General Stolypin wore both his uniform and his decorations with the casual elegance that came easily to one of his tall, slender build. He held back the patriarchal gray beard with his left hand as he bent to kiss the child.

Natalia, a beautiful girl of twenty, was the daughter of Stolypin's brother. She had been left an orphan in her uncle's charge; but proud and noble by nature, she had preferred, even though residing at the Kremlin, to earn her own living. She taught school for the orphaned daughters of Russian nobility. Natalia caressed the softness of the baby's cheek with her own and smiled.

The General's 27-year-old son, Peter, was glad to get this business over with. Now they could return to a splendid feast which had been prepared in honor of the occasion. The tables would groan with the weight of food, and with a champagne toast, they would launch little Valodia well into his future.

Kings, queens, and emperors sat firmly on their thrones in that year of 1890, and the court life of London, Berlin, Vienna, and St. Petersburg dispensed glamour, fashion, and entertainment. National theatres flourished under royal subsidies.

The almost 300-year-old rule of the House of Romanoff had all the appearance of permanency. Students who had tried to organize insurrections were imprisoned or sent to Siberia where they declared hunger strikes and sang forbidden revolutionary songs. But this had the quality of a musical comedy and was considered ineffectual by those in power.

It was a great creative age for Russian art. Tchaikowsky, Rimsky-Korsakov, and Rachmaninoff were the lions of the musical world. Young Fokine and the child, Pavlova, were beginning their meteoric careers. Feodor Chaliapin and his friend, Maxim Gorky, roamed the country like two tramps, obtaining occasional jobs in choruses of provincial opera companies.

In the town of Odessa, a ten-year-old boy with unruly black curls was entering school. His family name of Bronstein was later supplanted by Trotsky. In the Caucasian city of Gori, a mother was sending her little boy of eleven to a parochial school to prepare him for the priesthood. Joe Djugashvili was glad to leave the home where he was often beaten by his drunken father. In later years, he would be known as Joe Stalin.

In London, George Bernard Shaw was making a name for himself as a music critic, and in San Francisco, little Isadora Duncan danced barefoot to amuse her parents. In Rochester, New York, a strange little man, George Eastman, peddled a magic box that would build an empire called Hollywood. Isolated people in different parts of the world were to be woven into a fabric which would embrace the life and career of the infant who made his lusty debut that year in the home of the St. Petersburg lawyer, Sergei Rosing.

Vladimir was given a Christian name which meant "to own the world," and inherited a surname brought by a Swedish officer to the field of battle where Peter the Great decimated the armies of Charles XII in 1718. The young officer, who had been wounded, recovered, succumbed to the charms of his Russian nurse, accompanied her to the altar, and bequeathed the name of Rosing to future generations. Vladimir's father, Sergei, a stocky, broad-shouldered man with thinning hair and generous warm features, had distin-guished the name with his eloquence as a barrister.

Zinaida's gift of distinction to the child was her maternal grandfather, Baron Sivert, who was of Russian-Baltic origin. The Baron's charming daughter, because her father was frequently away on gambling and drinking sprees, found it necessary to negotiate with the Jewish merchant who held her father's mortgage. The two fell in love, but marriage was out of the question between a Jew and the daughter of a baron, even though the former was the wealthy owner of a large real estate and mortgage firm and the latter was impov-erished.

When the romance was discovered, the Jewish merchant barely escaped lynching by a pack of noble barons who were guests at a gambling party of Sivert's. The Jew offered Sivert a game of cards in which the stakes would be the mortgage on Sivert's estate against permission to marry his daughter. It was not an uncommon procedure, and the drunken company hilariously approved the sporting proposition. As a result, Sivert lost his daughter, but gained his mortgage. Later, after Zinaida was born, the couple moved from Rovno to St. Petersburg, and eventually Zinaida met a promising young lawyer, Sergei Rosing.

So, great-grandson of a baron and equipped with distinction, wealth, a link to the Kremlin, and a healthy pair of lungs, Vladimir merited the champagne toast which defined his name and deposited the world in his pocket: "To Vladimir; may he own the world!"

Chapter 3

Switzerland

I saw Switzerland for the first time with Val. He was so excited when we approached Montreux, where he had spent his early childhood, that he single-handedly grabbed up all of our luggage before the train stopped, as though the moment might vanish unless he rushed in to capture its reality. Of course, he *had* to drop something, and to this day my cosmetic case holds its grudge with a lock that resists stubbornly and then releases with a surprising sting.

He was impatient for me to share scenes which his memory had embraced all those years: Lake Geneva with the Alps mirrored in its emerald waters; the Dent du Midi — its white-capped range cutting the jagged pattern of a molar tooth; lights flickering over the slopes of the mountains at night where little ancient villages nestled; the Castle of Chillon jutting out over the water; and Glion, reached by the *funiculaire* which rose at an abrupt angle from the earth where two cable cars did a balancing act — the one at the top filling with water so that its weight, going down, would pull up the passenger-laden one from the bottom. He also shared more memories.

Before Val had reached his third birthday, his father's eloquence was one day reduced to incoherence as a sensuous blonde client entered his office. Zinaida, who was not about to be reduced to such indignity, reacted by packing the three children and their German governess off to Switzerland.

Valodia, at his age untouched by the tragedy, was fascinated with the journey by train, the drive through Berlin in an open carriage, the crossing of what seemed like a monstrously high bridge, another train, awesome mountains, and a lake all before they had arrived at the villa of Vevey which was to be their home.

The family of four expanded to include Zinaida's older sister Matilda, her husband, and his two sons by a former marriage. Matilda moved easily into the bustling, domineering role of a sister blessed more with intelligence than with beauty. She staunchly supervised the kitchen, projected maternal warmth, and bickered with her husband.

Their crowded villa opened its cobblestone courtyard and private gardens to the lake, and there the family bathed and boated. They picnicked in the mountains where the children helped the peasants gather grapes from terraced vineyards. When the weather was too warm at their lakeside home, they stayed on in the mountains at Chexbres, Glion, or Caux. In the winter they skated and bobsledded. The Castle of Chillon struck terror in Valodia's heart as he viewed the torture chambers and peered into the well which cradled the knives used to carve prisoners to pieces. It was his first realization of the cruelty of human nature.

Of Valodia's two sisters, Liuba was his favorite. She was only four years older and, therefore, still young enough to play with him. She was sweet, generous, and loving, and the childhood affection between them always remained. His other sister, Vera, was already fifteen and spent much time going about with her mother.

Of his mother, Val would say in later years, "Her eyes were of a golden brown such as I have never seen since. And I can never remember seeing her angry or hearing her say anything unkind. She was the essence of dignity and was loved and admired."

At the age of five Valodia apparently began grooming himself for the theatre. He had climbed a ladder leading to the roof of their two-story house and would have fallen to a stone courtyard below, had his foot not caught between the ladder rungs. The future tenor was found wailing resonantly for help, as he hung upside down.

One afternoon a *Thé Dansante* was planned, and Valodia was removed from being underfoot by a family friend who took him walking in the mountains. It was a hot afternoon, and the two thirsty pedestrians stopped at a little railway station for a drink. Only beer was available, and Valodia downed a tankard of it, then polished off his companion's while she was in the ladies' room. Unable, thereafter, to navigate his legs, he had to be conveyed to his home in a carriage. But while his legs were useless, his vocal equipment was greatly enhanced. To the delight of his mother's guests, and to her own horror, he arrived home singing with all the gusto of a drunken sailor. His beer binge may have launched his vocal career, but it also made him violently ill, and his loss of taste for the beverage was permanent.

When Val was six, he almost died from a severe attack of diphtheria.

However, he greatly enjoyed the convalescence during which his bed was covered with toys that had been rendered unrecognizable in their mutilated condition — he was extremely curious.

That same curiosity led him to demand of his mother how chickens were made, to which she replied, "A fowl sits on the egg and hatches the chicken."

This, he thought, was a magnificent affair, and he decided to hatch chickens himself. Since he was heavier than a fowl, he reasoned that he could not, of course, sit directly on the egg. So he placed it under a footstool beneath the dining room table and sat thereon for hours, constantly looking down to see if the chicken was emerging yet. The family was delighted with his occupation and urged him to have patience. He soon deduced that if an egg could produce a chicken, a glass of milk should produce a cow. So he abandoned the egg for the greater project and sat over a glass of milk. His failure and disappointment were compensated only when his mother finally gave him a toy cow.

Arriving home from kindergarten one day, Valodia was greeted by his godfather, General Stolypin and his niece, Natalia. The Governor of the Kremlin was tall, noble in bearing with his long white beard, and handsome in his uniform covered with decorations.

Natalia was lovely with soft, white skin, dark eyes and brows, silky hair, a beautifully shaped aquiline nose with sensitive nostrils, a rather trim but kind mouth, and a charming smile which revealed pearl-like teeth. Valodia thought he had never seen anyone quite so beautiful. He was even more impressed with the gifts they brought.

He loved playing with the Governor's medals while the grownups talked. And how they talked! His mother couldn't hear enough about the orthodox ceremonies surrounding the death of Tsar Alexander III, the visiting kings, queens, and princes, and the red and gold carriages draped in black that carried the family through St. Petersburg to the cathedral where the tsars were buried.

She wanted to know all about the wedding of Alexander's son, Nicholas, to Alexandra, which had followed within a week. Natalia described the wedding dress of silver brocade with the gold ermine-lined robe and train. Stolypin spoke of the crowds that had lined the streets, first for the funeral, then to greet the wedding party as it left the Winter Palace for the Anitchkov Palace where they would live temporarily.

The excitement ended all too soon. In a few days, the Governor and his niece departed, and the calm that followed was broken only by the constant quarreling of Aunt Matilda and her husband.

After two winters in Vevey, Zinaida, tired of running a villa, moved her brood to the Hotel Victoria in Lausanne. In its lovely gardens, Valodia pretended to be a soldier commanding armies and fighting battles with another little boy on a steep hill. Eleven years later, he was shocked to discover it had an elevation of less than three feet. Evenings in the hotel frequently sparkled with entertainment. The magicians, in particular, held Valodia spellbound.

Even at the hotel the quarreling continued until Aunt Matilda's husband and his two sons disappeared one day; Valodia never saw them again. Some time later, the governess, Pauline, announced she was leaving to be married. For Valodia this was a tragedy. He wept and promised that if she would only wait, he himself would marry her when he grew up. She had been not only a governess but also a friend to his mother, his sisters, and himself.

Four years after they had moved to Switzerland, when Valodia was seven, a letter came from his godfather Stolypin, persuading the family to return to Russia and live in Moscow. Matilda sanctioned the idea, and in a fever of excitement they made preparations.

A locomotive with a chimney like the inverted skirt of a woman hurtled the little family back through Switzerland and Germany. At last they reached the Russian frontier where tall, bearded soldiers watched every person who entered the Tsar's country suspiciously.

Chapter 4

A Touch of Royalty

Endless plains of cut wheat yielded to virginal forests of pine and white birch with sporadic villages. It was a warm August morning when the little group arrived in Moscow. A brilliant sun shone on the gold cupolas of a thousand churches, and the smell of Moscow permeated the air. It was a combination of tar, hay, and horse manure in such proportions that it amounted to a secret formula, not to be duplicated or emulated elsewhere.

Stolypin, creating a minor sensation, met the train. The stationmaster, his staff, the conductors, and the porters all bowed and vied with each other to serve and please. These same conductors, Valodia recalled, had not been nearly so polite on the train.

Two royal carriages waited at the station, attended by coachmen and footmen whose uniforms were adorned with gold braid and stamped with the double eagle. Valodia was lifted into his godfather's carriage to join his mother, while Liuba, Vera, and Aunt Matilda shared the other carriage with Natalia.

They were to stay at the Kremlin for a few days until an apartment could be found, and as they approached the Tsar's gate, Valodia was awed by the beauty of the churches and palaces and by the hundreds of cannon that surrounded the Kremlin walls. "These cannon," his godfather explained to him, "were captured from Napoleon or abandoned by him during Napoleon's invasion of Russia." He pointed out the imposing towers on the walls. "From those towers," he said, "Napoleon's approach to Moscow was observed, just as the advancing hordes of Tartars had been observed four hundred years before that."

As they entered the gate, Stolypin pointed out the Tsar's cannon to Valodia. "It is the largest in the world," he said. "It was built to protect the city, and it has never been fired." He showed Val the Tsar's bell and explained that when the city of Moscow had caught fire, this bell, which was the largest in the world, had fallen to the ground as its supporting beams burned. "A piece broke from its side as it fell," he said, "and the bell has never since been moved."

Valodia was too excited to sleep. The days that followed were ushered in and out by a bowing, scraping army of butlers and lackeys. Accompanied by one lackey in a gold-braided, double-eagled uniform, Valodia roamed throughout the palace as though he were part of the Royal Family. He toured the great halls where Court was held, the mammoth dining rooms where banquets took place, and the dungeons where Ivan the Terrible had performed his hideous tortures; he even peeped into the Tsar's apartments.

Much too soon an apartment was found. But it was close enough for frequent visits back and forth. Stolypin extended a beautiful love and devotion to Zinaida and her children and added comfort and happiness to their lives.

One day an unfamiliar man arrived at the apartment, and Valodia was introduced to his father. He was stolid, broad-shouldered, and soft-spoken. Valodia liked him straight away, and the gift of ten rubles endeared him even more. There were special offerings from the kitchen, and in the evening, the entire family went to the theatre to see Strauss's *Orpheus in the Underworld*. It was Valodia's first visit to the theatre, and he was thrilled, even though he understood nothing.

When summer arrived, Stolypin took Zinaida, Matilda, and the children to his country place outside of Moscow, on the shore of a lake, surrounded by a forest, and away from railway stations and populated areas. To Valodia the furniture seemed dark, massive, and overpowering. And the servants were amused by his accent. He was having difficulty relearning his native language. In Switzerland he had spoken only French, and the French "R" remained with him always.

The summer estate was not far from the humble home of Leo Tolstoi, a controversial figure at the time. The invitation for a visit, which came through a mutual friend, stirred up a debate. Zinaida wished to visit the great old man, but her sister felt it might compromise their host; she was adamantly opposed. After all, the church had bitterly attacked Tolstoi's views on religion, proclaiming him an atheist. By the ruling classes, he was considered a traitor to the Tsar because of his dangerous, utopian ideas.

Stolypin, himself, settled the debate by insisting that Zinaida go if she so wished. She accepted the invitation and took Valodia with her.

After a two-hour drive on barely navigable roads through forest land, they arrived at Liesnaya Poliana. On a clearing in the forest stood a simple frame house surrounded by a garden. An old man with a long beard was chopping wood. They mistook him for a house servant before realizing it was the great Tolstoi himself. They learned that it was his adopted mode of life to dress and work as a simple peasant. He received his guests with kindness and hospitality. While serving tea, he questioned Zinaida regarding the Swiss peasants and their amazing agricultural feats. He was curious to know of the methods they used to accomplish the cultivation of every inch of ground on their mountainous slopes.

Valodia soon became bored, and if any pearls of wisdom were dropped, they were wasted on him. But for days following the visit, there were intense discussions between his mother and Stolypin. Zinaida carried a message from Tolstoi which he wished to have relayed to the Tsar. Stolypin refused to deliver it. Zinaida was convinced it *should* be delivered. His godfather turned to Valodia and smiled, "Well, what do you think Valodia?"

Valodia bit into an apple and answered with a full mouth, "*Je ne comprends rien.*"

Chapter 5

A Devil Emerges

On the family's return to Moscow that fall, Liuba developed scarlet fever, and seven-year-old Valodia was sent to stay with a friend. Every effort to entertain him met the same response, "I want to go home." He rebelled. The decision was made to send him and Vera to stay with their father in St. Petersburg until Liuba recovered.

Sergei engaged a governess whom Valodia tolerated only because he was forced to do so. What really fascinated him was the gorgeous blonde who had a place in his father's home. He liked the way she dressed and the perfume she wore, and he couldn't understand why the governess would not allow him to be too friendly with her. When he was older, he learned that a triangle is a situation involving three persons, and that this woman was the third person in his family's triangle. He would never understand why people had to "buy" the right to separate from each other. It seemed it should be the other way around. But grownups had strange ideas.

Here he felt a new freedom and independence, and since the governess was quite occupied with Vera and her lessons, he moved rapidly from his cocoon and applied himself to his new world of opportunities. His angelic nature quickly became a thing of the past.

From the balcony overlooking the street, he could watch, unnoticed, the bobbing heads of passersby. He wondered if he dropped something from the balcony, could he hit a moving target? He decided to experiment. Working up a mouthful of saliva, he popped up from his hiding place, quickly made his calculations, let fly, and ducked again into concealment. But as his target moved, the wind caused his missile to drift, and it missed. He tried again. Each bobbing head provided a new challenge, and eventually success came with practice. After one particularly successful aim, he was spellbound by a certain familiarity in his target. Frozen, his eyes filled with horror as they met those of his father!

Restriction from the balcony forced him to find a new source of entertainment, and he found it in an old trunk which held hundreds of letters, each with a design at the top in gold, silver, and beautiful colors. An especially beautiful one had a large "N." He decided to make a wonderful scrapbook to take back to his mother. He found a pair of scissors and was working away when Sergei's secretary passed through the room with a tea tray. She screamed and dropped the tray as she grabbed for Valodia. But he escaped and took to the stairs with a syncopated rhythm that caused him to crash-land. He pulled himself up and circled the heavy oak table, but it seemed to rise up and attack him. Defeated, he lay on the floor while the household staff surrounded him. It was alarm he saw on their faces. They seemed to relax only when they were able to get him on his feet.

Upstairs on the floor lay his father's famous collection of historical missives, each flashing its royal and noble crest — and lo, Napoleon's topped the rest. They formed one massive jigsaw puzzle, completely freed of national prejudice and social stigma. For his elders, the incident began to fade into a philosophical acceptance of fate. As for Valodia, he was still trying to find an identity he could wear with comfort.

One evening when Vera appeared for dinner dressed in a lovely evening gown, Valodia asked, "Where are you going?"

"To the theatre," Vera responded.

"I want to go, too," he said. She denied his request, and he was offended. Twice refused, he was indignant and infuriated. When Vera said "no" a third time, he gave vent to his rage by grabbing one of the delicately sculptured meatballs and hurling it at her. The horrified governess started for him, but he stopped her in her tracks with additional ammunition. His beautifully groomed sister was an unbelievable sight by the time he made a dash for the bathroom and locked himself in. No threat from his victims could extricate him, and he resolved to remain there indefinitely. He held a trump card since it was the only bathroom in the house, and from that vantage point he dictated the terms of his armistice. He would emerge *only* if he would not be punished, *and* if he were allowed to go to the theatre! When it was established that there would be no indemnities, that there would be unconditional pardon (no cut in allowance), that he would be permitted to go to the theatre, and that they would swear to it on the Bible, Valodia unlocked the door.

They would have kept their promises, but Valodia's father came home.

When he had heard from all sides, Valodia received the only thrashing of his life, his allowance was cut, and he was not taken to the theatre. He kicked and yelled, and as soon as he was left alone, he demolished everything in his room. His father decided not to repeat such punishment; it was too expensive.

Zinaida's inquiry after her son met with the response, "My Dear, you don't have a son; you have a devil!" With great relief, his father returned him to Moscow.

It was the autumn of 1898 and time for Val to enter gymnasium. The prior summer was supposed to have been spent preparing for entrance exams, but the allure of summer games, swimming, and boating had taken precedence. Though he tried for the First Class in two of the gymnasiums and for the Preparatory in a third, he completely failed them all. His mother was ashamed but determined. In desperation, she made a final effort, and through her influence, he was accepted in *First Class* of a gymnasium which was established especially for children of Caucasian parents. Since the school was anxious to have a certain percentage of Russians enrolled, Val was accepted in spite of his lack of knowledge. The important fact was that since he had skipped the preparation class, he would finish his schooling in eight years instead of nine. Because of that, he would return to Switzerland in his ninth year, an event that would change his entire life.

His first lesson in school was learned not from the teacher, but from other boys. Though sworn to secrecy, he raced home in a highly excited state of mind. No one was there to greet him, so he went to the bedroom and rang for the maid. When she appeared, he took a deep breath, and with a tone bordering on command, said, "Come in and let's make love." The maid took one look at his descending trousers, shrieked hysterically, and disappeared convulsing with laughter. Val took his defeat badly and attempted no further conquests through his newly acquired information.

Here he was introduced to politics and world affairs. The Spanish-American War was on, and he sided with the Americans. Then came the Boer War, and his sympathy lay with the underdogs. Kruger and Smuts were his heroes, and he thought the siege of Ladysmith was a great event. He particularly hated Commander-in-Chief Kitchener, with his mustachios, and a war correspondent by the name of Winston Churchill.

Not only did seven-year-old Val fancy himself an expert on Russian politics, but he was a devout Monarchist and a religious fanatic. He especially anticipated communion and sometimes would stand through two services, for there were no pews, to receive a double portion of the holy bread and wine. He was sure that the more wine he imbibed, the more saintly he would become. And no one could deny that there was a great deal of progress to be made.

Chapter 6

A Royal Treat

In 1900, the Tsar and his family came to Moscow from the Winter Palace in St. Petersburg, and Val learned that these were real people, not some faraway heavenly beings. The streets were illuminated with colored lights, as was the custom on all birthdays and all name-days of each member of the Royal Family. Many houses wore attractively lighted signs, and throngs of people paraded the streets to see the Royal carriage go by. Valodia envied the three little girls who sat proudly in the carriage so far removed from all the people.

A great gala performance of *Eugene Onegin* was to be given at the Bolshoi Theatre in the Tsar's honor. Because it was necessary for Stolypin to accompany the Tsar and to be in attendance at the Royal Box, he gave to Zinaida and her children his adjoining box, that of the Governor of the Kremlin.

Ten-year-old Val was warned before leaving home to stay clear of the trailing ball gowns, and since they were omnipresent, he dared not raise his eyes for a moment to the great columns that preceded the stairs, or to the stairs themselves which rose majestically to the mezzanine and the Royal Box. The family was escorted to the Governor's Box by a lackey bursting his gold buttons with importance. Once there, with his feet firmly planted beneath him, Val surrendered himself completely to the dazzling spectacle.

A great crystal chandelier hung in space like a galaxy of stars spun together with magnetic magic. The glitter of gold and silver braid and epaulettes, the sparkle of diamonds, and the profusion of furs and trains wove a spell that was broken only by the orchestra playing the national anthem as the Tsar and his family appeared.

Moments later, the Royal Family was in the adjoining box, smiling benevolently on all their subjects. The Tsaritza was a heavenly vision of beauty under the halo of her sparkling tiara. Val wished he could kneel at her feet and kiss her hand. What must it be like for those children to live in the same palace with Tsar Nicholas, whom God had appointed in some celestial ceremony to represent Him in Russia? And how could these holy creatures have children like ordinary humans?

As they were seated, the lights went down, and the orchestra began the overture. Royalty was not only in the audience tonight, but also on the stage — operatic royalty. The famous tenor Mazini was singing Lensky, and "King of the Baritones" Battistini was performing Onegin. The soprano was Ziegrid Arnoldson. These three leads were singing in Italian while the remainder of the company held forth in Russian. Valodia wondered if they could understand one another. Perhaps opera was a mysterious sort of thing that only singers were supposed to grasp. But the conductor must be in on the secret, too, he reasoned, because the singers would often stride to the front of the stage and sing directly at him alone. He wondered how much the children in the next box understood, and convinced himself that they were only making a great pretense.

During the final act, the voices took on a peculiar manner of receding and then jumping at him, startling him, and making his head jerk spasmodically. He cast furtive glances at the next box where the proud heads of the children were poised high above their stiff little backs. Their endurance, or his lack of it, he was not sure which he hated more.

Chapter 7

Lord of the Manor

It was a creative period in Moscow. There were concerts by Koussevitzky, women swooned over Sobinoff, Stanislavsky had created the Moscow Art Theatre, and Chekhov was a rising playwright.

At the breakfast table, Val heard his mother and Vera excitedly discussing the marvelous concert of the previous evening. He tried to repeat the artist's name and stumbled over the pronunciation of Chaliapin.

That winter Val was taken to hear *Les Huguenots* which thrilled and excited him. His father came several times to visit, and his parents seemed to be negotiating a reconciliation when something occurred to transform the course of their lives. Natalia Stolypin's uncle, Prince Vorontzoff-Dashkoff died and left her a small kingdom composed of three estates totaling 37,000 acres. It made her the wealthiest woman in Russia. Natalia asked Zinaida to intercede with Sergei on her behalf, hoping he would handle her inheritance. Sergei accepted the responsibility and eventually became so engrossed with it that he gave up his private practice. Natalia reimbursed him with ten percent of the land, which they held in joint ownership, and the Rosings were suddenly shifted from a "well-fixed" status to wealthy landowners.

A reunited family went to spend the summer on its newly acquired estate, Theofilovka. It was a trip across Russia that Val would never forget. He would often say, "You must invest in beauty; you will draw on its resources all of your artistic life." He had a vast reservoir of it himself, and many times described to me the scenes of his childhood and youth.

As the train carried them farther and farther from Moscow, the forests of the north were replaced by the steppes of the south; villages of abject poverty gave way to the extraordinary beauty and wealth of the Ukraine, and whitewashed earthen huts clustered under thatched roofs. Forests stood on the horizon like ships, and Val was intoxicated by the smell of the black earth and the scent of cherry orchards.

Southern Russia was a strange mixture of Ukrainian peasants descended from the Cossacks, landlords who were mostly Poles, and Jewish merchants. Jews were barred from living in the north unless they had government permission or were university graduates. Only two percent were accepted in the universities, and no Jewish singer, actor, musician, or dancer was engaged in the Imperial theatres. They were also barred from being officers in the army and the navy, although they were conscripted for service. The government deliberately blamed them for the misfortunes in Russia.

Each time the train ground to a stop, Val would bolt from his seat, inspect the station, and purchase a chocolate, a sandwich, or an orange.

All of their future employees met the train at its final stop where they enjoyed a sumptuous lunch at the station buffet before departing in a long procession of carriages for the final three-hour drive to Theofilovka. Sitting in a victoria drawn by four horses abreast and attended by lackeys in livery, Val was amazed that every villager they passed swept off his hat and bowed low to the ground. The peasants, though freed from serfdom 33 years before, had not lost their servile attitude. But the feudal system was in its final spasm.

The estate covered 20 square miles, and thousands of peasants lived in its three villages. Theofilovka was the central village, and the owner's mansion was a mile away on top of a hill. Jumping down as the carriage stopped at the front gate, Val could see the tennis courts and stables off to the left, and stretching away to the right, a landscaped park which descended to a lake. There on the beach, two boats rocked gently on the rippling water. With one sweeping glance, he concluded that this was to be, by far, the most exciting summer of his life.

Val immediately headed for the stables where he counted thirty head of horses. One of these would be his very own. He would wear high, patent leather boots, and he would learn to click his spurs. In fact, he would be the greatest horseman in these parts. He would explore the surrounding country on horseback, and the villagers would look at him with admiration in their eyes as they bowed and scraped.

Though it was summer, they were actually taking up residence in the winter mansion which was well equipped with modern conveniences. Not until the following summer was the family to realize its preference for the summer mansion, seven miles away in the village of Djulinka — the largest of the estate's three villages.

Sergei was indignant at some of the inhumane practices that were still in existence. He forbade child labor, established nurseries where mothers could leave their children, and prohibited lashings by overseers. Eventually he would build hospitals to care for the sick, but for the present his good deeds were heaping upon him all the repercussions with which he could cope. County officials were aloof with disdain, neighbors furiously accused the Rosings of having revolutionary tendencies, and even the peasants were bewildered and suspicious. They whispered that there had to be a reason for such apparent generosity. Perhaps Mr. Rosing was trying to charm them into selling what little land they owned. These things were discussed at mealtime, so Val was aware of the veil of doubtful acceptance.

Meanwhile, life at Theofilovka was a boy's paradise. Val learned to ride and spent all of his available time in the saddle, inspecting the fields and paying visits to the neighbors — particularly to the priest in Djulinka who had a family of three sons and three daughters.

The sea of green wheat turned to billowing gold, and it was harvest time. Since there was insufficient machinery, and since those peasants who owned land had to attend to their own harvesting, proprietors were given permission to hire army regiments to augment the work force.

Three thousand soldiers hired by the Rosings bivouacked in the fields while the officers were guests in their home. Evenings were a time for revelry. Behind the lighted windows, there was gambling, drinking, dancing, and romance. But Val preferred to be in the fields. Great giant torches lit the sky with a heavy red glow to accommodate the night shift. The men who were resting from the day shift sat about bonfires romancing the village women. And always, day or night, there was that miracle of sound issuing from a thousand throats, swept into a mighty ocean of song and borne on a sigh of wind across the steppes until it hung suspended on a single thread of tone.

Summer was at an end.

Chapter 8

Putting Away Childish Things

After that first summer, the family established a winter home in St. Petersburg. They returned there each August, for the beginning of the school term and remained until the middle of May. Val enjoyed the three heavenly months of vacation in the summer.

Val entered the second class in a new gymnasium where he impressed his classmates with his knowledge of horsemanship by casually observing that passing horses were geldings, mares, or stallions. His admiring classmates conferred upon him the title, "Cavalerist" — the Cavalryman.

St. Petersburg contrasted greatly with Moscow. Spread out on the banks of the Neva and just a few miles from the Baltic Sea, it had been built as recently as 1700 by Peter the Great to become the new capital and to be Russia's "Window on Europe." Its streets were straight, wide, and long compared with the narrow and intricately curved streets of Moscow. The architecture was Europeanized, giving it a unique beauty and charm. Its culture was rich, and its social life was exhilarating and perpetual.

The Rosings had a spacious apartment on Nickolaegorky Street with a balcony overlooking it. Their home soon became a center for artists and intellectuals and a representation of the more liberal segment of the aristocracy.

By September, the cream of society had returned from summer vacations spent in Europe, at the beaches of Crimea, or on the Baltics and Finland. It was a time for sharing summer romances, scandals, and gossip, and this required daily parties. Impressed by the British "five o'clock tea," Russian hostesses sent out invitations to "come to my five o'clock tea at four."

Then would come the New Year with its intoxicating whirl of festivities — lunches, dinners, after-theatre suppers, and dances — which lasted until Lent began. The week before Lent was called "butter week" and butter, cheese, eggs, and meats were done without. But there were compensations in the form of caviar, salmon, sturgeon, and other fish delicacies; the champagne flowed as usual.

On Easter Sunday every church had a gala service, and for some of the very elegant ones it was essential to have tickets. Exactly at midnight on the Saturday before, the priest would proclaim, to the accompaniment of all the church bells in the city, "The Christ has risen!"

The congregation would respond, "Indeed He is risen!" followed by general congratulations and, most importantly to Val, a ritual of kissing, which he bent to his personal advantage. That wonderful custom lasted for three days, and Val devoutly conformed to the orthodox tenets of the church at this time of year. Weeks or months earlier, he would have established the object to whom his religious fervency would be communicated. On Easter he would approach her and say, "Christ is risen!" to which she was obliged to respond, "Indeed He is risen!" Thereupon she could be kissed three times upon the cheeks, but his third kiss was contemplated to miss the mark. Unfortunately, it was a two-way street, and sometimes fanatically religious men with huge, bushy beards would walk up to Val and say, "Christ is risen!" There was nothing to do but submit and endure.

As was the Russian custom, the Rosings kept open house, which meant that friends could drop in to dinner anytime they wished. When Val later went to England, he was surprised to learn that people must have a specified date to visit and dine. In Russia one would say, "Do come to dinner sometime," and often there would be fifteen unexpected dinner guests. The Rosings had a wonderful cook, and Val spent a good deal of time in the kitchen watching and tasting. He was an adept pupil, and, in later years, was able to entertain friends in England with Russian cuisine.

Sergei came home one day carrying a monstrosity — a large box with a horn-shaped device attached to it.

"Well, don't stand there gaping, Valodia; come and help me."

"What is it?" Val stammered.

"It's the payment for Ivan Malchanoff's divorce."

Val had never understood why people were willing to pay so much for the privilege of not living together. He understood *this* even less.

His father grinned, "If I can persuade you to hold the door open for me, I have a real surprise for you."

"What have you got?"

"It's a Gramophone."

"What's that?"

"A new invention; it reproduces sound. You're going to hear our favorite singer, Figner. Remember that evening?"

With the enthusiasm of a ten-year-old, Val helped his father assemble the strange contraption. It was a monumental task. The horn alone was seven feet in length, and its suspension to the machine was a very difficult affair. Having no mechanical abilities whatsoever between them, they cursed the inventor, an American man by the name of Edison. Finally, Sergei placed a thin black disc on the mechanism, wound the handle, and stood back. Val gasped at the unmistakable sound of a human voice, but it was a strange, regurgitating sound. Sergei reset the speed, and the voice became hysterical. But when it was all properly adjusted, Figner's voice poured forth, and Val realized it was not a trick his father was playing; it was a real miracle!

The Gramophone was to become an instrument of torture for the family, for Val not only played it all day, every day, but he also sang each selection along with the performing artist. He mimicked the dramatic tenors, Figner and Mazini, and the baritone, Bragin; he trilled with the coloratura, Baronat, and rumbled with the bass, Chaliapin. He mastered the complete operatic repertoire of the six records which accompanied the Gramophone.

His vocal enthusiasm knew no bounds. He demanded to be taken to operatic performances. And he joined the school choir. Singing high notes, he experienced a sensation of complete abandon during which he imagined he was soaring vocally over an orchestra and provoking an ovation from the audience.

Instead of the expected plaudits, though, Val's exhibition was interrupted by the chorus master who said politely, "Rosing this is a chorus, not a solo competition; you'd better return to your class."

The chorus master simply did not recognize real talent! But Val's irrepressible ambition outweighed his injured psyche, and he continued to vocalize in the corridors and in the lavatory where the acoustics were superior.

* * * * *

Natalia was an important part of the St. Petersburg scene. She never cared to spend much time at the summer estate, nor to take much interest in its administration, but in St. Petersburg and abroad she lavishly spent her income. Such was the manner of most Russian landowners. However, Natalia, like her cousin Peter Stolypin, now Governor of Gradno, believed the peasants should have the right to own land. Peter would later become famous for his land reform program.

Natalia and Aunt Matilda developed a close friendship, and she was constantly at the Rosing home, adding a great deal of gaiety. Although she was 20 years his senior, and his godmother to boot, Valodia adored this beautiful creature.

One evening Aunt Matilda, Natalia, and Val stayed quite late in the evening at the home of a neighbor. It was a chilly evening, and as they drove home, Val slipped down from the front seat of the carriage and sat on the floor at Natalia's feet, resting his head on her knees. With her satin-soft hand, she gently stroked his head, and it kindled in him a feeling he had never before experienced. He wanted to kiss her hand; he wanted to kiss her feet, but he dared not move lest he break the spell. Did she sense his feeling? She took her hand away, but soon it was back, and he laid his cheek softly against it, touching it with his lips. He remained in a trance for two hours. From that night on, he became her servant. At the table, he looked on her with adoration, and he would wait for hours just to kiss her hand good-night. He dreamed of Easter, but it was months away.

Spring ushered in its maddening white nights — those languid, sleepless, romantic, and sensuous nights when a silver light permeated the city until an hour or two before streaks of pink appeared in the sky to announce the dawn. And Val took his languishing heart to Djulinka, to the sun-warmed earth, to the open steppes that he loved so, to his horses, to his pack of fifteen mongrel dogs. Oh, those beautiful summers!

Chapter 9

Life Begins at Thirteen

That second summer, 1903, the family moved from Theofilovka to the 300-year-old summer house on the shore of the Southern Bug River in Djulinka. A half mile tree-lined drive led from the outskirts of the village to the porch which was supported by four urn-shaped columns. The long one-story structure with wine cellars below was surrounded by 15 acres of lilacs. A network of paths meshed through the thickness of bloom and fragrance, opening frequently into green carpeted clearings. Val fell in love with it.

After leaving Russia, and for as long as he lived, he dreamed of seeing Djulinka again. One day in 1944, while serving as Entertainment Director at Camp Roberts in California, Val opened the morning paper and read a terse communique from Stalin: "Yesterday our troops, in the battle of Djulinka, defeated the Germans. We were thrown across the River Bug, leaving 2,000 dead." Val's anguish was indescribable. Others who read the news rejoiced over another German defeat, but Val visualized his home burned and gutted, the gardens destroyed, and the beautiful peaceful village, so dear to his heart, demolished.

On the nearby Crimean peninsula, the best restaurants opened their summer places, and every night the elite drove in their elegant carriages under the shade trees, observing who was with whom, and whispering the latest scandals. Val joined the pedestrians longing for romance and adventure.

So life went until he was thirteen. That summer he consumed life in great gulps. An important event was taking place. His sister Vera was to be married to Baron Von Sivers, and elaborate preparations were under way. In the garden area, a tent accommodating 300 people was set up for the wedding feast, and all of the best peasant houses were leased for guests, for the celebrations would continue for three days.

For three months, Val had been collecting fireworks for a particularly spectacular display. By the day of the wedding, he had filled a two-and-a-half by six-foot trunk to the brim with various colored rockets, sun wheels, fountains, Roman candles, and bombs. He was very proud of his collection.

He had been granted permission to taste the wine on this occasion, so he began tasting early in the morning, and before the 11:00 a.m. ceremony, he had downed five glasses of champagne. On returning from the ceremony, his thirst was acute, and everyone was far too occupied to notice that he consumed another five glassfuls.

Arranged along the *hors d'oeuvres* table in the tent were thirteen bottles of vodka — each a different color. There were yellows, ranging from the palest lemon to deep gold, blues from the shade of a summer sky to the royal blue of his mother's Crown Derby china, ruby red, and emerald green. How could he choose from among them? There was nothing to do but to sample them all. Thirteen jiggers of vodka later, dinner was announced.

Val felt somehow detached from his feet and consumed with an inner fire. In front of his plate at the table were two bottles of wine, one madeira and one port. To quench the fire, he drank a tumbler of madeira and, feeling no improvement, followed it quickly with a tumbler of port.

The head butler was behind Val's chair. "Vladimir Sergeevich, will you see if the arrangements for the coachmen's dinner meet your approval?"

Oh yes, the coachmen's dinner; he had forgotten it was his responsibility. Excusing himself from the table, he turned to follow the butler. Suddenly, as though from a mallet, there was a skull-splitting blow on the back of his head. Darkness swirled in around him, and his knees crumpled.

Later, in his bedroom, the return to consciousness was accompanied by such a violent upheaving that he prayed for his return to oblivion. Death would be a welcome relief. But neither oblivion nor death extended such kindness.

Six hours later, a group of youngsters headed by his sister Liuba shook him out of his stupor and reminded him that it was time for fireworks. The fireworks, my God! He could not shirk his responsibility for the evening's entertainment!

"Leave me so I can dress," he said. "Liuba, ask the servants to carry the trunk to the field." He fumbled into the jacket of his parade uniform, staggered to the door and made his way to the field. In darkness, he groped toward his trunk full of treasures.

His arms felt heavy and awkward, and his hands trembled as he opened the trunk, picked up a match, and struck it. He accidentally dropped it, so he reached for another. But at that moment, an explosion rocked the universe. In the confines of the trunk, bombs and rockets ignited and fought a thundering battle. In a matter of seconds, there was an artistic exhibition of fantastic proportions. Flares of every imaginable color, shooting skyward from the Roman candles, spotlighted two bare legs beneath a dress parade jacket. Awareness of his miraculous escape came on the sound of laughter which plunged him from the brink of death to the depths of humiliation.

For several years after, Val could not bear the smell of liquor, and never as an adult was he able to consume more than a jigger or two of alcohol amply mixed with ginger ale, or a small amount of wine diluted with water.

The next morning, when the floor of his room no longer resembled the ocean, and the paintings on the walls came into focus, Val observed the tent which remained as a hollow monument to the recent festivities. Why couldn't he use it for a dramatic production? What an opportunity! He could be producer, director, and actor — all three. He decided that in the role of the sixty-year-old servant of Chekhov's *The Bear*, he could flaunt his ability as a comedian.

Within days, the stage was erected, some 200 guests were invited from 20 or 30 miles around, and never was a waiting bride more atremble than was thirteen-year-old Val the night before his dramatic debut. With profound solemnity, he paced the moonlit gardens and contemplated the great responsibility of his artistic future. The fire of genius was smoldering.

He was redeemed. From his point of view, it was a performance that far surpassed his sister's wedding.

Nine months later, back in St. Petersburg, Vera produced a son, Arkadin, and Val produced Gogol's *The Inspector General* for his class.

When Vera's son left the bosom of his nurse, a very pretty young girl named Amalia was engaged to help care for him, and they all spent the following summer at Djulinka. Amalia was a Baltic-German girl of about twenty-two with a cute pointed nose and attractive fox-like face. She devoted her spare time to Val in helpful little ways, such as turning down his bed at night and hanging his clothes. Sometimes she would sit on the bed as they chatted and laughed. One night Val teased her, and they began to scuffle. As their faces came close together, she planted a kiss on his mouth and ran from the room. Val found the sensation most agreeable, and he waited impatiently the next evening for an encore. Amalia chafed at his absorption in the art of kissing. There was much more to learn.

One evening when the world was bathed in silver moonlight and heavy with fragrance, they strolled into the garden. Serenaded by crickets, they followed a path which led to a secluded spot surrounded by lilacs.

Val could feel his heart pounding in anticipation of the mysterious experience that was about to unfold. Amalia quickly dismissed his introductory kiss;

she had something more advanced in mind. But it was all happening so fast for Val that the dreamy elements of his fantasies were fading. It seemed to him that it was suddenly broad daylight, and that sequestered among the lilac bushes were numerous pairs of astonished eyes. Terrified, he ran from the scene. His crossing of the Rubicon was a clumsy one, and his retreat lasted for two weeks. But a return to the knowing arms of Amalia was inevitable. From then on, he moved in a forward direction.

Chapter 10

Opera in the Grand Manner

Within a few months, Val would be fifteen. Another summer had passed, and it was time to return to St. Petersburg. His recent experience had given him an edge of superiority, and he felt ready to enter the intellectual and artistic life of the city.

Much of his time was devoted to ice skating. He also learned to play *Vist*, a Russian card game similar to bridge — only more difficult. It fascinated him to watch the grownups play, and he soon became a *protégé* of one of the best players. Aunt Matilda, who adored the game, often kept him up till two or three playing double dummy, and to her great annoyance, he invariably won. She would balk at paying him and usually settled her debts by giving him some of the very expensive fruit which she kept in her room.

The previous summer Val had persuaded his father to take him to Odessa to hear a baritone, Titta Ruffo, who had made a sensation there. But their timing was off; Ruffo had already departed, and Father was upset. That summer Ruffo came to St. Petersburg where he was an instant success. Val heard him as Tonio in *I Pagliacci* and was confronted with a difficult decision: Should he be a Caruso or a Ruffo? In his own eyes, he was becoming a great authority on opera and voice, and he was wildly jealous when he discovered that an aunt — who was unquestionably the greatest snob of St. Petersburg society, and whose daughter Julia was a great beauty — had penetrated Ruffo's dressing room and invited him to dinner. Ruffo developed a crush on Julia, but would not succumb to marriage. He departed, leaving an array of broken hearts.

Twenty years would pass before Val would hear him again and observe a sadly depleted vocal capital.

That fall, Natalia became engaged to Prince Kochubay, who was brother to the Administrator for the Royal Estate, and since all of the Royal Theatres were under his jurisdiction, the family's opera tickets were obtained through him.

Traditionally subscriptions to the opera were handed down from generation to generation. Occasionally someone would sell a subscription for 1,000 or 2,000 dollars, but this merely established the right to purchase tickets.

That winter Chaliapin was singing Mephistopheles in *Faust* at the Maryinsky Theatre. One night a week it was open to public attendance, and Val decided to purchase his own ticket rather than to ask favors. He played hooky from school, and at 7:00 a.m. took his place in line in front of the theatre. When the box office opened three hours later, there was a drawing to see who would obtain the 150 numbers that would place them in a new line for the right to buy a pair of tickets. Val drew no number at all, so he didn't even have a place in line. Then the man who held number 149 said he would sell his place at the end of the line. When he reached the window, he was sure he could not have stood in the bitter cold for another moment. Like a slap in the face, he heard the words, "No more tickets." Infuriated, he assailed the box office clerk with a tirade of schoolboy profanity.

"Well," the clerk said, "there *is* one seat left, but it is on the front row; the price is ten rubles."

Val knew that these seats were the most expensive in the house, and that they were usually reserved for generals and high officials. He knew also that the smug clerk was confident of his inability to come up with ten rubles.

"I'll take it," he snapped, "but I'll have to make a deposit and go home for more money."

He went home and borrowed the money from Piotre, the porter, who was always glad to oblige, for they had a confidential arrangement which gave Piotre 100 percent return on his money.

During the first act of *Faust* he was spellbound. The majestic figure of Mephisto, clothed in red velvet, strutted the stage, and Val knew his own destiny was cast. It was an ambition never to be completely fulfilled, for Providence had mistakenly endowed him a tenor instead of a bass. However, he would eventually sing many of the same songs that were in Chaliapin's repertoire, and in London *The Observer* would report that George Bernard Shaw wrote to him saying:

> When I was a boy, I used to sing like you, that is to say, I did not bother about being a tenor or baritone or even a human being. I sang soprano or basso profundo, piccolo or drum, cor anglais or

trumpet, just making the sort of noise the music wanted. You [are] not a singer at all; you [are] a whole band.

As the applause slowly subsided, he realized that the generals and guard officers had risen from their seats and were on exhibition. Well, he had paid dearly for his ticket, and he would absorb all the benefits of it. The short stocky boy in school uniform approached the orchestra rail, leaned against it, and imitated the other pretentious figures reclining there.

With such an infusion of inspiration, he could no longer merely stand by a Gramophone and sing. His concept of opera took on new dimension, and he began to stride about in the grand operatic style with wild, melodramatic gesticulations. He wanted to act, and he did. He acted out scenes from operas, improvising words and melodies. He was versatile; he could play Nero one minute and follow it with Desdemona the next. Tragedy was his specialty, and he usually chose those scenes involving death and murders. He drafted his younger cousin, Sergei, to play all the subordinate roles.

Val's ambition grew, and his company moved from the bedroom to the larger arena of the dining room where they gave performances for the servants and a few guests. Frequently there was laughter where there should have been tears, but Val was undaunted.

Cousin Sergei felt somewhat cheated by his minor roles, so Val promised him an important part in their next production, Rubenstein's *Nero*. As a matter of fact, he even allowed Sergei to perform all of the various roles of Nero's victims. Nero, of course, was played by Val. Nero's first victim was poisoned; the second, stabbed; the third met death through opening of the veins; the fourth was tortured on the rack; the fifth suffered offstage decapitation; and the sixth met with strangulation that was far too realistic. Insulted and indignant, Sergei refused any further roles; he had been pushed too far.

It was the irresistible bribe of a box of chocolates that finally induced him to accept a return engagement as Donna Elvira in the opera, *Don Giovanni*. This production had the added attraction of public performance in the dining room with music and cardboard scenery, both improvised by Val. Behind the cut-out window sat the benign and bewigged Donna Elvira devouring chocolates.

Val longed to become a producer. In his imagination, he formed two opera companies. One was composed of all the great singers he had heard, and the other was made up of his schoolmates. While other boys applied themselves to their textbooks, Val covered sheets of paper with potential casts for various operas. Someone with a lesser imagination could have suffered severe limitation when it came to casting an opera from his classmates, for Russian schools were not co-educational until the university level. The effeminate or less robust boys would never have forgiven him had they known they were his prima donnas.

For graduation, he persuaded those in authority to allow him to produce Pushkin's *Boris Godounov*, playing Dimitri, the Pretender, himself. It was a great success, and he fashioned himself, at fifteen, a second Stanislavsky. Later in life, he would find himself at odds with Stanislavsky's method of acting. Val scorned the idea that it was necessary to wring emotions out of the body each time one portrayed a character. He taught body sculpture and used it to re-create the author's concept of character.

Val could see that his vocal and acting abilities stimulated his parents' pride in him. Yet they were concerned about his absorption with a singing career, and they tried to impress upon him the instability of the artistic life.

"A singing career is beneath the dignity of a man unless he is a celebrity," said his father.

"But I will be a celebrity," Val assured him.

"You have a beautiful voice, but you could lose it," cautioned his mother. "Then what will you do?"

"Why would I lose my voice?" questioned Val with youth's virgin confidence.

"It has happened to others."

"But it won't happen to me."

Chapter 11

Troubled Times

Val had passed from class to class by the skin of his teeth, chiefly because of his natural ability for mathematics and his knowledge of French. But Latin was his nemesis, and he didn't take any honors in Religion either.

The religious ceremony in the Russian (Greek Orthodox) Church was very impressive with its excellent choirs elegantly robed in gold brocade. It was theatrical, but it was tiring to stand during the entire service and a relief to kneel. The Bible was taught literally in school, and it seemed illogical to Val that the world could have been created in six days or that Eve could have been created from the rib of Adam. Consequently, he was easily propelled into atheism by a student who had been engaged as a private tutor to help prepare him for exams. The majority of students were Socialists (though socialistic parties were illegal) and bitterly opposed the Church which was under the control of the Tsar's government. The universities were the center of ferment.

The times were disturbing. A year earlier, during the winter of 1904, Japan, provoked that Russians had freely gone into Korea and established concessions for themselves, torpedoed Russian ships in the outer harbor of Port Arthur. This act of aggression resulted in a great wave of patriotism — the last of such for the Romanoffs. A tremendous procession of Russian workers, students, and citizens marched in the streets and paraded flags in front of the palaces singing the national anthem. How dare those mosquitoes attack the Russian bear!

Val organized his neighborhood and joined the main procession, leading the singing with his lusty voice. Singing for hours on a bitterly cold January day gave him terrible laryngitis, and he was voiceless for weeks — which may have been a relief to his family, but Amalia consoled him.

To the amazement of the Russians, the Japanese produced long-range guns and destroyed the poorly equipped Russian army and then the fleet. With each defeat, criticism of the government became louder. The Revolutionaries raged. But extreme Monarchists called "The Black Hundred" removed the blame from the Tsar and placed it on the Jews. The Black Hundred traveled from town to town executing pogroms.

Val and his father were on a train traveling south. Every station vibrated with tales of horror told by escaping refugees. The two arrived in Kishinev soon after the massacre of many Jews and learned that the Governor, the Commander, the General, and the army and police forces had stood by for three days before getting involved. Val saw plundered houses and shops and heard stories of women being raped and killed, of people having been ripped open and filled with feathers from pillows. The experience haunted him day and night. How could such hatred be possible? An inner rage began to possess him as the pogroms spread to the north.

There were rumors that The Black Hundred was planning a pogrom in St. Petersburg on January 6, and that all of the Jewish apartments would be marked with a cross, as on St. Bartholomew's night in Paris when the Huguenots were massacred. Panic seized the Jewish inhabitants who were a minority because of the restrictions against them in northern Russia.

Within a few days, every liberal Russian offered his home as a hiding place. The Rosings sheltered the Menaka family whose son was a schoolmate of Val's. Val had a revolver and two hunting guns. After loading the guns, he helped barricade the two entrances with furniture, partook of a buffet supper, and settled down for an all-night bridge game to camouflage their vigil. Their actions froze at the slightest suggestion of a sound. It was a nerve-wracking but uneventful night.

At the same time, among factory workers, great discontent was breeding, and they found a sympathetic leader in an Orthodox priest, Father Gapon, who organized a march to the palace to petition the Tsar for better working conditions.

Val was forbidden to leave the house that Sunday, but before anyone else awoke, he pocketed some sandwiches and took a tram toward the workers' quarters. He joined the crowd of unarmed workers, which gathered momentum at each corner until it reached the Winter Palace Square where it found armed troops stationed in front of the closed palace gates.

In anticipation of the Tsar's appearance, the crowd sang the national anthem and lifted their icons. The sun blazed down as if to bless the event. Then an order rang out for the crowd to disperse. Thinking that the officers would not shoot down defenseless women and children, the crowd did not move. The officer counted: "One, two, three," but the crowd did not stir except for a few people who knelt in prayer. The infantry raised their rifles, and the command came, "Fire!" The first volley went into the air, and children who had climbed trees in the surrounding park to witness the event fell like shattered birds. The second and third volleys fell into the solid mass of people. There were deafening screams, and the crowd broke into a stampede. Another volley was fired at their retreating backs, and a cavalry of Cossacks and dragoons bore down on them with sabres and lead-tipped whips.

Fortunately, Val was on the outer circle of the crowd, and he broke into a run. Finding a doorway, he squeezed in and hid behind a pillar. After the fourth volley, he ran again, trying to reach a side street. He stumbled over a stone and someone fell over him. He felt something warm and sticky on his face. The boy who had fallen on him was bleeding, but it was not serious, and together they fled to a side street, the Millionaya. Once out of the crowd, and momentarily forgetting he was an atheist, Val thanked God.

His knees were still weak from shock, but he could not resist going back to the main street, Nevsky, to see what was happening. It was still patrolled by Cossacks who quickly dispersed any gathering. He paced the streets for hours, ate his sandwiches, and finally returned home exhausted. His parents met him with a mixture of joy and wrath, and he forfeited his allowance for a month. That day was to be known as Red Sunday, also called Bloody Sunday because of the bloodstained snow.

Val grew up that winter. He surrendered his loyalty to the Tsar and his government and became outspoken in his opposition to the views of his aristocratic friends who still sympathized with the regime.

Revolutionary fever was epidemic. Strikes spread to every industry, including the *corps de ballet*. There was no transportation or postal service. Even the banks were closed.

Students struck also. The Council of Students, to which Val was elected secretary, took over the school, intimidated the teachers, and introduced new rules. Attendance in class, they said, was not obligatory, quarterly exams were abolished, and smoking was permitted in the lavatories. They became the headquarters for gambling and *risqué* storytelling. Val was president of the gambling syndicate and ran the roulettes. Skipping afternoon classes, they would spread a green cloth on the lavatory floor, and Val would hold the roulette on his lap while sitting comfortably on the middle "can." The players squatted on the floor and used real coppers. An occasional silver stake produced great excitement.

All went well until the day the school director suddenly appeared. The players scattered like rats leaving Val perched on the can with the roulette wheel on his lap. Two weeks before, it would have meant expulsion, but now the director gently took the wheel from him and philosophically advised him never to try to win back his losses. The roulette wheel became the possession of the director for use of the faculty.

The University Council used the Student Council of the gymnasium as messenger boys. Between delivering messages, they attended the session of the Soviet (council of workers' deputies) where Val and another student had attained the status of deputy. Attending the Soviet and organizing his production of *Boris*, Val was much too busy to attend classes.

By the time the Rosings returned to Djulinka in the summer of 1906, the atmosphere was tense. Social Revolutionaries preached destruction of the large estates and distribution of the land among the peasants. They persuaded the mostly illiterate peasants that the Tsar had issued such a decree and expected them to carry it out.

There was no police protection in the country, and frequently the horizon glowed crimson with the flames of burning estates. Most of the landlords abandoned their homes and fled to the cities. Those who were foolish enough to remain, slept with their guns. Sergei refused to leave his property. He had faith that because of his liberal reforms, the peasants would know he was their friend.

One morning shortly after the family returned, they were having breakfast on the balcony when they heard an ominous rumble of voices, and the white-faced butler rushed out to inform them that the peasants were pouring in through the gates of the driveway. Sergei was recovering from an illness, and Zinaida was terrified. Unarmed, and without hesitation, Val ran to meet the intruders, ignoring the cries of family and servants begging him to return. Cheerfully he said to the crowd, "What can we do for you? My father is not well, but I will convey to him a message."

Taken aback, some in the front ranks took off their hats and explained that the Tsar had issued a new decree declaring that the land was to be divided among them.

Seeing a number of well-to-do peasants in the crowd, Val laughed and said, "If that is the case, then the order would also have applied to you, Ivan, Stephen, and Kraus. You, also, should give up your lands to those who have none."

They began to argue among themselves, and those peasants who owned land decided there was probably some error. It was possible, they decided, that the decree could have been concocted by Revolutionary students. They retreated.

Val was hailed as a hero by his family. His father put an arm about his shoulders. "You must study law, Valodia; you have all the potential for a fine barrister. You wait and see, you will one day be a deputy to the Duma."

"You be a deputy, Father; I want to be a singer."

Chapter 12

New Beginnings

The agrarian revolution was crushed by the government, and Russia settled down with its Duma into a sham democracy. The election brought in an overwhelming majority of liberals. Valodia was very disappointed that his father was not elected deputy to the Duma; he was defeated by a coalition of landowners against him.

Gregory Rasputin, a sensuous, greasy-haired, unkempt monk, was appearing in St. Petersburg society and had been introduced to the Tsar and Tsaritza.

Peter Stolypin, Natalia's cousin and son of Val's godfather, had become Governor of Saratov province where some of the most violent uprisings in Russia took place. He would often walk alone into the villages and talk the insurgents into laying down their arms. He believed strongly in land reform, but terrorism had to be eliminated first. Tsar Nicholas was impressed with Peter's success.

Natalia and Prince Kochubay were quietly married and remained frequent visitors of the Rosing household. Natalia and Aunt Matilda bought a villa in Montreux so they could spend a part of every winter there.

Liuba was also married that spring, and Val now became the sole recipient of his parents' affection, allowing him more freedom and a greater allowance. When he was not at the skating rink or playing bridge, he lived and breathed opera and dreamed of singing *Mephisto*.

Well, why dream? For five dollars, he could engage a hall at a small club and give a concert! He would include the Mephisto aria. Great idea! He engaged the hall, announced the concert, and offered the tickets for sale. There was only one problem — no one bought the tickets. Well, he had committed himself, so the next best thing was to invite some of the fellows and have them bring their sisters. Piotre would loan him the money — at 100 percent interest.

He made the round of voice teachers, hoping their interest would inspire his parents to finance a vocal career. After each audition, he would say, "Well, I guess I will wait until my voice is more mature."

With the exception of the great throat specialist Avaeff, who claimed his vocal cords were those of a baritone, the teachers all proclaimed him to be a tenor. He eventually became a tenor with a baritone quality which would later exonerate him when he purloined songs from bass and baritone repertoires.

One day Val came home from school to have the door opened by a new maid. Aunt Matilda said, "Your mother and Amalia had a quarrel."

"What about?" Val asked.

"Never mind; she has been replaced."

"She didn't even say good-bye."

"Your mother told her good-bye."

His mother's face told him nothing, and he dared not reveal the extent of his interest. Apparently the relationship between Amalia and himself had been discovered. But how? And had his mother also seen to it that she left no message and no hint of her whereabouts? At night he waited for his door to open quietly, bringing him whispered syllables, teasing hands, softness and warmth. But he never saw Amalia again.

* * * * *

Soon it was time for final exams, to be followed by a night of festivities — smoking, drinking, gambling, and women. It was time to emerge into manhood, time to enter the university of a military school. Val struck a hard bargain with his father. If he could study voice, he would agree to take up the study of law. He chose the most expensive voice teacher, Tartakoff, a famous baritone of the Imperial Opera Company.

But first, the exams. His teacher of French and German apparently assumed he spoke German as fluently as French. After all, he had a Baltic-German grandmother, and there was no need to have him showing off in class. So his German was ignored.

While he was worrying about German, the exam in Religion approached, and his knowledge of theology was skimpy. The Bible had to be read in archaic Russian, and certainly that had been a bore. Add to that the fact that the examiner turned out to be the priest from his own church; maybe he had perceived an ulterior motive in those multiple communions. The first question came: "Explain the word 'Providence.'"

How could he be stumped on that word? He was completely befuddled. The priest was impatient. Well, the word *did* sound similar to "province," so he would make a stab at it. "It's a sort of heavenly region."

The priest's face registered spiritual rape, then his hands made a gesture and he roared, "Go away!"

If Val failed another subject, he would have to remain an extra year in gymnasium. He would, of course, fail German! He would never get to wear those beautiful university uniforms that had been ordered. He headed for what felt like his execution and trembled as he waited to be called to the examination table.

Just as his name was called, his teacher, having full confidence in Val's knowledge of *der Deutsche*, responded to the urge of nature and left the examination table. He gestured good luck to Val and proceeded to the lavatory. This left only the second examiner at the table, a very old gentleman who was hard of hearing. A stroke of genius seized Val; he began to sneeze and cough violently and hoarsely, uttering probably the only German words he knew: *"Ich habe eine grosse kalt."* That magnificent phrase ended in a new spasm of coughing; and the old teacher, terrified of the unleashed germs, looked up Val's credits, duplicated them and said, "Get out."

It was a miracle! He had passed the gymnasium. He celebrated by purchasing the most expensive opera ticket available.

Chapter 13

Beau Brummel

Val liked what he saw in the mirror. The new university uniform was beautifully tailored from excellent fabric. The uniform could have varying degrees of elegance, depending upon a family's ability to purchase a better fabric and secure a more expensive tailor. He missed Amalia's approving eye.

Since that first summer in Djulinka, the sons and daughters of the village priest had been Val's companions. They had played together, and now they partied and danced together. The new uniform seemed to signal adulthood, and returning from a party one summer night in 1907, Lenotchka, one of the priest's daughters, declared to Val that she loved him. Surprised and flattered, he responded by declaring his long-concealed and eternal love for her, and they sealed it with a kiss. After that, he saw her every night until his return to St. Petersburg. They would meet by the river or in the garden among the lilac bushes, but Val resisted temptation, for he could not take advantage of his childhood friend unless he fully intended to marry her.

He returned to St. Petersburg that autumn, where a family friend soon arranged for him to sing for the great Battistini! Val could feel wings sprouting as he burst from his enveloping cocoon. This would settle the question of his future and convince his parents that he was to have a great career as a singer.

He was only seven when he had first heard Battistini. In the ensuing years, he had heard him as Tonio, Rigoletto, Valentine, and Germont, and would hear one of his final recitals at the age of sixty-six which, in Val's words, "was the miracle of a great technician. His voice sounded as young, fresh, and pliable as if he were in his youth. He sang with the style and finesse of a great vocal aristocrat which he was in life and on the stage . . . (wonderful for Germont — not so good for Tonio the clown, and Rigoletto the court jester)."

Val's sisters fussed over him excitedly. "I wonder if he will say you are a tenor or a baritone?" one asked. "Imagine singing for Battistini himself! I wonder if he would teach you if he lived in St. Petersburg?"

Shaved, groomed, perfumed, and clothed in a magenta velvet dressing gown, the great baritone welcomed the influential friend and Val and served them morning coffee. There was conversation between the two men that was difficult to recall afterwards, for Val was silently staging his performance and tranquilizing his fluttering heartbeat. Battistini displayed a diamond-studded gold watch with a double eagle on the face, given to him by the Grand Duke Constantine, a great lover of art in the Royal Family. Finally, the conversation seemed to settle down enough for the two men to remember why they were meeting, and Battistini turned to Val, "Well now, let's hear this young fellow."

While his friend walked to the piano and opened the music, Val cleared his throat and prayed he would do justice to this once-in-a-lifetime opportunity. He sang the aria he had selected, and when he had finished, he looked to Battistini and saw a smile on his face. For an exhilarating moment he tasted success and waited for the accolades due him.

"Yes, yes . . . well, thank you very much. That's very nice. A good instrument you have there, my boy." Battistini then turned to the accompanist, thanked him also, and then apologized, "I'm afraid you will have to forgive me, but I have an invitation to lunch at the Ducal palace and must be on my way."

Was that all? Was he going to say nothing more? Were they being dismissed? The vitality drained from Val, leaving him hollow. How could he go home? What would he tell his family?

Well, he did go home, and he did what he had to do. He invented a mass of answers to disguise his bitter disappointment.

Val was in love with the reigning queen of the opera, the *lyrico spinto* Rugnesbova and wrote her a love letter. But he received no answer. He was also in love with her rival, the *lyrico coloratura* Lipkowska, who was an exquisite blonde. He moaned for her in the solitude of his room, but his love for her was so poetical that he would never have dared to write to her.

But alas, life must go on, and at the university it was lunging ahead. The universities reflected all that was happening in government, and it was the duty of every student to register in one of the political parties. In Val's university, which had been built by and had served the administration of Peter the Great, this was especially true. He hastened to enroll in the liberal party, that of the Constitutional Democrats, and had the distinction of being appointed one of the deputies.

By this time, Peter Stolypin had been appointed Prime Minister, and Tsar Nicholas wrote to his own mother, "I cannot tell you how much I have come to like and respect this man." Stolypin immediately set up tribunals to sentence terrorists to death. Then he put his land reform program into effect, making it possible for peasants to own their land outright instead of sharing it on a communal basis.

Only a month after taking office, Stolypin was targeted for assassination. A bomb exploded at his country home outside of St. Petersburg, tearing away a wall, killing 32 servants and visitors, injuring his small son, and permanently maiming his daughter who was Natalia's namesake. A day and a half later, Stolypin resumed the Ministers' Council with complete calm and self-control.

Political activities monopolized the scene for Val. There were also hours spent perfecting his skills at the skating rink. And, of course, there were nightly parties following the opera or theatre, which lasted until 5:00 or 6:00 a.m. One time a bridge party began at 5:00 a.m. and ran until nine the following evening. Food was served to the players, so they needed to stop only to answer nature's demands. Obviously, there was no time to attend school lectures.

By December, this heavy routine was wearing on Val's health. After a severe attack of the flu, his parents decided to take him along to Montreux, Switzerland, where Sergei had business to discuss with Natalia. Natalia and Aunt Matilda had acquired their villa, and it was decided that Val would stay on with them for a rest after his parents returned to Russia. Meanwhile, he stayed with his parents in the hotel by the lake.

Val was surprised, in spite of the luxuries to which he was accustomed in Russia, to realize that his homeland seemed almost primitive in comparison to Switzerland, where childhood memories lurked around every corner.

On their second evening, a retired British general invited Val to be a fourth at bridge. The players were mediocre, and he was bored until there appeared in the doorway a young girl of such loveliness that he caught his breath. To a youth accustomed to the heavy, sculptured faces of Russian women, her delicately chiseled Grecian features gave her the appearance of a goddess. She was introduced as Marie, daughter of one of the players, Mrs. Falle. Aware of her fascination with his uniform, Val expanded his chest and introduced himself as an officer of the Russian guard.

When Marie left for the ballroom, the card game lost all interest for him. If the others played badly, he played worse. He was glad to lose his rubles in order to end the miserable game. Hurrying to the ballroom, he found Marie already besieged with partners. Before the evening was over, he learned that she was twenty-three. But when he discovered that she played the piano and violin and sang, his hopes ballooned in spite of the fact that he was not yet eighteen and still dependent upon his father.

In the days that followed, Val did everything that a Russian in love could do. He rented a boat, arranged a concert, planned a toboggan party and a masquerade. His parents had returned to Russia, and Natalia and Aunt Matilda saw little of him.

One evening Marie invited him to join her and her mother, Count Prashman, and a French couple from Paris, for a séance in her mother's room after dinner. "Do you believe in Spiritualism?" asked Marie.

Val considered himself a militant atheist, so he laughed and said that he, fortunately, did not believe in God or the existence of spirits, but he was anxious to accept the invitation, for he did not want to miss an opportunity to be with Marie.

When he joined them that evening, they invited him to sit with them at the table. Val begged off, offering to sit outside the circle and record whatever was dictated to him as the table tapped out its messages. All conversation was in French — his *premiere langue* — the only language he had spoken in his early childhood. The lights were lowered, and the five joined hands, creating a so-called "magnetic circle." They concentrated silently and solemnly with bowed heads, looking, Val thought, like children playing a serious game. Suddenly the table gave a shiver, and they all sat up. Mrs. Falle asked, "Are you a good spirit? If you are, tell us who you are, and if you are not, go away."

The table tapped once (one meaning "yes;" two taps meant "no") and then spelled out a name. This was accomplished by Mrs. Falle saying the alphabet as the table tapped. It stopped tapping at the letter it wanted selected. It was a long process which Val thought amusing. But he didn't mind, since he was happy just to be in the same room with Marie. He wrote down the letters dictated to him.

The first spirit identified itself as an old friend of the Falle family, Marie's godfather. His table taps were gentle, and they conversed tenderly as he gave them some personal advice and then left. The table became immobile. Then it became agitated again, increasing its violence until it was beating out letters with tremendous force. Val naturally suspected that either the Frenchman or Count Prashman was using his strength to move the table, but he was confused by their equally serious interest in the subject. This spirit gave his name as Danton, the great orator of the French Revolution.

That jolted Val out of his complacency. He emitted loudly, "Oh really, that is too much!"

The Frenchman turned on him with a "*Taisez-vous!*"

But Val was persistent and kept Danton waiting while he sarcastically asked, "Why would this famous tragic Revolutionary come to such an unrevolutionary group of people as are at this table?"

Rather heatedly, the Frenchman responded, "Because he is one of my ancestors in whom I take great pride. And now, will you kindly remain silent?"

Marie's sweet voice pleaded, "Don't interrupt, please."

Val complied, and the conversation between the group and Danton took an interesting turn. Prashman asked how he had felt when guillotined.

"I deserved it and accepted it with dignity," the spirit replied. It was Desmoulins who died crying like a woman."

"Why did you deserve it?" asked Prashman.

"I was responsible for the terrible September Massacre and the execution of the King and Queen; I could have saved them all, and I should have, but it was too late." The table gave one huge plunge that almost overturned it and then became motionless again.

Val thought the Frenchman had staged that little episode quite brilliantly, yet he evidenced such genuine elation that he obviously believed it. Well, maybe Prashman was responsible, for it certainly took real strength to move such a heavy table.

Then a new spirit came and began some kind of dribble that no one could understand. The letters that were dictated were: TISLISHKOMCHOR-OSHAYADUSHASHTOBIBITATHEISTOMVERNISKBOGY. The message was undecipherable. Eventually growing bored, all except Val turned to other conversation. Then, with a flash of excitement, he realized the message was in Russian, and he was the only one who knew that language. Since his presence had not been anticipated, he knew there could be no chicanery. He broke the letters into words as follows: *Ti slishkom choroshaya dusha shto bi bit atheistom vernis k Bogy*. In Russian it read: "You're much too good a soul to be an atheist return to God."

Val was shaken by the experience. He tried unsuccessfully to reason it away, and eventually decided to give God the benefit of the doubt and return to His fold.

In the meantime, he took courage and declared his love to Marie. Before acknowledging her own feelings, she asked, "What will your parents say?"

He concealed his embarrassment. In Russia a declaration of love did not mean a proposal of marriage; apparently in England it did. He stammered, "I'm sure they will be delighted." Well then, he was engaged while in his first year at university, without ever having earned a penny in his life, with full confidence in his parents' disapproval, but full of youth and an abundance of courage.

He disclosed nothing of his engagement to Natalia and Aunt Matilda, but continued living his days of freedom and happiness. Time and money, however, were running out, and examinations, for which he was once again totally unprepared, were approaching. It was essential to return to St. Petersburg. With tears and eternal vows, he and Marie parted. Even his first sight of Paris, which he had so anticipated, meant nothing to him. Every turn of the wheels decimated him, but as he approached St. Petersburg, his courage and determination revived.

The family was delighted with his return and welcomed him with a sumptuous breakfast, since his train arrived at 8:00 a.m. After warm greetings, he dropped his bombshell. His parents were at first vastly amused and thought he was joking. But he announced his intention to leave for London, where Marie lived, immediately after exams.

Sergei was the first to realize that he was serious. "And where," he inquired, "are you obtaining the finances to support a marriage?"

Val calmly answered, "You have given my two sisters a large dowry; I think I am entitled to expect the same."

His father smiled benevolently and said, "I have no intention of so endowing you; I do not even intend to give you funds to get back to London."

"I will find them somehow."

Zinaida was very upset over his being in love with an English girl. "The English are false and treacherous," she warned. "In time, you will get over it, Valodia."

Only Prince Kochubay was sympathetic and secretly expressed his best wishes, but he did not dare offer help.

Exams were a disaster. Val failed in practically everything except international and criminal law. But he knew he could always take the exams over again, so he took care of priorities and set out to acquire some money. The only thing he knew how to do was gamble, so he went to a gambling club. There he lost what little money he had, but he owned a gold watch, gold links, and a few other such valuables that he pawned the next day. He was invited to a party to play macao, a gambling game similar to baccarat. Blessed by phenomenal luck, he cleaned everyone out, winning an amount at that time comparable to $2,000.

It was daylight when he arrived home, and he immediately started packing. He needed only to renew his passport, get university permission, and book a sleeper, all of which would take him two days. So at breakfast he announced that in two days he would be leaving for London.

His parents' placating smiles froze when Val spread his money on the table. In their wisdom they decided to withdraw their opposition and give him additional help. A trip to England would be a good education for him, they decided, and it might cure him of the whole affair.

Chapter 14

Out to Conquer on All Fronts

The great metropolis of London dwarfed Russia's provincial cities. There were no taxis, as in Paris, but she was unique with her thousands of hansoms, two-wheeled covered carriages pulled by a horse. Near the great Crystal Palace, the vast iron and glass structure built for the first International Exhibition in 1851, Marie lived with her parents.

Val was welcomed warmly into their home, but before he was introduced to their friends as Marie's fiancé, her mother said, "There is something we must discuss."

Val's heart sank. Were they going to ask him to disclose his financial status?

Mrs. Falle began, "We know that you and Marie are very much in love, but I am sure you will understand that we also love her and wish to do everything in our power to insure her future happiness."

He swallowed hard and waited.

"You have a beautiful voice, and we know you are intent upon a musical career."

Oh, God, surely he wasn't going to have to fight that battle all over again.

Marie's father explained, "It isn't that we are asking you to give up a musical career, only to avoid the theatrical stigma — well, you know, the operatic stage."

Val was stunned. "But there are great singers on the operatic stage!"

"Yes, but it really compromises the dignity of the singing profession."

Val felt crushed. How could he surrender his desire for the stage? It was an obsession with him. Were they testing his love for Marie?

He answered slowly, "Since I can remember, I have wanted an operatic career. But I want Marie more than anything else in the world. I would sacrifice anything rather than give her up." After all, it was not as though he had to tear up a contract. So Val promised to limit his ambitions to the concert stage and was then introduced to family friends as Marie's fiancé.

The weeks flew by, and additional funds had to be sent from Russia, for Val spent lavishly entertaining Marie and her family. But his parents were mute on the question of marriage, and planning a marriage became an awkward subject. Eventual bankruptcy made a trip home essential. Three months had elapsed when Val and Marie tearfully separated, Val promising to return as soon as he could settle things with his parents.

He went by boat to St. Petersburg and then to Djulinka. His meeting with Lenotchka was a little awkward, but on the whole she took it very well. It was her mother who was unforgiving. His parents were versatile in their ploys to divert him — parties, theatricals, a trip to Uman. But not until they suggested he give a first concert in the neighboring town of Cherson did they capture him. Large posters were printed and hung on every station. He was eager to sing and thrilled at seeing his name in print.

His voice was big, but his technical knowledge small. Any inadequacies, however, were covered with enthusiasm, and his success that night made him sure of two things — his future would at least be that of a Caruso, and he could now marry Marie because a financially successful career was surely guaranteed.

After his concert, Val skied the slopes of success. His parents were not blind to his vocal endowment and were generous with their praise. His father was ready to make a deal.

"Son, it is time for you to take an uncluttered view of the future. We will support your efforts, and we will be proud and happy parents if you are fortunate enough to have a future in music. But to at least ensure a future, we are asking you to return to St. Petersburg to take the exams you failed in the spring. There you can continue your vocal instruction *and* the study of law."

Well, he had promised to ensure Marie's happiness; now he must ensure his father's confidence. Obviously, there was only one way to go.

Sergei, believing the romantic crush had resolved itself, made a giant mistake. He entrusted Val with enough money to cover tuition, rent for an apartment, upkeep for three months, and fare to St. Petersburg.

Val sincerely battled temptation, but on his arrival in St. Petersburg, he found that a few cholera cases had spread to an epidemic, with 500 people dying each day. If he got cholera, he would never see Marie again. There was only one thing to do; he wrote a melodramatic letter to his sister who was in the city (asking her to explain to his parents) and fled. He was no longer afraid of

Left, Vladimir Rosing (at nineteen) and his family, 1909. Fourth from the left is his English bride.

the future. Hadn't he established himself as a professional singer?

Val was enthusiastically received by Marie and her parents. Sergei and Zinaida sighed and withdrew their objection to the marriage. He was allowed to keep the money with which he had absconded, and a comfortable living allowance for the future was granted to him. His sister and her husband came to represent the family at the wedding, and in a little Russian church in Welbeck Street, Val was married to Marie on November 3, 1909, two months before he turned twenty.

In London, Val studied with Sir George Power, pupil of the great Lamperti. Sir George praised and encouraged him, and Marie, accompanying him, was embarrassed to realize the mistake she and her parents had made. She released Val from the promise never to sing in opera.

Shortly after their wedding, Val took Marie to Russia. After three days and nights of travel, they were greeted at the station by his family and escorted home through four feet of snow in a four-horse sleigh. Marie easily captured St. Petersburg society with her beauty, delicacy of manner, and musical talents. Reception followed reception, for it was a fashionable novelty to have an English lady as a guest of honor.

Early the following year, they returned to London for the birth of their son, Valerian. But Marie was intoxicated with Russia. Not only did she and Val plan to make it their home, but she also persuaded her parents to return with them and reside in Padolia on one of the Rosing estates. Valerian captured the hearts of all, and Val sprouted from adolescence into fatherhood.

That winter Val was engaged to sing at one of Mrs. Rubenstein's "at homes." She was a wealthy aristocrat who liked to introduce rising artists to St. Petersburg society. The same evening, she presented a little boy, a violinist of nine with curly hair and large eyes who opened the concert. Val was amazed at the depth of his tone, the perfection of his technique, and the abandonment of his temperament. His name was Jascha Heifetz, and he was making his first public appearance in St. Petersburg.

Val continued his university studies, took his exams, and fenced politically with Comrade Abram, whose real name was Krylenko, and who was destined to become Commander-in-Chief of the Armed Forces under Lenin and the Chief Prosecutor for Stalin's purges — until he himself was purged.

Abram, in the past, had badgered Val about his family's landowner status. "I hear you have three hundred working horses and another thirty just for yourselves," he once said. "Think what that would mean to the peasants who have no working horses at all."

As Val entered the council room for the first time after his return, Abram led his Communist friends in the singing of the wedding march. Then he needled, "Now you will have two women — your mother and your wife — to look after your Elegance, in addition to all of the peasants who support you by the sweat of their brows."

Val shot back, "I will earn my own living by singing! But if what you say is true, then I prefer to live by people's sweat than by their blood! You Bolsheviks are financed by blood money. You have killed hundreds of innocent people!"

The Liberals gave him an ovation, but the shocked Bolsheviks threw aside their copybooks and rushed at him. He was quickly surrounded by his own party, and the Bolshevik section had to retreat in view of the superior forces of the Liberals.

* * * * *

Having passed his exams, Val was more absorbed now with his artistic life. To his repertoire acquired from the Gramophone records plus the arias from *Pagliacci*, *Martha*, and *Rigoletto*, he added the songs of Debussy and Duparc and the arias of Tchaikowsky and Borodin. With Marie accompanying him, he entertained guests and was invited to sing at parties and charity concerts. He began to study seriously with Maria Slavina, the great mezzo-soprano of the Imperial Opera House and Cumersinger of the Tsar. Through her position, she was able to obtain for him a private audition at the Imperial Opera House.

Everything seemed to be happening at once. Pavlovsk, a summer place near St. Petersburg, was the setting for Russia's national roller-skating competition. Val was very proud of his roller-skating expertise. He was able to do special figure skating and to perform on the two wheels of one skate — skilled accomplishments which always brought applause. He was in the finals, and the hour of his triumph was approaching. And then it happened: He was the roller-skating champion of all Russia. At the age of twenty-one, it seemed he would fulfill the meaning of "Vladimir" — to own the world. Well, almost.

His scheduled audition for the Imperial Opera House was the following day. An audition number had been chosen which would best portray his beautiful vocal quality and casual delivery of high Cs. Alas, the skating rink which had claimed countless hours to perfect his breathtaking skills had also claimed his voice. The vocal cords emitted a sound like spinning cotton. He stood in the center of that sacred stage where Chaliapin, Battistini, and Titta Ruffo had stood, diminished and humiliated as his high Cs splintered like glass. A young conductor, Albert Coates, who had just made a brilliant debut of his own, accompanied the *Faust* aria. "Better one next time," he remarked in a loud voice, and Val plunged from recent glory to degradation. He was further humiliated the next day to read in the *New Times* that the tenor Rosing had sung an audition and had made no impression whatsoever. Slavina felt disgraced and promptly discharged him as her *protégé*.

* * * * *

That September in the Kiev Opera House, the Tsar, together with Peter Stolypin, watched Rimsky-Korsakov's opera *Tsar Sultan*. The pressure of Stolypin's work had wearied him and affected his health. He had argued heatedly for his own resignation. No such precedent had been set; an appointee of the Tsar stayed in office until dismissed by the Tsar. And Nicholas knew that the government had made progress under this Prime Minister. Unwittingly, Stolypin had made an enemy of the Empress Alexandra by banning from St. Petersburg the uncouth peasant monk who reveled in seducing wealthy socialites and titled women. Alexandra had accepted the monk as her mentor and as the healer of her son who was afflicted with hemophilia. She never forgave Stolypin for his condemning of Rasputin, and Nicholas refused to override Stolypin's decree.

The day that the Tsar and Stolypin were in Kiev, Rasputin was there also, and he called out after Stolypin's carriage, "Death is after him!" That night at the opera, Stolypin left his seat during intermission and stood with his back to the stage. From his box, Nicholas heard two shots and saw Stolypin make the sign of the cross, then sink to a chair in his bloodstained uniform. A shocked Nicholas, at the risk of his own safety, refused to leave the city. Stolypin died five days later, the victim of a terrorist's bullet.

The progress made by the government under Stolypin now halted, and the Revolutionary movement began to revive. Rasputin became the subject of such public scandal that it dominated the political scene.

The Rosing household was rocked by the tragedy.

Chapter 15

The Sting of Success

Val soon found a new teacher named Madame Katjeva. Under her instruction, he began to develop an outstanding style and beautiful pianissimo. He possessed a voice of unusual range and color, and was called "the young Caruso." After six months, she presented him to the director of the Music Drama, a new opera house which was to open the following year as a rival to the Imperial Opera.

This time it was a brilliant audition, and it was repeated publicly a few days later. He signed his first contract and became the leading tenor of the Music Drama. He would debut as Lensky in *Eugene Onegin* followed by Walter in *Meistersinger*.

Cast in two operas, he rehearsed the entire day, and because he lived on the far side of town, he did not get home between rehearsals. Exhausted, nervous, and short-tempered, he decided to indulge himself with a new horse and carriage in order to commute to the opera house. This attracted a surge of females, which involved him in some rather innocent flirtations. But, innocent or not, Marie took a firm dislike of his actions, and after a few explosive rows, Val left their apartment and returned to the home of his parents.

One day a phone call came from Fred Gaisberg of the Gramophone Recording Company who was going from capital to capital recording the best artists of the time.

"Valodia," he asked, "would you like to record duets with Lydia Lipkowska?"

Lydia Lipkowska! Lipkowska was performing at the Imperial. She was the vocal goddess of his adolescent years. When he was a student in the gymnasium, he had called in a carriage to escort her to a charity concert, and she had hardly noticed his underdeveloped manly charm. A second time, when he sang with an opera chorus, she had graced the performance with her presence, and he had outdone himself, hoping she would ask, "Who is that talented young man in the chorus?"

"Valodia?" Gaisberg broke into his thoughts.

Val's heart stood still as he inquired which duets.

"'The Madrigal' from *Romeo* and the first act duet from *La Traviata*," Gaisberg responded.

Val said he knew them both and would be delighted. A few days later in the recording studio, he was standing next to Lipkowska, touching her hand, singing as an equal with her. As their voices blended together, all of the adoration he felt for her poured into his singing. He was still in love with her poetically.

She complimented him, "You have great feeling for your music."

He wanted to say, "No . . . no . . . it is for you!" But he remained tongue-tied. He knew he would use those tones again in all of his love scenes; they would be his Lipkowska tones.

Val's first recordings for *His Master's Voice* also included an aria from *La Tosca*. His friendship with Fred Gaisberg lasted for many years. And ten years later, when Val was thirty-two and had become a star in England and a rising one in the U.S., there was a reunion between Lipkowska and him in New York. His preparation for that appointment was very emotional. With a palpitating heart, he was ushered into her living room. As he kissed her hand, he realized that time had not stood still, and his adolescent love adjusted itself to reality. They reminisced about the old days, mutual artist friends, and the tragedy that had befallen Russia. Val was always grateful for the exquisite pleasure he had found in her singing and for the inspiration she had given to his own.

The Music Drama was organized by a great director, Lapitzky, who had gained support to create an opera company patterned after the Moscow Art Theatre. Unlike the Maryinsky (the people's opera) with its operatic greats, few rehearsals, and old-fashioned stereotypical form of acting, the Music Drama would rehearse for three months at half salary stressing modern dramatic acting, for a season's repertoire of three operas: *Eugene Onegin*, *Sadko*, and *Meistersinger*.

One night during a performance of *Eugene Onegin*, Val was inspired to incorporate something new. It was the scene in which he, Lensky, accused Olga of infidelity. Earlier, she had given him a flower for his lapel. He tore the flower from his lapel, threw it down dramatically, and crushed it with his foot. The contralto admired the bit of strategy, and Val thought it was a real stroke of genius. After the performance, he waited for high praise from Lapitzky. Sure enough, the stage director rushed backstage. But to Val's amazement, Lapitzky accosted him in rage. "You are a dilettante — absolutely irresponsible!"

Val was crushed by such insults. In his bewilderment he stammered, "But did you not think it was a good thing I did?"

Lapitzky snorted back, "It is not a question of whether it is good or bad; it is a question of principle. If every artist on the stage introduced his own new business, nothing would be left of the original production. It would disintegrate."

I wonder what Lapitzky's reaction would have been if he had met with the response Val, as director, would later receive from a baritone in a Chicago Lyric Opera production of *Lucia*. The Italian baritone responded to Val's stage direction with, "But, Maestro, how do I know where I will be on stage at that time?"

After Lapitzky's verbal thrashing, Val decided to leave the company where his individuality was not appreciated! The next day, he was presented with a renewal of his contract, assigning him the roles of Don Jose in *Carmen* and Herman in *The Queen of Spades* for the following season. He hastened to sign it.

His voice could not stand the strain of rehearsing the Wagnerian role of Walter. He began to push, and the famous Caruso-like top register was slipping. Instead of admiration, he was getting sympathy and advice. He resigned the role of Walter and sang only Lensky.

Meanwhile, the Rosing household was not diminishing in size. Vera's German baron turned out to be a tippler with a roving eye, so both she and Val were at home with their parents. And Marie's brother Bertie, who had been in India during the period of Val and Marie's marriage, came to stay with the Rosing family as well. Bertie was a wonderfully refined man, the essence of dignity, honesty, and kindness. He learned to speak Russian and acquired a very good position with an English business firm. Bertie and Vera instantly fell in love. And it was Bertie who patched together Val and Marie's marriage. At the end of the opera season, he persuaded them to meet at the station, be reunited, and go together to Switzerland.

A few weeks before leaving for Switzerland, Val became Russia's first bridge editor, publishing his column in St. Petersburg's largest newspaper, the *Evening News*, under the name of Gnisor (Rosing spelled in reverse). The assignment compensated Val for his disappointment at the Music Drama. It would be a little awkward to run the column from Switzerland, so he appointed Liuba's husband as his assistant.

It was heartwarming to be back in Switzerland. Val gave two concerts; one was at the Montreux Kursal with a young conductor, Ernest Ansermet. Val was supposed to be preparing his roles for the fall opera season in St. Petersburg, but in spite of successful concerts, his voice had not really recovered from the *Meistersinger* rehearsals. He went to Dr. Mermot in Lausanne for throat treatment, but it didn't seem to help. Finally, he canceled his contract with the Music Drama and returned with Marie and little Valerian to the home Marie's parents maintained in London, in order to resume his study with Sir George Power.

At Drury Lane Theatre, Chaliapin was performing a season of Russian opera for Sir Thomas Beecham, and Val and Marie attended a performance. The Russian chorus was angry at the bass for his miserly treatment of them, since Sir Thomas was paying him 250 pounds per performance. His eccentric penny-pinching defied explanation. The chorus, armed with scythes, had plotted to attack him during a revolutionary scene. When Val, who was seated in the first row, saw what was happening, he leaped over the orchestra pit, onto the stage, and stood in front of Chaliapin. The singers dropped their scythes, the curtain fell, and the performance ended.

Under Sir George's tutelage, Val's voice returned, and Amy Woodford Finden, whose songs Val sang, was so impressed that she arranged for him to meet Nellie Melba who was looking for a tenor to tour Australia with her.

Melba was the queen of the operatic world and the most illustrious star he had met. She was so idolized that on several occasions her fans unharnessed the horses of her carriage and pushed it by hand.

Val expected to see an ethereal beauty *à la* Isadora Duncan; instead he saw a might-have-been beauty on whom time had left its mark. But it was Melba, and in his exhilaration, he sang as he had rarely sung before. As he finished the aria from *Bohême*, Melba rushed to the phone and called the great English impresario, Lionel Powell, asking him to come immediately to the Claridge's Hotel and hear this tenor sing.

Powell came, listened, and offered Val a London debut on May 13 at Albert Hall, the great concert hall which seated 10,000 people. It didn't matter that he was not offered a fee; to be so introduced was to become an instant celebrity. He was to be presented in joint recital with Mischa Elman, the violinist who had just returned from a highly successful tour in America.

The week preceding the concert, Val became ill with the flu, was miserable beyond words, and was ordered to bed by the doctor. Inhaling machines were installed, electric massages were instituted, pine and eucalyptus sprays were used, and special foods were prepared. Val was indignant with God for allowing this to happen. Was this just reward for his return to the faith? He argued the point. Maybe God had not gotten the message. Well, he demanded the return of his voice! He did not get instant feedback, but by Saturday morning when Val was taken, as though to his execution, to the terrifyingly large hall to try his voice, the Almighty seemed to capitulate. After the first few notes, Val found his balance and sang very well.

On Sunday afternoon, he arrived at Albert Hall clad in his best Prince Albert coat. His presence was ignored by Elman until Val's singing of the *Tosca* aria which evoked excessive applause from the audience. Val took three bows while his accompanist searched for the encore music. Eventually, it was discovered under a chair where Papa Elman, taking a dim view of any competition for his son, had concealed it. Val's father-in-law (also a crafty individual) was backstage and resolved the hide-and-seek game in time for Val's crippled generosity to respond with an encore.

A few weeks later, Val was engaged by Melba to share a concert at Tunbridge Wells. He was not in good voice, and the handsome tenor Cicolini was engaged to join her on the Australian tour. But Val's success on the concert stage led to many "at home" engagements, and he was offered a tour of Switzerland and the south of Russia for the following season.

Chapter 16

Whom the Gods Wish to Destroy They First Make Mad

Wimbledon and its galaxy of international tennis stars occupied London during May, June, and the first week of July. Then society dispersed, nobility retired to ancestral homes and castles until the hunting season was over, and all Londoners, except the very poor, crowded the beaches and watering places.

Fortunately, it was a recess from concertizing. On the verge of attaining a spectacular career, Val's voice again seemed to have deserted him. Terrified, he began to lose health, confidence, concentration, and memory. He had tried doctors in Russia, London, Paris, and Switzerland. He took Marie and the baby to a hotel in Lausanne to try the invigorating air. Nothing helped. After a game of bridge where he, the expert, had trumped his own trick, he was ready for suicide.

Sitting on the balcony, he absorbed the emerald green of Lake Geneva and the towering Alps which encircled it. The peace and beauty of nature seemed to accentuate his inner despair.

An American visitor to the hotel asked why he was so dejected, and when he related his woes, she said, "You should see Dr. Vittoz, the great Swiss brain specialist."

"Brain specialist!" Val exploded. "There's nothing wrong with my brain! I'm a bridge editor, chess player, horseman, roller-skating champion of Russia — I even dabble in politics."

"Nevertheless," the American persisted, "Dr. Vittoz performs miracles that can change one's entire living process."

The temptation haunted him. What did he have to lose? He made the appointment and entered the doctor's office with a sizable chip on his shoulder. He had respect for general doctors, specialists, and surgeons, but a complete disdain for anything bordering on the psychological. He was prepared for the pomposity and superficiality that he assumed awaited him.

The thin little man to whom he was introduced took Val off guard. He was surprised to find himself exposing his wounds. The little man had hardly spoken, yet Val sensed a warmth of understanding.

When he spilled it all out, Dr. Vittoz said quietly, "Your problem is shared by most people to some degree or another. If you have determination and patience, you can conquer it, and you will be infinitely better off for having gone through these two unhappy years of your life. You can look upon them as the raw material of change.

"The answer is within yourself," he went on. "The moment you step outside yourself to seek the answer, you separate yourself from it. It is the Consciousness within you which is your unlimited power, energy, and success. You must recognize it, tune into it, and claim your inheritance."

This was a brain specialist?

Dr. Vittoz continued, "The body is a great and wonderful instrument, but *you* are not to be confused with your physical body. *You* are its master, and you can dictate and transmit orders; you can improve, destroy, enslave, dominate, or develop your human self."

Val felt a door opening. Was there really hope? Could he make a comeback? He recognized in this man a sincere and caring individual. But was there something more — what was it? Did it have religious overtones? Well, whatever it was, he felt it reaching for him.

Dr. Vittoz went on to describe what he called "the two working centers of the brain:" the conscious, or objective, and the unconscious, or subjective. "The subjective brain," he said, "is the source of ideas and sensations, and the objective brain focuses them. A man in a normal state of health keeps a balance between the 'two brains.' And this control depends upon three things: One must be conscious of what he does and thinks, he must learn to concentrate on each act and idea, and then he must learn to project and control his actions and thoughts by proper use of the will. A brain in control is *active*, but an uncontrolled brain is *passive*. A passive brain can be semiconscious and tired, wandering, over-excited, confused, worried, depressed, or greatly distressed."

He spoke of relaxation, of developing order and cleanliness in the mind, of eliminating unnecessary and unpleasant thoughts, and of controlling the five senses. He gave Val some exercises in concentration. "When the brain is concentrated on something definite, it will become less and less troubled," he said. And he described the physiological effects of concentration. "You can influence the vaso-motor nerves, changing sensations of numbness or cold; you can change your heartbeat, regulate breathing, cure stomach spasms. You simply concentrate on that part of the body you wish to influence."

Dr. Vittoz leaned closer and spoke more slowly. "The most important part of this training is exercising the will. You must first define your wish. It must be in the realm of possibility, and it must be honest and genuine. It is a lack of honesty in ourselves which accounts for most failures. We must resolve to do something and accomplish it in a fixed time. A patient with passive, uncontrolled ideas is inclined to weigh considerations too carefully when confronted with alternatives. He takes refuge behind difficulties, and loses sight of principal reason, attaching too much importance to secondary considerations which pervert his judgment. He should be taught to decide quickly as soon as an idea is clearly defined. This quickens mental recovery.

"Only you can rid yourself of your suffering," Dr. Vittoz concluded. "The universe is yours — you need but to accept it." He placed a book in Val's hands. The title of the book was: *Traitment des Psychonévroses par la Rééducation du Controle Cérébrale* (Treatment of Psychoneurosis by the Reeducation of Brain Control). The author, Dr. Roger Vittoz.

In Val's own words: "It is difficult to believe that one hour so completely changed my life. When I left Dr. Vittoz's office, I was a different person. I walked with firm, strong steps, and energy began to flow throughout my body. Since then, I have never stopped building, developing, and improving myself, my thought, and my art. The success I have had as a singer, director, and producer, I owe to him, and if I have helped others to succeed in life, they can thank him, too."

Val knew he still needed a good voice teacher to get him back on the track vocally, but he was certain now of his future. He would take command of his life and would not tolerate less than total cooperation from his human self.

Dr. Vittoz had said, "The universe is yours." Well, that is what *Vladimir* meant: to own the world. When he walked out of the doctor's office that day, he removed his dark glasses and carried a new set of tools.

Chapter 17

Turning Point

Val and Marie soon left for St. Gallen where Val was to sing a concert and perform in *Faust* — a production in which Marie was to make her debut as Marguerite. The engagement came through a wealthy St. Gallen lace manufacturer — or rather through his two daughters who had heard Val in Montreux the previous season and who had brought pressure, through their father, on the director of the opera house. Val had insisted that Marie be included, and they were to be the houseguests of the manufacturer's family.

They found themselves in an enormous mansion with long corridors and game rooms of various kinds. It was a house where one could easily lose himself. Val was surprised to find that he and Marie were given separate rooms that were not even connected.

No sooner had he changed his clothes than there was a knock, and in came the eldest daughter to see if he wanted anything. Apparently *she* did, but Val did not want to be disloyal to Marie, so he terminated the amorous encounter with a few kisses which, he rationalized, a gentleman could not deny a very attractive and passionate lady.

She left, and he was on his way to join Marie when out of one of the doors to a billiard room popped the younger daughter, cute as could be. She took him by the hand and said, "I am so glad that at last you are here; you don't know how long I have waited for this moment." With that, she led him into the billiard room, closed the door, sent the billiard balls scurrying from the table, and threw her arms about him. He was terrified that someone might enter and begged her to be prudent, but she was a little ball of fire. Val's vanity was flattered as the girls vied with each other to corner him, but he restrained his ardor and was almost relieved when it was time to return to Montreux, where he belatedly wondered if he should have taken advantage of the opportunities.

The concert was a great success. However, the production of *Faust*, for which he had acquired beautiful costumes while in London, could have been better. He was nervous for Marie who was a fine dramatic artist, and who looked the reincarnation of Marguerite, but whose voice could not carry over the orchestra. They mutually agreed that her operatic career should end with the same performance which had initiated it.

There were concerts in Montreux and Lausanne, and then, with six weeks to go before the tour of South Russia, they went to Paris so that Val could study with the great tenor and artist, Jean de Reszke. De Reszke charged 100 francs a lesson, an exorbitant price for four of the dozen lessons that were to render magic for him.

Val and Marie registered at the Hotel Majestic. The famous de Reszke occupied a palace in the Rue de la Faisaderier which contained a small theatre where he presented his talented pupils. There Val met him, already portly, but still very handsome, cultured, and elegant. He had retired at the height of his sensational success on the operatic stage, at a time when the drawing power of all tenors was surpassed by Caruso, to take up a teaching career. He had brought to the stage great singing and beauty of movement. The latter was the same semaphoric style of the time, but at least it was done with plastic beauty and finesse.

De Reszke put Val at ease. "Your voice reminds me of my own in my early career," he said. "Until the age of thirty-four, I sang as a baritone." He called to his brother Edouard, the great basso, "Listen to this passage. Doesn't it sound like my own voice?"

After Jean's own first performance, which was a fiasco, he had gone to Giovanni Sbriglia, undoubtedly the greatest vocal teacher in the second half of the nineteenth century, who in six months had transformed him from baritone to tenor. He produced singers such as Nordica, Lasalle, the three de Reszkes — Jean, Edouard, and Josephine — and the French bass Plançon whom Val would eventually hear at the Metropolitan.

Hearing Jean and Val from the next room, Marie could sometimes not differentiate between their voices, particularly in the middle range. Sometimes Jean would coax his wife, "Show Vladimir how to sing an open ahhh." To Val: "She can show you better than I." Each time Val went for the high notes, Jean would say, "*Accrochez le plafond!*" Anchor it to the ceiling!

After four lessons, Val presented his second 400 francs, but Jean, with a grand operatic gesture, refused. "I don't want any more money from you." Then, putting his hand in his pocket, he said, "Do you need money yourself? I will be glad to help you." Val was touched by his generosity and faith, and continued to anchor his voice to the ceiling.

After the last lesson, he returned to the hotel and sat, dejected and desperate, in a corner of the lobby. His soulful seclusion was interrupted by a voice with a mid-American twang. "Cheer up; it's not the end of the world."

"It might as well be," he said, recognizing one of the hotel guests with whom he usually exchanged daily greetings and weather reports.

"What's wrong?"

"My tour of South Russia is three weeks away, and I have no voice left. It is on the ceiling of Jean de Reszke's studio."

The American had the audacity to laugh. "It serves you right," she said. "Why didn't you go to his teacher, Sbriglia?"

What a stupid question, but the poor woman was from St. Louis. How could he expect her to know? His answer was to the point, "Because St. Peter has long had him in custody. It would be impossible for him to be alive today."

But the irritating female chuckled and said, "Oh, he is very much alive; I took a lesson from him today. He is still a wonderful teacher and still takes a few pupils. But he would never see you if he ever suspected you had been to Jean. He refuses to repair damages inflicted by him. My advice is to forget Jean — pretend you never heard of him and go to Sbriglia. Cheer up! All is not lost."

One of the last great voice teachers of the golden era, Sbriglia, was still alive? A lady from St. Louis was giving him vocal advice in Paris? Well, things could be no worse. So the next day, he and Marie, disguised as English tourists, went to pay their respects to the great singing master.

For half an hour they waited. Then the door opened, and the 94-year-old man with hair and moustache dyed jet black shuffled in on a cane. Gruffly, he questioned, "Singers?" They both meekly replied in the affirmative, and, after casually inspecting Val as one would inspect a horse, he said curtly, "Well, don't waste time; let the man begin."

Val produced the aria from *Bohême* and proceeded to pin his high C to the ceiling.

The old man sat majestically with his chin poised on his cane, face devoid of expression. He now gave a grunt of pain and said, "If you take a top C like that again, you will drop dead. Go away, I won't teach you."

Val was shocked; even in his worst student days, he had never been turned down. He was too upset to respond. He gathered his music and gave Marie his place.

Pleased with Marie's voice, the Maestro said, "*You* I can teach," and gave her an appointment for five days later. Marie tried to console Val, "When he hears you again, he will change his mind." But Val felt his singing career was at an end. He concentrated on the principles he had learned from Dr. Vittoz.

What did all of this mean? Should he cancel his concerts and think about practicing law? He must maintain a constructive viewpoint and discover his life pattern.

Marie came down with the flu, and Val was obliged to go to Sbriglia's house (since the old devil did not have a phone) to cancel the lesson. Sbriglia shuffled into the waiting room, inspected Val from under his bushy eyebrows, and rather than lose the price of a lesson, said "Alright, I'll give *you* a lesson instead." After a few minutes he became so enthused that he said, "I think I can help you." Then he scheduled Val for daily lessons.

The first phase of his vocal analysis was: "You are lodging support in the neck instead of in the bones of the chest." For three weeks Val practiced Sbriglia's famous exercise of attacking the sound while holding two fingers below the trachea on the bone (never above the whisper of a tone), playing the notes downward on the bone as the scale went upward and vice versa. It was a pleasant sensation, a kind of overtone in the chest. When he was finally allowed to sing a song, he was amazed to find a new voice. He was able to sing, to shade, and to control. He felt power, sweep, and expansion without strain. The voice which had been dark and muffled began to open up. Sbriglia bullied, insulted, and mocked him, but he had saved him vocally, and Val promised to return upon the completion of his Russian concert tour.

The first concert was in Kishinev, the capital of the Province of Bessarabia. There Marie developed a cold and high fever, and, after a brief encounter with the doctor, was confined to the hospital with measles. There was no hint of luxury in a primitive hospital in a provincial Russian town, but there Marie stayed while Val gave his concert. It was a tremendous triumph, and the press wrote that, while it didn't like to make comparisons, it had to admit that Rosing had sung comparably better than Smirnoff who had performed there two weeks earlier. To be so compared to the greatest Russian tenor was a great victory, and Val spent the next day sending out press notices to St. Petersburg.

After attending a huge party in his honor, he was ready for a short-term romance with the local beauty queen. She was willing to cooperate, and they went boating on the local river, but he reacted to her embraces with chills and realized it was his turn for the measles. If he had to be hospitalized, it was not going to be in this place, so he decided to escape from Kishinev that very night on the Paris Express. For two days he generously spread his germs and arrived in Paris with a burning fever. The doctor ordered him to the hospital, and Marie, by now recovered, followed him. With complications that arose, he was hospitalized for three weeks.

When he was well, he continued his work with Sbriglia. Then he returned to London for his second concert at Albert Hall. He was enjoying great popularity and was in much demand for "at homes."

Diaghilev soon brought to London the Russian Ballet and Opera, which

included many of Val's friends. The Russians were very much "*à la mode*"—
at the forefront of things. And then, Val's agent, Alexander Khan, arranged for
him to sing in Paris for the director of the Vienna Imperial Opera.

Val was engaged as its leading tenor and given a six-year contract. His
career was going international, and his future was set. He was to make his
debut as Cavarodossi in *Tosca* on September 10, 1914.

Val and Marie returned to London, filled five trunks with costumes, furs,
and clothing for the coming season, and departed for Ostend where they would
relax for the summer while Val learned his repertoire in German. Within a
week, they were bored and discussed whether they should go ahead to Vienna
or return to Paris and Sbriglia. "Let's toss a coin," suggested Val. "Heads to
Vienna; tails to Paris." It came up tails, so they registered their trunks ahead to
Vienna and took the train to Rambouillet where the Maestro gave a summer
class at his chateau.

On June 28, 1914, an Austrian Archduke was assassinated in Sarajevo, a
problem for Austria-Hungary and Serbia to resolve. Val was busy preparing
his fall repertoire for a career that was ready to take off in high gear.

Chapter 18

The War Years

Within a week Val's pianissimi and high Cs were drowned out by the sounds of bombs and guns and by the cries of the wounded and dying. Decades of inspired hatred turned men into animals as Austria mobilized her army to punish the Serbians, and Europe became an armed camp. Russia came to the aid of her Slavic brothers, but all Russians caught in Vienna were interned in concentration camps. This included the Russian dancer and choreographer, Nijinsky, who spent most of the war years there, only to be confined in a mental institution when he was freed.

Sbriglia, who had witnessed the horrors of the Franco-Prussian War, insisted that Val and Marie depart for London immediately. They left their remaining luggage at the Maestro's chateau and fled to Dieppe where they encountered throngs of people pursuing the same course. As they sat in the station restaurant where train after train disgorged fleeing visitors, Val was overwhelmed with a sense of tragedy quite apart from the loss of his six-year contract and the small fortune contained in his five trunks. It was the horror of what was in store for the world that caused him to weep unashamedly.

The wind was howling as though all the demons in existence had been loosed, and a packed boat hardly provided standing space. Val had always been a poor sailor, but this was by far the worst challenge he had ever faced, and he was determined to invent a method for conquering seasickness. For an agonizing six hours (instead of the usual three that were required for the crossing), he ascended and descended the steps between decks in a pattern that opposed the mounting and plunging waves. He was sure he had discovered a scientific principle. Some thought he merely dissolved anxiety through his excessive activity. But for the first time in his life, he avoided seasickness.

When they arrived, London appeared to be celebrating some kind of festival. Cars carrying people on their hoods crowded the streets. Class snobbishness had given way to a great camaraderie with singing, shouting, and waving of flags. Theatres were packed, restaurants were full, and city-wide parties celebrated the departure of soldiers. Frequent notices were issued from the War Ministry and the State Department; and Lord Kitchener, who had been appointed Secretary of State for War, was the hero of the hour.

Val was appalled at such madness, but it seemed that everyone was trying to do something to help in the war effort. As an only son, he was exempt by Russian law from military service, and he decided to go to Bournemouth where, with the local symphony, he arranged and participated in concerts to promote a "Serve in the Red Cross" slogan. The London division of the Red Cross quickly summoned this dynamo to the big city and adopted his services.

There, as he was reading postcards from Russian prisoners of war one day, he came across a shocking situation. The Serbian army's 60,000 men, defeated in the first few days of the war, were starving in army prison camps while Germany ignored the Geneva agreement.

Immediately Val went to the Russian Ambassador, Count Paul Benckendorff. Benckendorff was a typical diplomat of the old school, a narrow ultra-conservative, and with the usual pomposity, he declined any responsibility. So Val appealed to the British government. Within half an hour he was at the Foreign Office, and by the end of the day, he had received the necessary budget to provide daily rations to the 60,000 starving men. With the help of the Serbian embassy, he established contact with the units and provided them with foods that ensured the essential calories and nourishment. He presented charity concerts to provide additional aid, and was decorated with the Serbian Order of St. Sava for saving thousands of Serbs from starvation.

His connection with the British government increased Val's popularity with the Russian Embassy. The Russians in England hoped that their country's alliance with the western democracies would bring liberal reforms to Russia and make her, like England, a constitutional monarchy. This inspired Val's dedication to his work and to his artistry. From the best available talent, he organized charity concerts and theatrical activities in which he also participated. From 8:00 a.m. to 5:00 p.m. he was in the office; evenings were devoted to concerts and to entertaining troops and munitions workers. Sometimes it was 5:00 a.m. before he retired. He began to feel that he had a real mission in the world.

When artists left London to concertize, it was necessary to obtain a police permit registering their destination. After the concert, a return permit was required, and the report was finalized upon arrival back at the London station. Sometimes, if the sergeant at the desk was involved with other red tape, it could be a time-consuming affair.

Val's reputation grew, and he received an invitation to sing for a police benefit concert in Queen's Hall. He was delighted. He loved the English police, and besides, being better known by them might facilitate quicker exit permits.

The day before the benefit concert, Val was scheduled to perform in Hull. Combating a heavy schedule, he dashed to the station with no time to spare. At the desk was an obstinate red-headed Irishman, Sergeant Day, busy with some complications concerning an Irish girl. Val's interruption irritated him, and he rudely commanded him to wait his turn. After a third interruption with Val repeating, "I have a concert in Hull tonight, and I am going to miss my train," Sergeant Day took Val by the collar, threw him out, warned him to stay out, and slammed the door.

Val's pride and dignity were outraged. He telephoned the incident to Scotland Yard and said, "I am leaving for Hull without an exit permit, and I have no intention of singing for your concert in Queen's Hall tomorrow."

On his return to London, he found a huge basket of flowers from the Minister of the Police, stating that Sergeant Day would be present at Queen's Hall prior to the concert to personally extend a humble apology if only Mr. Rosing would reconsider his decision.

The Minister himself brought in the much chastised sergeant, but before he had time to say a word, Val threw an arm about him and said, "Sergeant Day, I must apologize for interrupting your work yesterday." The incident dissolved in laughter, and a bond of lasting friendship developed among the three.

Mrs. Matthews, called "Loving Mully" by her friends, had a salon which skimmed the most interesting and celebrated people of London. There Val enjoyed great popularity, and there he met C. P. Scott, owner of the *Manchester Guardian*. He later said of Scott, "He was truly a wonderful man, and his friendship is one of my most cherished memories." He also acquired a special friendship with Prime Minister Asquith, with Lord Reading, and with Sir Alfred Mond who became Cabinet Minister. These men drew on his knowledge of Russian affairs to the point that Val was becoming somewhat of a political figure.

One night while having a sumptuous dinner at Coomb Bank, the home of Alfred Mond's brother Robert, the alarm sounded. Ordinarily everyone would have dashed to the cellar, but because the sky was so brilliantly illuminated, curiosity drove them to the roof. Searchlights were trying to locate a Zeppelin that was approaching London, and suddenly it was well defined in the deep blue sky. Guns from an English plane attacked, sending silver specks into the darkness. Flames burst from the Zeppelin, and within seconds it had disinte-

Vladimir Rosing's London opera debut in 1915 as Hermann, in Tchaikowsky's *Queen of Spades.*

grated. It was a dreadful sight as the searchlights accompanied the debris that, fortunately, fell outside the city where fire engines extinguished the flames. A somber group returned to the dinner table, pondering the greater damage that could have been done and, at the same time, finding it impossible to deny compassion for the enemy.

Not long after that, there was a reunion and a wedding between Val's sister

Vera and Marie's brother Bertie, after which Bertie went off to war, never to be seen again. Vera returned to a small son in Russia.

* * * * *

Covent Garden was on the verge of closing, and Val jumped into the breach. His schoolboy dream of being an opera producer was about to be realized, but its path would be different from his expectations.

Oscar Hammerstein I, the great impresario, having been paid off by the Metropolitan Opera Company to relinquish his competitive Manhattan Opera Company in New York, confidently launched the London Opera House. But he had made a miscalculation. In London, the opera public was an elite society faithful to its own traditions at Covent Garden, and it refused to patronize Hammerstein. In his anger, he had rudely insulted some faction, an act which put the finishing touch to his venture.

Young, naive, and fearless, but knowing that Covent Garden was closing and that he could rent the London Opera House, Val found the temptation irresistible. A young English broker with whom Val had become acquainted at the bridge table was infected with enthusiasm as well and added 5,000 pounds to Val's small amount so that the operatic morgue could be rented, and Val announced an opera season to London.

He plunged in with exhilaration, gathering singers from all of the allied nations for what he called his *Allied Opera Season*. Marguerita Silva was a great Carmen, and he introduced for the first time a Japanese prima donna, Tamaki Miura, as Butterfly. He reveled in the inspection of scenery and props, and confident of the ticket receipts which would guarantee all of the money needed, spent most of his funds on the first three productions.

The season was to open on Saturday night with Val singing Herman in Tchaikowsky's *Pique Dame* (*The Queen of Spades*). At the final rehearsal, according to the famous accompanist Ivor Newton in his autobiography *At the Piano*, "Rosing (everything about him was larger than life) brought a party of bearded, strangely robed priests, with incense and holy water from the Russian church, to bless the scenery."

Before the second act, the machinery balked, and the audience alternately shuffled and clapped while Val raged. After a long interim, the curtain agreed to rise, and the production was a success. Val's performance roused considerable enthusiasm, as much for his ability as an actor as for his voice, and the company spent Sunday basking in its success.

Monday night went well with *Lakmé* which starred Mignon Nevada, the daughter of famous Emma Nevada who came out of that state and wore its name. Tuesday was to be a repeat of *Pique Dame*, and Val was taking an afternoon rest when he heard the strains of the Rachmaninoff "Prelude in C

Sharp Minor." It was the voodoo of his life, the one thing that could drain the color from his face instantly. Two days after hearing Rachmaninoff himself perform it, Val had nearly drowned when his ship foundered on a rock in a calm sea. (In 1960 its strains came through an open window in Mexico, and Val *knew* I was going to leave him!) Now fear gripped him and settled into a depression which he tried to shed as he ate an early dinner. Suddenly, from without, came the roaring and wailing siren of the first air raid. As the alarm signal pierced the air, civilians ran for the air-raid cellars. It was their first contact with real ammunition. The raid was over by 7:10, and by 8:30 the curtain went up for *Pique Dame*, but only a few brave souls had dared to come out. The following evening was Tamaki Miura's *Butterfly*, and the public, especially the Japanese colony, could not resist; but after that, theatres and streets were deserted at night.

It was a heartbreaking artistic setback and a total loss of his own and his friend's capital.

That summer the Tsar ordered all the Second Reserves to join the Color; this had not been done since the war with Napoleon in 1812, and it meant Val's return to Russia. The Serbian Red Cross considered him indispensable because of his efforts on their behalf, and the Serbian government requested that Russia transfer him back to London.

The British government availed itself of the opportunity to entrust Val with secret papers from King George V for the Russian government. Under oath never to let them out of his hands, he was proudly impressed with the importance of his mission.

The government made all of the arrangements for his travel. The only way to get to Russia from London was by British ship on the North Sea which was under attack by German submarines. Rumor had it that the submarines stopped the British ships, removing all enemy passengers, and then let the ships go because they knew them to be reinforced with German spies. Val kissed his wife and six-year-old son good-bye. Then he hid himself in the ship's hold for 36 hours, but the ship made it through to Norway without being stopped.

It was a great relief to be in a neutral country. In Norway there were no *wagon* restaurants, but there were magnificent smorgasbords laid out at certain railway stations that were announced in advance. However, with hordes of hungry passengers, Val's one-handed struggle for food was hopeless. Finally, he decided to lock the papers in his compartment and concentrate on the station buffet. The smell of food was intoxicating, and he had heaped his plate and was beginning to indulge his appetite when, to his horror, he saw the train pulling out. Dropping everything, he gave pursuit, yelling in every language he knew at the conductor who was standing at the rear of the train.

The conductor merely laughed. Val had lost the precious documents with which he had been entrusted! How could he go to Russia? How could he return to England? Exhausted, desperate, in mental agony, there was nothing to do but return to the station.

There, switched to a different track, stood his train! He had been chasing the wrong one. He was the laughingstock of all, but his dispatches were safe! He even forgot his hunger.

Val found St. Petersburg a different city from the one he had left four years earlier. Russia, disliking the German sound of thé city's name, had changed it to Petrograd. It was a city of gloom where food was scarce and violent flu epidemics raged. Val carried tragic news to his sister Vera. Bertie had been killed in the Dardanelles. Everything seemed to be disintegrating. Natalia was dying from a strep infection of the liver, Aunt Matilda was in terrible distress, Father wasn't feeling well, Liuba and her husband were on the point of divorce. It was a sad return.

The Russian army was retreating, and no one knew how or when the German army could be stopped. The streets were full of beggars and soldiers who had no place to go. The War Minister, Sukhomlinov, was accused of betraying the Russian army and was imprisoned. His aid, who used to visit often in the Rosing home, was hanged. The Tsaritza was accused of being pro-German and of favoring a separate peace. Rasputin was at the height of his power. His orgies became more and more offensive. The aristocracy was turning away from the Tsar, and the Tsaritza, blind to the rising storm, was obsessed by religious fanaticism and idolized the dirty, disreputable monk whom she considered a minister from God. Thus the illiterate monk actually dominated the Tsar through an uncanny influence over his wife.

The Liberal party was mobilizing the majority of the country, and the minor socialist Bolsheviks spoke only in a weak voice. The Royalists were still loyal to the Tsar but were revolting against the Tsaritza. The patriotic Mensheviks and solid Liberals were trying to save Russia.

Though life was depressing in Petrograd, the theatres were still always full. The government, realizing the power of the arts, exempted all artists from military service. Consequently, theatrical life in Russia was not interrupted. Val visited his alma mater, the Music Drama, and saw most of his comrades who envied him for his London transfer.

He visited his university, and found that most of his liberal comrades were practicing law or were in the army. Comrade Abram had become an ensign.

After two months, Val bade a tearful farewell to friends and family. He was leaving a tragic country whose fate he could not have imagined. There was still no hint in the air of the revolution that would five months later demand the abdication of the Tsar. As he waved good-bye to his parents, the curtain descended for him on his beloved Russia. He would never see his country or his family again.

Chapter 19

The Madman

In the next compartment on the train a middle-aged man with bristling mustaches sat reading a book. Val identified the book as a medieval musical score and the gentleman as the great Russian conductor Wassili Safonoff who was on his way to London to conduct symphonic concerts.

The previous December, Safonoff, together with three other conductors — Thomas Beecham, Arthur Fagge, and Emil Mlynarski — had participated in one of Val's charity concerts for Serbian Relief. As they talked, Val and Safonoff decided on another one for the following month, December 1916.

It took place in Queen's Hall with the London Symphony Orchestra, Safonoff conducting the first performance in England of scenes from Glinka's *Russlan and Ludmilla*, together with Rimsky-Korsakov's *Sadko*, and Borodin's *Prince Igor*.

A few weeks later, on January 1, 1917, the monk Rasputin's body was found in the River Neva. The man responsible for his death was Prince Yussoupov who later attended Val's London concerts and described to him the bizarre events that had led to the murder in the cellar of Yussoupov's Moika Palace. Filled with poison and punctured with bullets, Rasputin had rejected death until his body was bound and pushed through the ice in Neva.

The Russian government was disintegrating; on March 12 it collapsed. Tsar Nicholas abdicated on March 15, and out of the March 17 Revolution evolved the Provisional government with Kerensky at its helm.

It was not long before news reached Val of the death of his father, and shortly after, his mother also was gone. His rich past crumbled.

Within months, the new Russian government had fallen and the Bolsheviks were in power. Val stared at the *Manchester Guardian*. C. P. Scott was the only editor in England who was taking a sympathetic view toward the Bolshevistic government. Val loved the elderly editor and had spent hours answering his questions and acquainting him with the political structure of the new parties that had sprung up with the Revolution. What a blow now to have him advocate support for Lenin and the Bolsheviks. Admittedly, Val himself had fought for a change — but under a constitutional party after all!

During this time, Val received a request from one of his sisters for a typewriter. A typewriter! After that he lost contact with his sisters. He had inherited his father's estate, but now that too was gone. And he was severed from his homeland — that land of stark and silent steppes, of luminous starlit skies under the aurora borealis, of lingering white nights, winding canals, golden spires, church bells, and samovars.

Some time later, Val's taxicab was passing Aeolian Hall where his name lighted up the marquee. In the box office window was a sign, "Standing Room Only," and people were still queued up for tickets. This kind of success could not but be gratifying; but by the same token, its responsibility was frightening. How could he ensure a continued surge of popularity?

He took immediate inventory of his assets. He had a tenor voice of beautiful quality with high Cs and a beautiful pianissimo. He was launching a career in England at a time when male singers stood like mannequins dressed in tails (or a Prince Albert if it were an afternoon concert), with white gloves, a stiff, immobile back, patent leather shoes, a carnation in the lapel, and a little black book in hand. Val, who used his little black book for other than traditional purposes, was a rebel against outworn forms and traditions and had begun to break them for the concert stage.

First, he had discarded the white gloves, the buttonhole adornment, and the little black book. Then, as he developed vocal colors, painting characters and human emotion in sound and achieving a body technique through which he could express himself, he had discarded the tails and accepted a lovely black jacket designed by Monsieur Poiret, the Dior of that period.

Had he played out his hand? What new dimensions could he reach? His mind drifted to his underlying depression. A flood of Russian artists was spilling into London: Gretchaninoff, Tcherepnin, Telinarsky, Safonoff, Coates, Diaghilev. What a deluge of artistic greatness! Was it possible that Russia's great nationalistic art might be the key to her restoration? How he would love to be her artistic Messiah! Through his art, could he portray his homeland so realistically that his audiences would see it, feel it, know it, and love it just as he did? Could he give them the heart and soul of Russia in song?

Val decided right then to inaugurate a new recital series and call it the *Soul*

of Russia! Through the music of great Russian composers, he would interpret
the love, comedy, satire, religion, and politics of his country! Fired with
enthusiasm, he directed the bewildered cab driver (who had drawn up to his
home address and was opening the cab door) to "Chester" at 11 Great
Marlborough Street. J. & W. Chester had the greatest supply of Russian music
in London, and there Val searched for and found songs to exploit the "soul of
Russia."

He launched into a study of his new repertoire — analyzing, visualizing,
finding the right physical form and the right vocal color to make the body and
the music become a complete blend of sculpture and sound. Whatever
potential of joy, sorrow, bitterness, laughter was in the music, he was
determined his audience must drain the cup along with him.

One of Val's "finds" was a song of Moussorgsky's called "Savishna." It
was the love song of a village idiot who had a spiritual significance in Russia
where he was called "oorodlivee." In a 5-4 rhythm, without the relief of a
single vocal rest, it psychologically portrayed a torrent of emotion spilling
forth in a hopeless jumble of words: How could one who was born for the
purpose of provoking mirth ever reveal that he had the same capability as other
human beings for experiencing love?

This, he thought, was an exceptional composition, but as he worked with it,
it presented a problem in the interpretation that stumped him. Obviously, it
meant the sacrifice of beautiful vocal tone to portray the emotion; still, he
seemed unable to find a vocal style to interpret it.

As he grappled with this problem, he suddenly realized, "It is not I who
must control the idiot; it is the idiot who must control *me*! And just as that state
of mind will produce a corresponding physical reaction on the nerves,
muscles, and joints of the body, likewise it should react on the nerves and
muscles which control and produce sound. Till now *I* have been trying to
create. *Now* I will let the village idiot create!"

Val did not need a prescribed atmosphere in which to work; he created one
wherever he happened to be. And this time he happened to be on a bus headed
for Piccadilly Circus. To give concrete shape to this exciting thought, he made
his mind feel empty and chaotic; his body sagged, his features drooped, his
eyes assumed a vacant stare, and his mouth dropped open. Softly, he sang a
few phrases of the song and found his voice was perfect for the character. He
was elated; it was the key to a whole new style of singing! So carried away was
he that he was only vaguely aware that a woman seated next to him got up and
changed her seat.

The following Sunday, he was invited to tea at the home of a patroness of the
arts. When the maid opened the door, she took one look and ran screaming to
her mistress, "Madame! The madman! It's the madman!"

When the maid was finally subdued and was convinced that Mr. Rosing was not a dangerous lunatic, the lady of the house apologized and explained that the poor girl had come home a few days prior, half frightened out of her wits because she had been sitting by a madman on the bus. She had thought Mr. Rosing was the same man.

Val lit up like a Christmas tree. "Ah, but she is right, she is right!" he cried. He could not have been more delighted with the total realism he had achieved. Not only did I hear this story from Val, but in 1962 Madame Pauline Donalda, the Canadian prima donna who shared the stage with Caruso and Scotti and formed the Montreal Opera Guild, related the incident to Val and me as told to her by the London hostess.

Another of the songs he discovered, "Song of the Poor Wanderer," was by an unknown composer, Nevstrueff. In it, the composer takes an allegorical figure, a starving peasant, through a series of miniature pictures as he wanders through The Steppes of Russia where he hears the wind howling, "Wanderer, it is cold . . . it is cold;" through the forests where the wolves are crying, "Wanderer, we are hungry . . . we are hungry;" through the fields of wheat which are moaning, "Wanderer, we are cold . . . we are cold;" and among the cattle on the range who are mooing, "Wanderer, we are cold and hungry." It was a brilliantly conceived composition — a tragic picture of the year of famine in Russia — and Val was elated with the anticipation of performing it. He worked relentlessly, sculpturing his body and demanding the correspond-ing vocal sounds to portray the wind, the wolves, the wheat, the cows, and the starving peasant. He locked himself into the song — into the kaleidoscope of pictures he was portraying.

Ivor Newton, Val's accompanist, in his book *At the Piano*, wrote:

> Rosing had one of the vividest and most magnetic personalities I had ever come across; rarely have I known anyone who could hold an audience in such a sheer ecstasy of enchantment through a whole recital. A Rosing audience was unlike any other. There was electricity in the air and people crouched forward in their seats as though they were watching some fierce and terrifying melodra-ma. . . . He acted every song; often he overacted it, sometimes he all but clowned it. The purists were scandalized. . . . He sang — his eyes closed and feet wide apart, like a blind goalkeeper — not only with his voice but with his heart, brain, body, hands and feet. If he tore a passion to tatters, you felt that particular passion was much more effective in tatters than intact. If he made a mess of a song, well, it was a glorious mess. Cyril Scott, then the white hope among the young English composers, said to me after Rosing had sung some of his songs, "I'd no idea I could write songs as good as that."

Gone was the tenor recitalist. The break with traditional concert singing was complete. Val introduced to England such songs as "Lord Randall," "The Volga Boatmen," "The Drunken Miller," "The Goat," "Song of the Flea," and others. Forty years later, he received a letter from a friend in Cornwall, England, saying, "I itch now as I write and recall your inimitable interpretation of 'Song of the Flea.'"

Many of his songs had been composed for baritones and basses. Val transposed them. This would later antagonize Chaliapin, back in Russia, who maintained they were "his songs," but Val sent him a message that the songs had preceded both the singing debut and the birth of the great bass.

While preparing his *Soul of Russia* series, his recitals continued on alternate weekends. Ezra Pound, writing for *The New Age* in London under the pseudonym of William Atheling, titled his April 18, 1918, review "ROSING THE MAGNIFICENT":

> He is, without varnish, a great artist. . . . He has the great style . . . we did not have "all of him" until he reached Moussorgsky's "Serenade" from the "Cycle of Death" . . . the serenade gave us major art.

On May 2, Pound called Val's recital:

> This week's treat, the feast of soul. . . . He displayed the great variety of his tone quality (may we call it voice-orchestration). He is full of sudden surprises, unexpected richness of expression. . . . One can't hear too much of him.

On June 13, Pound continued to rave:

> . . . His concerts are the main musical interest of the season. No lover of music and no one with any musical curiosity will willingly miss them. . . .

On June 27:

> It is pure folly for any music lover to miss Rosing's singing of Moussorgsky.

And on July 25:

> VLADIMIR ROSING is, as the reader now knows, one of our rare delights; but he should hatch his chickens in private.

At this time, Val had taken a young singer under his wing and had shared the concert with her. Through the years his generosity with subordinates would be a mark of his stature, and also a means of his undoing. Pound bristled,

> . . . His male-henish care for the chick under his wing, interfered with his singing . . . he is perfectly capable of filling the hall by himself, there seems no need of his jointure.

October 19 Pound noted

> . . . There is no one in London to interpret Moussorgsky as he does. . . .

Artists of the Royal Academy painted and sculpted Val. During one of his concerts, Glyn Philpot sketched as Val sang with closed eyes one of Moussorgsky's *Songs of Death*. It was developed into a portrait known as "The Blind Singer." His head was sculpted by Charles Ricketts who never missed a concert and thought Val could do no wrong. He always reserved the aisle seat on the second row and when especially pleased would render a triple "Bravo," which was to be interpreted as a command for the song to be repeated.

When Val felt he had extracted the utmost from "Savishna" (The Village Idiot) and that he was prepared to deliver it to his audience, he included it in one of his recitals. As he made his physical transformation, a gasp went through the audience. When the last note died away, he listened for that triple "Bravo." There was absolute silence! Had he gone too far?

Then a storming audience was on its feet shouting, and Ricketts's thundering "Bravo" led them on. Relief and gratitude brought tears to Val's eyes, and the audience would not release him until he had sung it three times. However, he did not truly realize the extent of his success until after the concert when admirers came to the Green Room to congratulate him. Said one English lady ecstatically, "You were wonderful! But oh, Mr. Rosing, the song that suits you by far the best is 'The Village Idiot!'"

On October 31, Pound titled his article "ROSING AND LAUREL CROWNS":

> . . . He was far too interesting to permit the critic to take notes. I mean exactly that — the orchestration of the voice was so subtle that one could not scribble and listen at the same time, there was too much going on. The four by six performer imagines, or . . . takes it for granted, that the scale contains thirteen tones and half tones, and that to sing consists in hitting (or approximating) the

"The Blind Singer" — oil portrait of Vladimir Rosing by British artist Glyn Philpot, 1917-1918.

note set down on the page. It seemed to me that Rosing never repeated the *same sound* through all the six songs of the opening group. . . . Note that the programme was arranged, built as skilfully as a good play. . . . I do not care how much music anyone may have heard, this Russian concert should be part of his musical education.

Then on November 2 came Val's *Soul of Russia* concert. It began with five folk songs from a collection by Philipoff, harmonized by Korsakov. The four successive groups depicted Oppression, Love, Suffering, and Gaiety and Satire. It was reviewed by Pound on November 14:

> . . . Rosing's recital . . . was probably the most serious Russian concert ever attempted in London. . . . He attempted to give, as far as possible in one afternoon's singing, the music portrait of Russia's subjectivity ("soul" is . . . the term used). He succeeded admirably. . . .

The first six recitals of 1919 were announced as: *Human Suffering, Soul of Russia, God and Nature, Moussorgsky, Love,* and *Historic and Fantastic Legend.* Pound continued his praise. He said that on the stage

> The *voice* of the actor should express the character portrayed. . . . Rosing does this, [conveying] mood . . . and character . . . by changes in vocal quality. He called it "impersonation by voice."

The year 1920 still embodied severe scars of war, and after one of Val's recitals, Pound wrote:

> Rosing humbly asked if he might sing Schumann in German. The audience greeted the proposition with enthusiasm, but Rosing sings two languages: Russian and Rosing. . . .

Val had thought it a clever strategy to salvage his German repertoire by using French translations. Ernest Newman, music critic for the Sunday *London Times*, however, compared it to the "morganatic marriage of a French poodle to a German dachshund by a Russian priest."

Ivor Newton also said:

> A Rosing recital was something new in the world of music. It was a kind of prolonged "blitz" of violent emotions, which left singer and audience (and frequently accompanist) limp and wet with perspiration.

When Newton once questioned Val's rhythm in a song, Val replied with great grandeur, "Perhaps it is not the rhythm of the composer but it's a real rhythm, although it may be mine."

Val once substituted for an ailing John McCormack in a concert tour of Ireland. When Newton discovered that he planned to sing the "Irish Famine" song in Dublin, he pointed out that for a Russian to go to Ireland and sing them one of their own songs dealing with a tragic period of their history seemed to be almost impertinent. "But," said Newton, "he persisted — and won. Dublin took him to its heart and wept over him. The 'Famine Song' was the high-light of the recital."

After Val's January 13, 1920, recital, Neville Cardus, music critic for the *Manchester Guardian*, took on the purists. In his book, *NEVILLE CARDUS Autobiography,* he wrote:

> Those of his critics present who, though they admit Rosing's interpretative genius yet deny him qualities of pure song, must have been considerably astonished at the amount of lyrical beauty he spilled over the music that craved for it. Duparc's "Extase" was given with a tone of such fugitive loveliness that the song floated through the hall as lightly as petals from a flower. Brahms's "Serenade," given as an encore . . . one has not heard done with so light a touch and so sunny a grace. . . . And in Grieg's rather drawing-roomy "Un Rêve" Rosing displayed a tenor voice of pure gold. [He] can, whenever it suits his purpose, serve out the full measure of lyrical sweetness.
>
> He chooses, however, more often than not to follow the inclination of his temperament. . . . As an interpreter of Russian song Rosing is . . . definitely a Primitive, aiming at a realism of extreme simplicity, his outlook one of naked innocence. . . .
>
> No other singer has so transcended the scope of mere specialized musicianship. . . . Last night Rosing sang the setting to Nekrasov's "The Wanderer," and at the passage where we hear the piteous lamentation of the starving peasant there was a miracle for the psychologists on the platform. Rosing's face was as though a light had been turned down inside; at the cry "Cold! Cold!" the cheeks, so it seemed, became sunken; the body contracted as though intensely chilled, the hands clenched, and surely, the voice itself was pinched. Like Chaliapin, Rosing is a great actor, his very stance on the platform is significant — the entire body alive with an eloquent animation, almost sculptural.

Of course, there were purists who registered musical rape. They thought Val could do everything but sing and that his performances were better for the fairgrounds than the concert hall. Ivor Newton wrote:

> Perhaps they were right, but it came off because, despite all his eccentricities, Rosing was never *cheap*; in everything he did there

was such an overpowering impression of stern, unflinching sincerity. The man simply threw himself into his music and its poem.

In *The Perfect Wagnerite*, George Bernard Shaw gave to Val the most treasured criticism of his singing career:

> . . . The two most extraordinary dramatic singers of the twentieth century, Chaliapin and Vladimir Rosing, aré quite independent of the old metropolitan artificialities.

Since the age of fourteen when he had stood all day in freezing weather to secure, with borrowed money, a ticket to a Chaliapin concert, Val had idolized the man as Russia's and the world's greatest artist. In 1919, when Chaliapin escaped from Russia and arrived in London, it would never have occurred to Val that there could exist a rivalry. But Chaliapin had said to a friend of Val's, "How dare Rosing, a tenor, sing my songs?"

A few years previous when the great bass had just been a colossal success in London, and when Val was recording for *His Master's Voice*, Fred Gaisberg of the recording company took Val to meet Chaliapin at the latter's home. It was noon, and the bass was still in bed, so Val remained downstairs while Fred went up.

In due course he was invited upstairs where Chaliapin was still lying in his king-sized bed. They were introduced by Fred, and Chaliapin said, "Forgive me for receiving you like this, but I am exhausted from last night's activities."

Val apologized for seeing him the morning after a concert. Chaliapin laughed, "I'm afraid my fatigue is a result of post-concert activities. The girl — no, no, not the girl — a *real woman* had what it took to deplete old Don Juan here. And that idiot Diaghilev calls a rehearsal at noon. Doesn't he know I can't even spit before noon?"

The next time Val and Chaliapin met was at the Gramophone Studios in Hayes. Val was recording a Russian song when Fred Gaisberg ushered Chaliapin in and said to him, "It's a beautiful voice, isn't it?"

"Yes," Chaliapin said, "but I don't like to make predictions. Once a baritone asked me what I thought of his voice, and I said, 'It is warm and soft — like horse manure.'"

After the Russian Revolution, Chaliapin, who had been a pet of the Tsar, had to bow to the Dictator of the Proletariat, from which class he himself had come. But the Lenin regime didn't appeal to him. He was able to get permission to leave Russia for a concert tour in Europe, and he never returned. During the war years, Val had become known in England as the greatest interpreter of Russian song. No wonder Chaliapin was outraged when he learned that a Russian tenor was singing songs from his repertoire.

Both singers made concert tours in America in 1921, and Olin Downes, who was then critic of *The Boston Globe*, stated his preference for Rosing's interpretation of "The Flea." That was the crowning insult for Chaliapin. Returning to London ahead of Val, he was given a big press reception at which a journalist friend of Val's asked, "Did you meet Rosing while you were in America?"

Chaliapin replied, "Rosing . . . Rosing . . . Who is Rosing? I never heard of him." But that evening at a reception, he paid a great deal of attention to an attractive lady who was a friend of Val's, and when she asked if they had met, he answered, "Oh, yes, many times. They call him 'The Little Chaliapin' over there."

A few years later, Hurok booked Chaliapin for a tour of the United States in *The Barber of Seville* and needed an understudy. By that time Val was developing The American Opera Company in Rochester, New York, and employed a six-foot-five bass named John Moncrieff who was a superb actor as well as a marvelous singer. Val presented him to Hurok who engaged him on condition that Chaliapin never know that he was one of Val's artists. Chaliapin liked Moncrieff and invited him one day to his drawing room for a bourbon. "Where," he asked, "have you been studying?"

Taken off guard, Moncrieff replied, "In Rochester with Rosing."

Chaliapin shook his head. "Too bad . . . too bad. He dared to sing my repertoire." Moncrieff did not receive a second invitation.

It was impossible for Val to view Chaliapin as a rival. He had idolized him from the age of ten, spellbound by that glorious voice that issued from his father's Gramophone. He had stood in the freezing weather for hours to buy a concert ticket with his borrowed ten rubles. He had witnessed the great bass's tenth jubilee in the Bolshoi Theatre with hundreds of laurel wreaths, a stage full of flowers and gifts, and an audience showering him with love and admiration. The pitch of enthusiasm that night had grown to such an extent that the horses were unharnessed from his carriage while his admirers, with their own hands, pulled it to his hotel.

When news of his death stunned the artistic world, Val mourned his loss, for Chaliapin was himself a whole epoch, an artistic giant among the vocal greats of the Golden Age of Opera.

On March 6, 1921, in Albert Hall, Val broke a record, giving his one-hundredth song recital in London. The *Morning Post* maintained, "Rosing recitals are like meetings of the only true believers." The *Daily News* added, "Mr. Rosing has become an institution in the musical world." The Sunday *Times* declared, "Rosing is unique. . . . [His] hold on the public is really extraordinary." The *Westminster* confirmed, "Famous Russian tenor enjoys extraordinary favor"; and the *Daily Telegraph* echoed, "A real triumph."

Val did not save his beloved country from the Bolsheviks, but he did bring popularity to Russian music. And from an emotional singer had come a great interpreter.

A tour of the provinces reaped prodigious praise, and each review seemed to transcend the one before it. It was a mad love affair between artist and audience. As the audience took him to its heart, he gratefully responded with complete abandon. The madman was monarch.

Chapter 20

Val and Isadora

While soaring on the currents of his fame, Val was invited to dinner at the home of Robert Matthias, Commissioner of Works, and his wife, a daughter of the Wertheimers who were deeply involved in the arts. Upon Val's arrival, Matthias announced, "Isadora Duncan is joining us after dinner."

Val thought it was a joke. "The goddess? Impossible!" He had idolized her from the time she had visited Russia in 1905. Then a lad of fifteen, he had observed this fantastic phenomenon as some kind of celestial being. Obviously Matthias was tuning in on his idolatry.

Much to his amazement, the door opened later in the evening to display a peculiar individual in a black cape and toreador-style hat. She was accompanied by a revolting individual with effeminate characteristics. It was the disillusionment of his life! What had happened to her extraordinary beauty? There were pouches under her eyes. Well, maybe it was poor make-up. But how dared she deign to be in the company of that off-beat looking guy?

Val politely greeted her before she was whisked to an upstairs drawing room. When Val later joined them, his hostess asked, "Will you sing, Val?"

Val was nursing his disappointment and replied, "No, I am sorry."

Isadora, stretched on a couch, said, "I, Isadora Duncan, ask you to sing."

Rather rudely, Val replied, "I, Vladimir Rosing, decline to sing." He would later regret his shameless attitude. As the party broke up, Isadora and a French officer walked ahead followed by Val and his friend Bonell, a bass, all searching for taxis which were difficult to find. Val decided to apologize. "I am sorry," he said. "I had eaten too much, and I don't like to sing after dinner. Maybe you will come to my concert?"

"Of course," responded Isadora, "but why not join us at my apartment now?"

It was a beautiful night, and the four walked all the way. Val was surprised when they arrived at a second-rate apartment on Duke Street. Isadora's rich past rested in an album which she shared with her guests. When they turned to a page portraying two lovely children, she explained, "Those are my children; a taxi plunged into the Seine with them." With this she burst into hysterical tears, burying her head on Val's shoulder.

A goddess past her prime had lost her two children and, obviously, her material resources as well. Val was consumed with regret for his earlier attitude. In his own words, "I felt as cheap as I had ever felt in my life."

At his invitation, Isadora attended his recital two evenings later. Afterward, she rushed to his dressing room and threw her arms about him crying, "You are the greatest singer I have ever heard!"

"If you really enjoyed my singing," Val replied, "I will arrange a special evening in your honor."

Mrs. Mully Matthews, who shared her war rations and her friends, and whose drawing room drew the greatest artists of London, offered her home and filled it with friends for the occasion. Everyone was agog in anticipation of Isadora's presence. When the goddess of dance arrived, she brushed everyone aside, hardly spoke to her hostess, went upstairs to the drawing room, had a sofa brought to the center of the room, reclined full length upon it, took Val's hand, and said, "You will sing for me now." She never moved from the sofa where her refreshments were, of necessity, served to her. Mully was infuriated.

For two years Val lost sight of Isadora. Then while concertizing in Paris, he noticed in the paper that she was performing at the Theatre de Champs Élysées. He invited his friend Charles Fol to attend the performance with him.

Charles questioned the intimate inflection in Val's voice. "You *know* her?"

"Oh yes, we are dear friends."

Val reserved box seats. There was no orchestra, only a piano. An extremely tall, handsome, god-like creature with long hair entered and proceeded to play Liszt *par excellence*. There were wrong notes, but he played like an orchestra. Charles enlightened Val. "He is the illegitimate son of Franz Liszt. He has become famous for his piano transcriptions of Wagner and Liszt."

When the performance was over Val said, "Come on, I'll take you to meet Isadora." Charles was nervous at the prospect, but Val assured him, "Don't be silly; she'll absolutely swoon with delight when she sees me."

They entered the dressing room to find her in her favorite pose, reclining on a sofa. Val approached her with great warmth, a broad smile, and an extended hand. "Hello, Isadora."

The smile froze on his face when she looked at him blankly and said, "Who are you? I don't know you."

Charles winced as he looked at his imposter friend, but Val was indignant. "Don't you remember me? I'm Vladimir Rosing."

"I don't know the name."

"Don't you remember the Russian tenor in London?"

She jumped from the sofa and threw her arms around him. "Walter, Walter, come here," she cried. "This is the greatest tenor in the world — the one I have always talked to you about." The grin reappeared on Charles's face as Walter Morse Rummel, the composer-accompanist turned to shake hands.

"Your friend is my friend," said Isadora as she was introduced to Charles Fol and embraced him. "You're both coming to dinner tomorrow night at seven, and I won't take no for an answer."

"But, Isadora, I have scheduled an evening concert for some friends of Charles's at eight."

"Oh, that's alright; we will have finished dinner, and we can go with you. Meet us at the Hotel Continental."

The Hotel Continental? The last time he had met her she was destitute!

The next evening they were ushered to her sumptuous, almost royal, suite. Walter, her "Archangel" appeared, and a friendship ignited between him and Val which lasted for many years, broken eventually by political differences.

Time passed, and Val was tense with apprehension. He was late for a concert appearance, and Isadora had not yet emerged. Finally at 8:20, she materialized, whereupon he had to beg her forgiveness and depart. A cold supper at midnight was a poor substitute.

Tea time at Claridge's Hotel was traditionally a time for the mellow exchange of ideas. Isadora, Walter, and Val met in a private sitting room. One afternoon as Val and Isadora talked, Walter improvised at the piano. Suddenly there was a passage that caught Isadora's attention. She jumped up. "Play that again, Walter." As he repeated it, she improvised.

Val was astonished. It was a difficult passage rhythmically, melodically, and dynamically, but she was extending it into a visual experience. "I can't believe it," he said. "I can actually *see* the music!"

"That is my art," she said. "Other dancers create motion from the music, but I let the music create motion in me. I feel the vibration of sound and melody in every fiber of my body. It automatically moves and shapes me. I register those movements I like best and combine and mold them into a plastic structure."

Val realized that this same principle applied to opera. Every movement, every gesture should be the result of the musical phrase or passage. He experimented, and his horizons expanded. A soft lyric passage or an allegro phrase moved the body accordingly. A single chord demanded a body freeze, and Isadora admitted that this was the most difficult accomplishment — to stand motionless. Body and music became a complete blend of sound and motion, every motion coming out of the sound, translating the emotion into motion. Isadora accomplished this with a single aid — that of a scarf.

Val was forever grateful to Isadora. Added to what he had learned from Lapitzky at the Music Drama, her contribution to his art helped to define the difference between ordinary operatic acting and the distinctive style he would develop. He would apply this technique not only to his own art, but to that of others who studied with him and who performed under his direction.

The secret to Isadora's seeming current opulence was that she had sold the palace which Singer, the inventor of the sewing machine, had donated for her Paris school. She was bringing six pupils from America and planning a party for eighteen pupils and satellites whom she would take on a trip to Greece. The trip would benefit everyone except Isadora, for by the time the group reached Venice, Walter Rummel deserted with Isadora's oldest and best student, the very attractive Anna. Isadora was inwardly devastated, for Walter was the great love of her life.

Val felt Isadora had unconsciously invited her disaster. When her dancers had arrived from America, she evaluated them as "cold as ice." "You have no emotion," she would say. "Now come say goodnight to the Archangel. Express yourselves with warmth." It was not long before all of the ardor had concentrated itself in Walter and Anna. Isadora was isolated with anguish.

That fall Val was concertizing in London when he received a call from Isadora who was spending the remains of her fortune at Claridge's Hotel. It was a sad reunion. She wept on his shoulder, bewailing the ingratitude of people. In less than six months, her group was reduced to three. She gave a series of matinees at the Criterian Theatre where Walter returned to accompany her. Their relationship had become solely artistic.

At her first performance, Isadora spied Val in the stalls. She was going to dance Wagner's *Träume*, and having heard Val sing it in concert, she suddenly called on him to come to the stage and sing while she danced. Val was embarrassed, but remembering the pain of a previous refusal, he hastened to comply. Sir Frederick Ashton, then seventeen, was in the audience and recalled the incident many years later.

Was Val in love with Isadora? I don't know. She was his senior by twelve years. Yet his notes say, "I fell in love with a Dancer, but I 'loose' her. Final break with Marie. Isadora goes to Russia."

Isadora's fame and fortune were dwindling when Max Rabinoff, who as general director of the Montreal Opera had brought Pavlova for her first American tour, persuaded Kamenev, a Russian communist leader, to invite Isadora to establish a school of dance in Russia. They gave her a palace where

Irma, the only pupil to go with her, ran the school for her. "The palace was beautiful, but there was no heat," said Irma.

Kamenev had also offered Val the directorship of a large theatre if he would return to Russia, but the offer apparently did not tempt him.

In 1922, it was announced that Isadora would make a farewell tour of the U.S. with her recently acquired Russian poet husband. She was to appear at Carnegie Hall. Val was touring America also, and, overjoyed at the prospect of seeing her again, left a welcome note and a request to see her at her hotel. Besides the joy of seeing her again, he was anxious to have news of his native Russia. But no answer came. Remembering his past experience with her, he thought she had again forgotten him; he was hurt and didn't attend her performance. That was the evening when her tunic fell from her shoulder, and she danced bare-breasted before a shocked audience. In spite of his personal hurt, Val suffered for Isadora. The tour, which should have been a tribute to her greatness as a dancer, was a failure. And her turbulent, unbridled, unpredictable husband abused Isadora and shocked the public with his behavior.

Val's concert tour took him to Paris. One beautiful spring morning as he walked near the Champs Élysées on his way to visit Walter Rummel's brother, he found himself facing a group of people which included Isadora, her husband, and some members of the Russian Embassy. There was no possibility of avoiding each other. Isadora visibly paled. Val tipped his hat and walked on. Suddenly he heard running steps behind him. Isadora, out of breath, said, "Forgive me, it wasn't my fault. When I received your note, Yessenin thought it was a former lover. He beat me and forbade me to answer it. I could never forget you."

She ran back to the group, and it was the last time he ever saw her. A few years later he opened the newspaper to read that Isadora Duncan had died of strangulation when her scarf caught and twisted in the wheels of her moving car.

Val cursed the irony of the scarf that had made her famous and was now responsible for her death. In later years he said of his friend, "All of the imitations which followed but made the original gem more precious."

Chapter 21

Opera — Too Damn Grand!

In *Living Musicians*, David Ewen quoted a 1921 letter from George Bernard Shaw to Richard Strauss as evidence of "how highly Rosing was thought of by leading musical and intellectual figures in London."

> My excuse for writing to you is that I want to call to your attention Vladimir Rosing. . . . Technically he is a tenor, but really he is more than that; he can and will do anything with his voice that will produce the right tone color to the passage he is singing. He behaves like an orchestra rather than like a singer.

Later the same year, while touring America, Val met with Strauss and Howard Taylor, Strauss's representative from the Judson Agency, at the Wellington Hotel and spent the afternoon discussing future possibilities, all of which dissipated with the departure of Strauss for Austria and Val's return to England.

At thirty-one, Val was at the peak of his career. He had given an unprecedented 100 London recitals, and his public was in love with him. What more could he want? He wanted to be a producer.

One day a friend brought to him a review of a Covent Garden performance of *Don Giovanni* in which the role of the Don was sung by Maurice Renaud. The review, written by George Bernard Shaw, said no one artist could perform this role; it would take the blending of two great artists — for instance, the acting of Sir Forbes Robertson and the singing of Vladimir Rosing combined would make the ideal Don.

Val wrote a note of thanks to Mr. Shaw. "But," he said, "you have never seen me act, and when you do, you will change your mind about saddling my voice into the body of Sir Forbes."

An invitation arrived asking Val to lunch at the Shaw home on Adelphi Terrace. It was a quaint old house facing the river. Nothing was ostentatious, nor was anything ordinary; it was comfortable, cozy, and unique. Val found Shaw "quick as lightning, energetic in his movements, and a gracious host — always amusing, sometimes bitterly sarcastic." Shaw deplored, as Val did, the old, outdated form of operatic acting — describing gestures as "semaphoric" and comparing the opera singers to "police bobbies regulating operatic traffic on the stage." He described a prima donna known to both of them: "Her voice wobbles to such an extent that it sings a duet with itself."

They had a mutual friend in Mully whose great salon was a meeting place of England's greatest talent, and sooner or later, included every luminary. She developed a crush on each new celebrity, and it was now Val's turn. He confided to Shaw, "She told me that I should not allow wartime rationing to deprive my voice of proper nourishment, and she insisted on secretly giving me some of her own rationed meat coupons."

"Well," said Shaw, "that is no less than a miracle, for she secretly and confidentially presented to Hugh Walpole, Charles Ricketts, and me those same precious rarities. I suspect that she knows someone we don't."

Shaw and Val took apart opera, the concert stage, and world politics and cited cures for all. They were lamenting the fact that London, financially depleted by the war, would have to forego the opera season. Said Val, "The trouble is that grand opera is too expensive."

"Yes," said Shaw, "It's too damn grand."

Val heartily agreed and declared that opera could and should be reduced to theatrical proportions. "After all," he said, "every opera is based on a great drama — *Faust* on Goethe's tragedy, *Butterfly* on Belasco's drama, *Traviata* on Duma's *La Dame aux Camelias*, *Tosca* on Sardou's melodrama, et cetera. None of these plays need a large chorus; it is mostly included for padding and, as you say, to make it damn grand."

"Right," said Shaw. "It should be eliminated or reduced to the minimum needed for the story."

"And the orchestra," Val said. "It's also a surplus. People are willing to hear a singer in recital with a piano accompaniment; surely they will go to see a good opera production with a small orchestra."

They enthused each other to the point of deciding to rent Aeolian Hall and present an opera season. Val would get Theodore Komisarjevsky, producer and director from the Moscow Art Theatre, to direct; he would secure Adrian

Boult to organize and direct orchestra and singers. Val would be the lead tenor. They would call their project Opera Intime.

In London, the *Observer* announced the project in a page-length column headlined: "INTIMATE OPERA: Mr. Rosing on His Experiment." It read,

> An interesting experiment is about to be tried in the production of a grand opera. Some of the big choruses are to be cut, and we are to have opera on as intimate a scale as that which we associate with the daintiest of comedies.

Val had stated that the way to present "grand opera" at that time, unless it was government subsidized, was with "simplified" production. That would develop the "psychology in the drama of the opera." The opera, Val thought, would positively "gain by the intimacy." The big chorus scenes could be eliminated without affecting its "musical interest" or its psychology.

After listing the cast and the operas to be performed, The *Observer* article continued by including a letter Val had received from Shaw which further reiterated his views that much of opera would be better served artistically in a small and private setting. Shaw closed the letter by wishing Val success with the project and saying:

> When they asked me whether I did not think you were a wonderful singer I told them that you were not a singer at all, you were a whole band. I hope your opera week will lead to something. When the next war leaves London and all other great capitals in ruins and we are all beggars we shall have some real music at last.

Sir Adrian Boult wrote in his autobiography, *My Own Trumpet*:

> [Val had] secured as producer none other than Theodore Komisarjevsky, who had also arrived in London, after many adventures, from the famous Moscow Art Theatre. He asked me to look after the music, and we decided that the intimacy of the whole production would be nicely caught by an orchestra of seven: five strings, a pianoforte played by Leslie Heward, and a chamber organ played by Arnold Goldsbrough. Both of these young men were then students at the Royal College.

Shaw organized a reception for London's elite at Claridge's Hotel where he made an opening spiel to launch the project. Mully helped him, and everything was going well. It seemed that half of London was there. Anticipation was high; Mully was in her element, greeting and flattering, receiving duchesses and celebrities. Admiring females surrounded Shaw and Rosing. Tea was served, and then Shaw took the floor to make operatic history. Val knew his presentation would be original, although he did not realize *how* original. Shaw described the new project and all of its practical aspects. Then he launched into a description of the opera to be performed. But something was terribly wrong. Val had proposed *The Queen of Spades* for their production, but who was this *queen* that Shaw was talking about? Queen of Sheba! How did *she* get into the act? Val was not familiar with Goldmark's *Queen of Sheba* which was a part of London's repertoire, while Tchaikowsky's *The Queen of Spades*, a more recently composed opera, was well known in Russia, but not so well known to the British. As soon as he realized the mistake, Val passed Shaw a note. It would be quite a predicament for the leader of a new movement not to know its opening vehicle — but not for Shaw; he stroked his beard, and with one of his Mephistophelian chuckles, said, "I have told you about the *Queen of Sheba*, and now Vladimir will tell you about the *The Queen of Spades.*"

After giving his version, Val returned the speaker's chair to Shaw who said, "Fortunately, for the remainder of our productions, there is only one *Barber of Seville* and one *Pagliacci.*" The audience, now realizing the mistake, responded with laughter and enthusiasm.

Val was not to be outdone. Singing three performances of *Pagliacci* in two days, he felt he should resort to the support of a corset, a habit to which many male singers adhered in those days. He was unable to find his own, and so struggled into his wife's, oblivious of the supporters attached. He also forgot to button his trousers, and when he removed his outer clown costume on stage, the two forgotten items coordinated themselves and brought down the house. Said one prominent socialite regarding Rosing and Shaw's *Intimate Opera*, "This is really quite too intimate!"

Ventured Ivor Newton in his autobiography:

> An act of complete madness, . . . Aeolian Hall . . . must have had the smallest stage in the world and necessitated that the chorus . . . should approach from various points all over the stalls. . . . But once Rosing began a scheme, he galloped away like a runaway horse. So an army of carpenters hammered away turning Aeolian Hall into an opera house. It was a most elaborate business. Komisarjevsky produced (when Rosing would let him), Adrian Boult conducted and Leslie Heward was chorus master. . . . There was nearly always in Rosing's ambitious schemes some ludicrous flaw or other. On this occasion the curtain refused to come down at the end of *Pique Dame*. Rosing, who was playing the lead, had died

in superb style and it rather impaired the effect when the corpse, after waiting about five minutes, had to get up and walk off.

There were the following reviews:

"Opera Intime" seems to be a success. And it is very "intime." The actors are within a yard and a half of the conductor's baton, and the audience within a yard of the conductor, which brings us all very near together and makes a very happy family of us. . . . Altogether there are to be eight days of this pleasant operatic intimacy. Make the most of it!

* * * * *

Under the heading "NEW KIND OF OPERA — MR. ROSING'S EXPERIMENT": . . . Grand opera (at its best) means for most people scenic pomp on a big stage a long way off, and a surprising volume of tone from the tiny-looking singers on that distant scene. What the actors are saying or doing precisely is mostly a mystery. The big voice, the unmistakable tune, the spectacular scene — in fact the *gros moyens* which, in literature, Henry James so amusingly deprecated — these are the things that tell in grand opera.

The "Queen of Spades" (1890) was not an obvious choice for a beginning. It boasts all the *gros moyens* with which the new form of opera might dispense and is not graced with the small refinements looked for. . . .

But those who waited for the latter scenes saw the why and wherefore of the choice. For then Mr. Rosing went mad with the utmost vividness, and, after the "thrilling" gambling scene at the end . . . stabbed himself and died gruesomely . . . and we saw him using effectively and legitimately the raging, storming manner which he has been apt to overdo in pure lyric song. . . .

* * * * *

Rosing's company not only play "The Barber of Seville" in English; they Anglicise him as well. . . . They make a good deal of fun out of it, so much that the Aeolian Hall resounds to the audience's mirth. . . . One wonders whether the barber has ever been seen in a tall red hat on a London stage before? Mr. Komisarjevsky has dressed the opera most effectively, and his

folding box scene seems capable of adapting itself to an infinite
variety of uses.

A dual bill composed of "Bastien and Bastienne" and "Pagliacci" was presented on Friday and Saturday. Mozart's little pastoral
is just right, given under "intime" conditions. . . .

From the formal little fantasy to "Pagliacci" was a long step.
Leoncavallo's opera was done without the chorus which plays such
an important part. It was surprising to find that the result of that
and of the other alterations and innovations — such as using the
auditorium as an entrance — intensified the dramatic element and
made the tragedy more vivid and vital than ever. Rosing's Canio
was powerfully acted and very well sung. . . .

                              * * * * *

Of all the Rosing productions at Aeolian Hall, "I Pagliacci," the
announcement of which aroused the most misgivings, has turned
out to be the best. For the two acts of the story the Aeolian Hall
stage represents that of the booth in which the Pagliacci perform.
First they are behind the scenes, some in mufti. Then the stage
performance proceeds until Silvio, in modern evening dress,
emerges from the auditorium too late to save Nedda. Curiously
enough, this way of presenting the story seems to fit some of the
lines better than the more familiar method. To mention only one of
them, it has always seemed absurd for Canio to sing "On With the
Motley" when he has it on already.

Rosing is unquestionably a great dramatic artist. His Canio was
powerful enough to recreate the illusion even in a stage-worn opera
such as this. . . . In the end it was Rosing himself who carried the
responsibilities, and to him the success of the evening was due.

That summer and fall Val took the little company to Ireland and Manchester. In his book, Ivor Newton tells how while in Manchester Val

produced a charity week of opera in which he sang *Faust* with
Mignon Nevada as Marguerite and Robert Radford as Mephistopheles. Rosing set out to break every tradition and even restored
the ballet, which had not been seen in England for years, appoint-
ing himself its leading dancer although he was already the leading
tenor. The "corps de ballet" consisted of sweet young things from
the Manchester dancing schools, their ages between fourteen and
sixteen, and Rosing leapt about among them with remarkable

vigour. It was not very good dancing, but like everything that Rosing did, it was whole-hearted. He bounded about the stage like a Faust possessed, picking up the terrified girls, throwing them over his shoulder, flinging them down on grassy banks and beds of flowers, till their mothers in the stalls began to look at one another in the utmost consternation. The result was, of course, that in the next act Rosing was completely out of breath and the final trio became virtually a duet between Marguerite and Mephistopheles.

I was present with Tetrazzini, who watched his performance from a box with utter bafflement; brought up in the hallowed traditions of the Italian opera houses, she could not understand these eccentricities.

The "hallowed traditions" of opera, according to Val, were well represented by a tenor who could interrupt a love scene with his leading lady and walk away in order to savor and prolong his high note, returning thereafter to his love-making.

More and more Val dreamed of his own opera company where opera would be theatre — where singers would be actors as well as painters in vocal sound. The idea became an obsession.

Chapter 22

American Opera Company

Val, Marie, and little Valerian lived in a flat on Baker Street where, according to Ivor Newton, they did a great deal of entertaining.

> Their friends seemed to include the intellectually great of the time
> . . . who enjoyed Rosing's company and conversation, for he was a fluent and excitable conversationalist, overflowing with ideas and ambition. He talked with eloquence and a passion for abstractions. He would also, after repeated refusals, sing, and at unusual length. The Rosings would spend every penny they had on a party and have nothing with which to pay the milkman next morning. That was their way; they were bohemian as only Russians can be.

Marie provided program translations for Val's Russian songs, rehearsed with him, and entertained for him. However, their earlier separation had set a pattern that was to be repeated. Whatever the difficulties, Val's frequent absences from home must have weakened the bond which had already suffered a previous break. Marie was not a globe-trotter. When I met her in 1958, she affirmed that she would *never* cross that ocean!

And in 1921, Val was to tour America. To his disappointment, his first crossing of the ocean was on the 19,000-ton *Cedric*. He had heard so much about the great ships and wished he might have taken the *Mauretania* or the *Majestic*, but Ed Barber of the Barber Steamship Lines was advancing him the money, and it was necessary to economize, so he took a smaller ship.

On the eighth day of the trip, he was to sing Moussorgsky's "Song of the Flea" for a radiocast. Amazing — to think that his voice would be heard 1,500 miles away! He would be called through the loudspeaker when the moment arrived. But something went wrong with the transmission, and the broadcast, originating from KFI in New Jersey, did not materialize until six weeks later.

In New York, Val stopped at the Carlton Hotel which faced Central Park and was immediately captured by the wonder and grandeur of America. Everything seemed to be conceived and accomplished on such a grand scale and with so much idealism. He hoped to be able to please the Americans, and of course he did, for he was vital, original, and fearless. He missed Ricketts's cry of "Bravo," but soon found a number of admirers, especially among females. It seemed that *they* ran music in America. There was a saying that in France a conductor must have lovers, and they will give him children; and in America he must also have lovers, and they will give him an orchestra. Well, Val was not a conductor, and he didn't need an orchestra, but he was receptive to attention from the opposite sex.

He gave a series of recitals in New York, Boston, Chicago, and then Washington where he sang before President Harding. New York was at first blasé, but Boston, led by critics H. F. Parker and Olin Downes, gave him some of the greatest notices of his career. Parker's was incorporated in his book *EIGHTH NOTES: Voices and Figures of Music and the Dance.* Under "Rosing the Russian," he called Val

an unusual, engrossing singer . . . not to be easily compared with any our concert halls have much known.

Mr. Rosing's voice is a tenor. Heard in stripped song, with neither characterization nor outpoured passion to cloak them, his tones are of clear Italian quality. . . . When he believes that pure song is voice to the music in hand, he sings with clear regard for well-shaped, transparent tone, sustained line, warm felicitous Italian phrasing, adept modulation, spun transition, plastic progress, apt climax.

Usually, however, Mr. Rosing prefers to make his song an insistently expressive art. . . . In his tones he would define and project character; summon picture and vision; evoke and convey passions of the mind, the soul, the body. And he would do all these things to the utmost. For such purpose, he bends or breaks rhythms, chops or fuses phrases, zigzags the melodic line, sharply changes pace or accent, emphasizes contrast, multiplies climax. To gain these ends he uses unashamed what the vestal virgins of song call vocal tricks — the falsetto, for example, or the long-sustained note, swelled, diminished, melted almost inaudibly into the air. . . .

A more personal concert than one of Mr. Rosing's is rare indeed. Not even Chaliapin's are more pervaded by a single spirit. . . .

It is the transmitting, the impassioning power of Mr. Rosing that conveys such sensation. There is rhetoric in such singing but an honest, living rhetoric.

According to Val's notes, he returned to England like a "Puffed Pigeon."

But opera was Val's first love, and while in America, he was eager to observe productions at the Metropolitan and the Chicago Opera companies. Already at the Music Drama, Lapitzky had discarded the old conventional routines and metaphoric meaningless gestures. But, even in the excellence of Lapitzky's productions, there was still something missing in operatic acting. Val was consumed with the desire to research and improve the art.

What he found, both at the Met where Gatti-Casazza ruled and in Chicago where the McCormick dynasty was gambling millions on Mary Garden's directorship, was a situation in common with European countries. With the exception of such great artists as Chaliapin, Mary Garden, Marcoux, Muratore, and Schipa, singers did not know what to do with themselves on stage; there was no artistic direction, and the old-fashioned style of acting was accepted by the press and public. Moreover, and contrary to European countries, the United States lacked a national opera company with opera sung by its own artists, in its own language.

At a party, Val met Serge Prokofiev who had been commissioned by the Chicago Opera to compose a new opera, *Love for Three Oranges*. Prokofiev played portions from the opera, after which he accompanied Val as he sang. Stumbling over the accompaniments of several songs, among them the "Song of the Flea," which Val had performed many times in concert, Prokofiev said, "Why don't you sing something you know better? Don't you know anything else?"

Val turned to Artur Rubenstein, who was also present (and who had previously accompanied Val on tour in England) and said, "Artur, maybe you could help." Artur played the accompaniments superbly, resolving an awkward situation.

Of course, Prokofiev was known for his bad-boy impertinence and sarcasm. He was also exceptionally precocious. By the age of twelve, he had already composed three operas. He was only thirty when *Love for Three Oranges* was produced in Chicago. It was a failure and was shelved after three performances "at a cost of $50,000 an orange." But its satire had been completely misunderstood. In 1949, produced at New York City Opera under Val's direction, the audience found it hilarious. Val had recognized its satire and style, and it was a resounding artistic and box-office success.

In New York, Val met Claire Sheridan, a wonderful sculptress who had just achieved fame by going to the Kremlin and sculpting two "untouchables," Lenin and Trotsky. At the same time, Bill Bullitt, a young journalist and reporter, had attended the Warsaw Peace Conference. Bullitt and Val were keen to meet each other, and Claire provided the opportunity. Though each held strongly to his own political opinions, they found great interest in each other's company. Spending almost every evening together, they paced the floor of Bullitt's library, trying to write a play on the Russian Revolution. Unable to agree on a plot, they finally gave up.

Claire and Val tried to spawn a romance, but between the efforts at playwriting and social commitments, it never evolved. Instead, they contributed all of their efforts to a special concert for famine relief in Russia, Val donating his voice, Claire donating a sculpture of the head of a child, and Bill officiating as Master of Ceremonies. It was a huge success. Herbert Hoover, who was in charge of administering Russian relief at the time, received 1,500 parcels of food and aid from them. In Russia, Val's sister received a food package at the distribution center and found Val's name on it!

By spring of 1922 their paths separated. Claire went back to London and Italy; Bill was divorced from his wife and married the widow of America's first communist, John Reed. Roosevelt appointed Bill as the first Ambassador to Russia in 1933. There was some correspondence between Val and Bill, but they were never to see each other again.

That spring and summer Val concertized in almost every capital of Europe and through England, Belgium, and France. His marriage to Marie was dormant, and Marie was being romanced by a Dr. West.

Val yearned for companionship, romance, and attachment. He was not properly insulated for celibacy. Every capital held fresh potential, and he rationalized his excesses: Didn't his mission in life need feminine inspiration? The penalty was a heavy amount of correspondence with his wife.

Then he met a beautiful girl named Hope in Boston, and the experience changed the rest of his life. He didn't marry her. He met her only six times. The first time, he was warned by the hotel management not to bring a lady into his room again. The second time, he was thrown out of his hotel at 3:00 a.m. The third time, the girl's two brothers came home unexpectedly at 7:00 a.m. and told him that the next time they found him there they would kill him. The fifth meeting took place in Paris. Val was ecstatic with anticipation. He would lock Hope into his heart and never let her go. From the first time he had met her, his future had expanded with happiness and, literally, hope.

Spending every possible moment in her presence, he entertained, caressed, cajoled, and charmed. Then, returning to his hotel after trying out the concert hall on the day of his concert, he received a telegram. It was a final adieu;

Hope's train had already departed.

He felt like a Christmas tree in a vacant lot after New Year's Day. How could he sing a concert? He was consumed with turbulent emotions — brilliant pain, loneliness, longing. And this life-sized opera had no props or supporting walls, no doors or windows for escape. He would somehow have to think only of the step ahead. He channeled his anguish into his songs. He did not know whether the concert was his best or his worst, but the days that followed were hollow and meaningless.

His final American concert was in March, and he was scheduled to sail the same day on the *Homeric*. Suddenly he discovered that the SS *Paris* was to leave two days later and would get him to London in time for his first concert. He immediately changed his sailing date and sped to Boston to meet with Hope for two last days together.

It was the altered sailing date that changed his life. At his first meal aboard the SS *Paris*, he discovered a number of friends; it was a boat popular with the musical elements of New York, Boston, and Chicago. He was besieged with requests to give a concert, and Ganna Walska, who was aboard, loaned him her large stateroom in which to rehearse. At midnight on the following evening, after he had concluded the concert for his friends, he went directly to the radio operator to cable a message to Hope. A young man, also sending a cable, introduced himself as Jack Warner, music critic from Rochester, New York. He was on his way to London to close the deal with conductors Albert Coates and Eugene Goossens for the Rochester Philharmonic Orchestra and for their affiliation with Rochester's Eastman School of Music, backed by Kodak king George Eastman.

"They are both friends of mine; tell me more about it," said Val. When Warner said it was hoped that Rochester would become another Bayreuth, it occurred to Val in a flash that this should be the home of the opera company which he wished to create. He lost no time in gaining Jack Warner's enthusiasm for his idealistic dream. In fact, he assaulted the man with it from five minutes past midnight until sunrise, at which time Warner relayed the spark by radiogram to George Eastman, advising him to cable Rosing an immediate invitation to Rochester. Val was in seventh heaven, wrapped up in his dream of an opera company with singers who would sing and act in accordance with his theories and ideals.

In London he was received as a conquering hero, and he kept secret his possible invitation from Eastman lest it fail to materialize. He met Marie's new love, Dr. West, and admired him to the point of adopting him as a best friend.

Four weeks later, in June 1923, he was giving a series of recitals at the Theatre Des Champs Élysées in Paris. Having heard nothing from Rochester, he surrendered his dream to disappointment. Then, just before going on stage one evening, a cable arrived: Would he be willing to come and discuss his opera plan with Eastman and — in any case — teach voice? It was not what he wanted, but he decided to take the chance. Surely they would come to a mutual understanding. He sent a cable of acceptance and canceled his July and August concerts. Within a week, he set sail on the *Berengaria*. He was not only gambling on his future; he gambled on everything in sight. And he could not lose. He even bet and won on the second they would enter the harbor. In all, he won almost $8,000 during the crossing.

In Rochester Val was met by the secretary of the Eastman School of Music, Arthur See. Arthur's wife was French, and this spelled instant friendship. But when Val conveyed the plan he expected to propose to Eastman, See had to admit that he felt it would never be accepted.

Val was to meet Eastman for lunch in the penthouse of the Kodak building. He went to inspect the Eastman School and the theatre which he found to be the essence of luxury and beauty. The theatre would rival the Grand Opera of Paris, and the school was a model of everything one could desire. There was also a small theatre, Kilbourn Hall, the most modern of the period, seating 600. In addition to the structures themselves was a $16,000,000 cash endowment for the school's theatrical and artistic activities. By the end of his tour, he was ready for any compromise as long as Eastman accepted the idea of creating an American opera company.

Val arranged his books of press clippings, immodestly admitting to himself that they were quite impressive. His plan was businesslike and well prepared. Precisely at 1:00 p.m. he made his appearance at Eastman's office.

Eastman was small in stature, unapproachable in manner, cold, and seemingly bored. He greeted Val politely, but not as one who had crossed the ocean for an important meeting. Val's immediate reaction was to withhold enthusiasm and let Eastman initiate the conversation. After a few polite remarks about the ocean voyage and inquiries as to whether Val had seen the school and theatre, the conversation ceased. "Well," said Eastman after a pause, "what can I do for you?"

"Nothing," Val replied. "What can I do for you? You have a building; it needs to be filled with great artistic activities."

This was obviously not the manner in which things were supposed to proceed, so the cards had to be reshuffled. Though Eastman's exterior was cold, he was a man of keen perception and understanding, so he responded, "Very true. Do you have a plan?"

"Naturally, or I would not have come all the way from England. Do you want to hear it?"

Eastman gave him a sarcastic smile, "Of course . . . of course, or I would not have asked you to come all the way from England."

So they began anew on equal terms. Val pointed out, "America is practically the only great country which hasn't its own national grand opera. Here opera

Val Rosing, producer and director of the American Opera Company, 1924.

is imported. In the realm of classical music, everything American is looked down upon as second rate. The Metropolitan is run as a social club for the elite. It is a rare exception when it has a star singer who is American born. German and Italian directors discount opera in English. The Society for Opera in English has made attempts in Chicago, but they were pathetic attempts. So, in your country the greatest art of all arts (for it is a combination of all arts) is in the hands of German and Italian directors, with French dominating the Chicago Company repertoire.

"I therefore propose that Rochester's Eastman Music School and Theatre form an American national opera company composed entirely of American singers who will sing in English, using beautiful English translations; that English diction will be on a par with the dramatic theatre; and that singers will be actors who will look the part of the roles they sing. I propose two years to train a company of twenty-five to thirty singers in my style of realistic and rhythmical action, blending music and drama as one entity. Instead of a bastard art built of compromise, opera could and should be the greatest artistic expression because of the blending of all its artistic components."

Obviously Eastman caught the artistic vision, but in his usual sardonic manner, he poured cold water on it. "And why do you think you have the ability to create such an opera company?"

Val brought out his book of press reactions. Nothing seemed to move Eastman to enthusiasm, but he murmured "Good . . . good . . . prepare the budget for your plan with Mr. See — he is a good man — and remember, I don't correct mistakes. Everything in the budget will be covered, and you will be responsible for all omissions. I will give you two days to prepare a budget for four years. The national operatic future of America is in your hands. I believe in you." Eastman then offered Val his hand.

Suddenly it dawned on Val that this was a *fait accompli*. He stumbled for words. "Thank you. From this moment I will dedicate my life to an American opera company."

In the next room Mr. See was waiting, and when he saw tears in Val's eyes, he was quick to sympathize.

"Oh, I am sorry," he said, "but I warned you. May I at least engage you for a recital at the school? Maybe next year he will change his opinion . . . he is tough."

"I am sorry to be an emotional fool," Val said, "but he has faith in my plan. This marks a dramatic change in my life. It is good-bye to England and hello to my new country, the USA, and to the cause of national opera here."

Equally moved, they embraced and pledged mutual support, a commitment faithfully kept through many difficulties during their eight-year working relationship. Their close friendship was permanent.

For 24 hours they worked at preparing a plan for the organization of an opera department which, after two years, would be transformed into an American opera company. The next step would be a three-year plan, a project of great magnitude, in which three national opera companies would be formed: an eastern one in New York, a midwestern one in Chicago, and a western one in Los Angeles. The purpose was to render tremendous cultural service to the country, its musicians, its singers, and its composers.

When the plan and budget were presented, complete with a diagram containing a multitude of squares used to correlate departments, Eastman was highly complimentary and secretly asked Arthur if Rosing really had prepared it. Arthur enthusiastically confirmed the fact, a two-year contract was signed, and the United Press delivered the news throughout the country, giving it front-page treatment and national importance.

Auditions were held in Boston, Chicago, and New York, offering a three-year scholarship with free tuition and $1,000 a year for expenses.

Val admitted, "My first blunder was to miscalculate voice teachers, who, of course, did not want to surrender their paying pupils. Since they were willing to give up only their non-paying students, much of the talent was second rate. However, there were some outstanding voices which soon came forward to add luster, and all together they became a dedicated group of American artists and operatic pioneers."

Twenty-four singers were accepted. One of these, Margaret Stevenson, related her experience to me. "The year before," she said, "I had been only a servant in a big household, washing clothes on a washboard, scrubbing bathrooms on my knees, etc. I was often so tired I could hardly climb the stairs to my room at night. I was doing this to save living expenses for myself and an unloved husband, the agreement being that I should have half of the saved money at year's end. In the meantime, I saw the newspaper notice of the auditions being held in Chicago, so I decided to try my luck, although I hadn't studied or sung for months. So I went to Chicago. The theatre was packed with well-dressed aspirants, and I felt conspicuous in my shabby clothes, but surprisingly I had a lot of confidence, and when my turn came I sang the 'Vissi d'arte' from *Tosca*. Val rushed up on the stage and asked me to sing more, which I did, and he gave me the three-year scholarship for the Eastman venture. He did like my voice, but he didn't observe that I was too tall for most tenors. This fact was a great drawback for me in the following years. But I was happy in Rochester."

The singers would receive their training under a staff which included Kermin, the vocal teacher of John Charles Thomas, and the newly arrived Albert Coates and Eugene Goossens. In Paris, Nicolas Slonimsky had accompanied Val on tour. Val sent for this phenomenal musician who spoke no English, but more than made up for it later. Slonimsky was capable of playing any score from memory, flipping the pages of a book which rested on the music rack (in order to keep up with his reading), and correcting the slightest musical mistakes of singers at the same time. No musical error got by him; it merely interrupted his reading. He would leave Rochester after three years to become an assistant to Koussevitzky with the Boston Symphony where he would also become the plague of the Maestro's life. After each rehearsal, Slonimsky would appear with a list of wrong notes each musician had played. He had begun by stopping the orchestra, but that proved impossible, so he adopted the alternate plan. Whatever he did, and however he did it, his phenomenal musicianship seemed to be interpreted by Koussevitzky as a reflection upon himself — and finally, the Maestro let him go. He went on to become conductor, composer, lecturer, teacher, and author.

Previously while in London, Val had been invited to the chorus rehearsal of a group of Russian refugees. After the rehearsal, a performer of magic tricks had been introduced. He was tall, dark, and pimply faced with magnetic eyes. A refugee from Moscow and Tiflis and a member of the Vahtangoff Studio (an Armenian offshoot of the Moscow Art Theatre Studio), he was a clever performer. Val had been impressed and had invited the man, Rouben Mamoulian, to his home. A friend of Val's was authoring a play, and Val, who was leaving for an American concert tour, recommended the direction be entrusted to Mamoulian. The script was mediocre, and neither rewriting nor Rouben's cleverness could save it, so Rouben had returned to a secretarial job.

Val now brought Mamoulian to Rochester to be his general assistant. He was brilliant, a great egomaniac, and an excellent stage director. Soon after he arrived, he fastened his hypnotic eyes on Val, waited out a penetrating silence and then posed the question, "Who is going to direct the operas?"

Until that moment there had been no question in Val's mind, but before he knew what he was saying, he stammered, "Well, I guess we can do them together."

"How?" Mamoulian demanded with the same fixed stare.

"Well, we could divide them by scenes."

"How?"

Val then proceeded to break down *Faust*, giving Mamoulian all the best scenes. Val couldn't explain to himself the hypnotic effect of Mamoulian's methods. It was as though his own will was paralyzed. Sometime later, Mamoulian admitted that he had both studied and practiced hypnotism.

When things went wrong on stage, Val and Mamoulian fell into an habitual pattern of eyeing each other and simultaneously saying, "*You* fix it." Mamoulian graduated to Broadway and then to Hollywood, and, at a time when Val's career was in shock after the wartime closure of the Royal Opera of Covent Garden where he was Producer-Director in 1939, he met Mamoulian in Hollywood and inquired about potential involvement in the world of films. Mamoulian replied, "Do you need help, Val?" and offered him $200. Val blanched, repulsed the money and withdrew.

Val had two assistants for teaching body movement: Martha Graham and Anna Duncan (one of Isadora's favorite adopted dancers). For English diction, he brought Mrs. William Carrington — American millionairess, sister of Walter Huston, and teacher of John Barrymore. Among the coaches were Emmanuel Balaban, Otto Luening Ernst Bacon, and Guy Harrison.

Paul Horgan, a student, had come to the Eastman School of Music to study voice, fortified with a letter of introduction from Richard Bonelli to Arthur Alexander, the vocal instructor, and with the promise of employment at a Rochester newspaper. He discovered that Alexander had moved to Los Angeles and that the newspaper in Rochester had been sold. He was penniless as he stood in front of a poster announcing the new American opera company. In his book, *Encounters with Stravinsky,* Horgan says:

> At the bottom of the poster a photograph of the director was pasted beside his name, and I looked, and looked again with confirmed amazement. He was the acclaimed Russian tenor Vladimir Rosing with whose singing and style I had fallen in love in Albuquerque two years ago through the phonograph.

Horgan went to the meeting in Kilbourn Hall to hear Val describe his plans for the future of the new opera company. When Val failed to make any mention of scenery or costumes, Horgan surmised that no plans for that important aspect of opera had yet been made. Although he had no experience beyond painting a simple backdrop for a cadet production at the Roswell National Guard Armory, he resolved to become the stage designer for the Rochester Opera.

> I returned to my garret and without an evening meal set to work. I drew and painted some scenes for operas I had never attended, but whose atmosphere and stories I knew from the Victor *Book of the Opera*, and from recordings.
>
> The next morning, I gained access to Rosing, he liked my drawings, assigned a few other test subjects, and in two days I became the artistic designer of the Rochester American Opera Company on the basis of desperation, confidence, and need which drove me to what amounted to be a swindle.

Horgan's self-appraisal is amusingly modest, but he had a "devoted familiarity with the books and reproduced drawings of Gordon Craig, Adolphe Appia, and Robert Edmund Jones" and he managed to produce sets of beauty that first year (by his own admission), particularly for the Pilgrim's

Scene from *Tannhäuser* and the Prison Scene of Gounod's *Faust*. Horgan's first published novel, *The Fault of Angels*, was based on his Rochester experience.

The underlying principle of the productions was to make the stage come alive dramatically in such a way that every movement, grouping, and reaction was so completely coordinated with the music itself that action and music both emphasized and enhanced each other. Nowhere should the illusion of dramatic life be lost; nowhere should a single bar of music lose significance.

Early on, Val became aware that he seemed to create actors in his own image and likeness. Out from under his directorial guidance, they ceased to be good actors. He searched and experimented to find a method of acting that would free them from imitation. And when he found it, he realized that he had a new and lasting technique.

Val's definition of acting was that it "is the re-creation of a character conceived by the author and brought to life through the medium of one's body." In contradiction to Stanislavsky's method, he said, "The mind is strong enough to re-create situations that have already been created. It is not necessary to re-live experience. Nor do emotions necessarily need to have been experienced in real life in order to project them."

Val scorned the "when I am in costume" excuse as a mark of the amateur. "When you develop your body language," he said, "you suddenly become a person — you speak! you dominate! — without apology." He did not try to illuminate subliminally or to offer general precepts for a groping game. He gave exercises in concentration, relaxation, visualization, and projection. But he also taught rules for the independent and coordinated action of the thirteen joints used in sculpturing body movement. He taught that every movement has a preparatory movement in the opposite direction, and that the retreat of a gesture is of extreme importance. He taught eye focus, head angles; he cut off waving arms and wandering hands, and he demanded that *every* unnecessary movement be eliminated! "MOVE and HOLD" he would cry. ". . . MOVE and HOLD as though a series of still shots is being photographed." There was a formula for falling, rising, kneeling, embracing; a formula for comedy attained by body distortion; for old age — shoulders drooped, head carried forward, knees bent, and feet shuffling; for drunkenness — lack of balance, uneven steps, and exaggerated gestures.

But he did not set patterns of action to music. He brought opera to its maximum effectiveness with dramatic interpretation resulting *from* rather than affixing itself *to* the music. The body and the music would become as one — a complete blend of sound and motion, with every motion coming out of the sound.

He built his entire principle of motion on this theory. It was a choreographic approach, but since ballet is mathematical and its motion continuous, the style was completely different.

I shall never forget the characters of Ping, Pang, and Pong, played by John Reardon, David Williams, and Paul Huddleston, in the 1957 production of Puccini's *Turandot* which Val directed at the New York City Center Opera. The trio was a gem of perfection — every movement coordinated into a stylized artistic unity. It was my first season of working with Val, and I was amazed. He said to me, "In this opera company you have young American singers who are willing to learn and will take direction, so it is possible to create."

In the following season, it was obvious that there was no possibility of repeating this type of composition in Chicago's production of the same opera. Each of the three Italian singers was on his own trip; only someone who had seen what it *could* be, knew what it *wasn't*.

"Thinking, feeling, and projection must be coordinated," Val said. "Great artistry is correct thought and deep feeling in a perfectly controlled and coordinated body, projected with corresponding energy, maximum clarity, and a minimum of effort."

Byron Belt, journalist, former assistant manager of the Chicago Lyric Opera, and the president of Chicago's Cosmopolitan School of Music, reminisced for the *Massachusetts Republican*:

> With his energy at white heat, Rosing demonstrated HOW to act, HOW to move on the stage and HOW to think through the WHYs. Few directors can accomplish as much in weeks as Val accomplished in mere moments. The man could communicate a soul and genius dedicated to making music come alive.

Mornings at Rochester were devoted to dramatic instruction. Afternoons were devoted to music coaching and rehearsing, and the latter spilled over into the evenings and weekends. "Days and hours," said Val, "did not exist. We worked as much as was needed."

Soprano Margaret "Stevie" Stevenson, one of the original members of the Rochester group, recalled for me those rehearsals when the cast would think, "*Finally*, we got through a scene without interruption," only to have Val charge down the aisle and leap up onto the stage with a placating "practically almost — practically almost."

The San Carlo Opera Company was paying its annual visit to Rochester where it performed in the Eastman Theatre. All members of the Rochester opera group were required to attend since, like other opera companies, the San Carlo represented the antithesis of everything the new group would come to stand for.

Rigoletto was one of the operas presented, and since the Rochester fledglings were working on the fourth act of that opera for their first assignment, they scrutinized every detail. Charles Hedley, one of the group's original members, recalled that all of the time Rigoletto was exacting his vocal vengeance over the receipt of the sack which supposedly contained the body of the Duke who had disgraced his daughter, the sack lay someplace upstage while Rigoletto was downstage wringing his heart out to the footlights. "All of this," he said, "was a matter of amusement and irony, but also an education for all of us young novitiates."

The Eastman Theatre with its large orchestra pit presented motion picture performances three times a day, interspersed with orchestra overtures and live entertainment. This was the setting for the Rochester group's first operatic sequences, before it moved to Kilbourn Hall.

The opera department, begun in 1923, was launched as the Rochester American Opera Company, November 20, 1924, with scenes from *Boris Godounov* and *Pagliacci* in the Eastman Theatre.

On January 15 and 29, 1925, *Faust* was presented. Prior to one of these performances, Val, Mamoulian, and Paul Horgan attended a séance at which Dr. Faust had promised to make an appearance during the performance. The incident, however, was forgotten when trouble developed with the lighting. Later, Val tried to find out what had gone wrong, but neither the lighting director nor the stage hands could locate the problem. They were in the habit of projecting the pattern of a cross at a designated time. The cross had appeared. But immediately something seemed to short out, yet nothing else was affected. Said the lighting director, "It was as though someone walked in front of the light." Val's and Mamoulian's eyes happened to meet, and in a moment of silent comprehension, the mystery seemed to dissolve.

Carmen and *Martha* were presented in 1925, followed by *The Marriage of Figaro, Cavalleria Rusticana*, and *Pagliacci* in the spring of 1926. Following their performances in Kilbourn Hall, they performed in surrounding cities and toured upstate New York and Canada. The company had become a group of singers who knew how to act, and who were cast for physical appearance as well as vocal ability. No fat prima donnas were playing romantic young heroines. Val had developed a style of operatic choreography which brought the blurred vision of opera into focus. He brought to it logic, sincerity, physical coordination, and rhythmical action.

One of the company's members, Brownie Peebles, would write to Charles Hedley in 1971.

> Who would know that the productions given in the Amphitheatre in Chatauqua under Rosing, with full stage lighting, costumes, etc., and the Rochester Philharmonic Orchestra would prompt Mr. Ralph Norton to contribute $40,000 to build Norton Hall. I can

remember his very words: "If we can have opera like THIS, I'll build you an opera house — with the stipulation that the singers learn to perform in English the way these singers do."

With the two-year incubation period at an end, what would happen? Would Eastman still support the project? Val went off to Seattle and Vancouver to teach master classes during the summer. In Seattle he was captured by the teachings of Yogananda and decided to become a yogi. In Vancouver his spiritual enthusiasm brought him invitations to "preach" in churches, and his spiritual proclamations produced editorials declaring him a "second Messiah." He was rescued from this lofty assignment — or, as he called it "near disaster" — by a summons from Rochester.

The New York Theater Guild had extended an invitation to the opera company to run for a week in their new theatre in the spring of 1927. Who ever heard of opera on Broadway?

In the meantime, fall performances in Kilbourn Hall for 1926 included *The Pirates of Penzance* with "Prelude" and "Ballet" from *A Forest Play* by Howard Hanson (conducted by the composer), and *Pagliacci* together with *The Sunset Trail*, an operatic cantata in one act with poetic text by Gilbert Moyle and music by Charles Wakefield Cadman.

Mary Garden, after fulfilling a concert engagement in the Eastman Theatre, was given a tour of the school and came upon the opera group in rehearsal. She was so impressed with what she saw that she affirmed, "Someday I must come and perform *Carmen* with this company."

She was pinned down on the spot with, "When?" Committing herself to February 7, 1927, she traveled to Rochester on three consecutive weekends for rehearsals. Tenor Charles Hedley chalked it up as a pinnacle experience to be her Don Jose.

> Most of the Carmens that played opposite me complained of the bruises inflicted by me, particularly through the struggles of the third act. The momentous challenge of singing with Mary Garden really chopped me down to size; I was nervous and inhibited. However, I was making progress in my technique of creating the illusion of physical struggle, and Miss Garden was so responsive and her muscular action so loose that it melted and blended into my every move.

Imagine his surprise when Miss Garden said, prior to the third act quarrel, "Now don't hold back in this scene; throw me down as hard as you possibly can. You cannot possibly hurt me. I know exactly how to stop myself with the flat of my hands on the stage."

So he took her at her word, and when rehearsing the part where Jose, in an outburst of fury, throws Carmen to the ground, Miss Garden hit the stage floor with a resounding smack that Charles felt could surely be heard out on the street. In alarm, he thought, "I have really overdone it!" He could feel the company behind him gasp and freeze, the action on stage coming to a complete halt. Even Goossens and the orchestra were transfixed, and there was silence throughout the auditorium. Everyone waited for the temperamental outburst. Nothing happened. Miss Garden lay prone, her face buried, for an eternity. Then slowly, from her prone position, she raised only her head and caught the eye of Goossens, "Isn't he wonderful?" she whispered.

And now for Broadway! The gospel, according to the Rochester American Opera Company, was to present opera in English with dramatic acting on a par with singing. It succeeded with both press and public.

Conductor Eugene Goossens, in his book, *Overture and Beginners: A Musical Autobiography,* said:

> We opened with a sparkling performance of *Figaro* in English which, I think, for perfection of style, *mise-en-scène*, and ensemble, can rarely have been surpassed. This was not a student performance, but a thought-provoking and entertaining exhibit by finished artists. The credit goes largely to Rosing, whose production was original and novel in a subtly detailed way. It certainly vindicated his theory that young American artists could adequately present small-scale productions of opera on original lines as opposed to the conventional ones featured elsewhere.

Goossens footnoted this by saying, "The Rochester venture undoubtedly paved the way for companies like the New York City Opera."

Speaking of *Butterfly*, which was presented the second night with Cecile Sherman in the title role, he said:

> Until then the harbour of Nagasaki had always appeared on the back-cloth, with the watching Butterfly silhouetted against the paper screens, as the curtain fell. Rosing reversed the procedure, with Nagasaki in the audience, and the silhouettes behind semi-transparent *shoshi* drawn across the proscenium arch. . . . A refreshing feature, too, was the elimination of much of the conventional and rather silly business with the relatives in Act I. . . . [The event] aroused the excited comments of the New York critics who lavished their hallelujahs on [it].

Up to this point, Eastman had paid the company's expenses but let it be known that his support thereafter would extend only to Rochester's city limits; it was time for the company to become independent. Many considered this limited support a mistake. Samuel Chotzinoff's headline in the *World* read, "George Eastman misses the boat."

A national committee was formed, headed by Mr. and Mrs. William Carrington, to take over the company and make it a national institution. The board of directors included Mrs. Christian Holmes, Mrs. Rockefeller McCormick, Mrs. Stanley McCormick (who generously financed the company's Chicago seasons), Otto Kahn, Nicholas Longworth (Speaker of the House of Representatives), and Mrs. Longworth.

Upon leaving the nest in Rochester, the group took up residence in an abandoned luxury hotel in the fashionable summer retreat of Magnolia, Massachusetts, just south of Gloucester on the Atlantic coast. Here they prepared for their big New York opening that would take place that fall of 1927.

For the following three summers Magnolia would be their home while rehearsing repertoire for upcoming seasons. Though vacant and unattended, the hotel had huge ballrooms and dining rooms which were perfect for rehearsals, and of course there were ample sleeping quarters for all. Next door was the new affluent hotel which had replaced the old one, and here the company dined in luxury on the American Plan.

Leslie Buswell, an Illinois patron, invited the company to perform at his North Shore estate in Gloucester where he had an English stone theatre, Stillington Hall. Performances of *Figaro*, *Pagliacci*, *Martha*, *Abduction*, and *Faust* roused such enthusiasm that the American Society for Opera in English was organized to partially sponsor the group. Buswell quoted Joe Leiter, a prominent patron of the arts, as saying, after the first performance of *Faust*, "That's the first time I ever cared a damn whatever happened to Marguerite."

Victor Roudin and his wife Mata met Val at this time, participated in plays which he was directing at Stillington Hall, and remained Val's lifelong friends. Years later they recalled those times with animation, interrupting each other with laughter and embellishments.

> We first saw him dining at a table next to ours in the very proper, fastidious New England hotel. We thought he was an Armenian rug dealer, a suspicion that was confirmed when we saw him drink tea from his saucer.

They recalled that

> for *Peter Ibetson*'s mystery effect he successfully used a semi-transparent gauze curtain, and for Mrs. Belmont's play about

miners, he achieved the effect of a descending elevator by having us gradually bend our knees.

Mata recalled Val's performance at one of the hotel's Sunday night concerts:

> Of course, there were Russian and French songs which he explained in English. Then came the English group, including the famous folk song "Lord Randall, My Son," which he also explained in English. But in what language was he singing it?

According to Ezra Pound, it had to be either "Russian or Rosing."

Mata said, "He always called me 'Dear,' and after some time I said, 'I think you call me Dear because you can't remember by name.' With an expression of simple delight, he congratulated my discovery—'You're right!' "

The gods were smiling on Val's operatic dream and on his personal life as well. He was in love again. Marie gave him a divorce, and on February 26, 1927, he married Margaret "Peggy" Williams, one of the company members. On March 16, 1928, he and Peggy were blessed with a daughter, Diana.

That December, the American Opera Company, as such, made its auspicious debut in Washington before President Coolidge, and on January 10, 1928, it opened its first season in New York at the new Gallo Theater with *Faust* in an English adaptation by Robert Simon. Scenery and costumes were designed by Robert Edmund Jones, and the new Musical Director was Frank St. Leger. Val cast two singing actors to characterize Faust; Patrick Killkelly represented the aged philosopher, and Clifford Newdall, the rejuvenated lover. Mephistopheles was the youthful, debonair, George Fleming Houston. Natalie Hall was the delicately beautiful Marguerite.

The *Literary Digest* for January 28, 1928, gave two full pages to the event under the headline "OPERA IN AMERICA FOR AMERICANS":

> Opera in English interpreted by American singers and presented from a fresh dramatic point of view, has been accomplished by the American Opera Company, and the sign of approval has been given by the most sophisticated opera people in the country. Opera . . . has come to us in the same manner as has long been demanded by French, German and Italian audiences of their singers. . . .

The article went on to quote Mr. Henderson of *The Sun* who, as an adherent to the tradition, praised the performance but cautioned the company about going too far in its "endeavors to cleanse old operas of some of their antiquated features."

Lawrence Gilman of the New York *Herald Tribune* said,

If anyone had told us that a performance of Gounod's "Faust" could be made prevailingly fresh and engaging we should have tried to smile politely and with an appearance of belief. . . . The American Opera Company . . . taught us that Gounod's banal and moth-eaten opus could be transformed into a music-drama which an adult playgoer might hear and witness without making apologies to his intelligence. . . . What happened at the Gallo Theater last night, in essence, was that the American Opera Company . . . showed us the ancient brigantine of Gounod, Barbier, and Carré freed of barnacles, fitted with a motor engine of the latest type, her spars and hull newly painted, cutting the operatic waters with a clean swiftness which was exhilarating to behold. . . .

Gilman said that "This is . . . a very different 'Faust' from that 'grand opera in five acts and eleven scenes' which has held the stage for almost seventy years . . . a new way of looking at old things."

The Arthur Judson office became the company's booking management, and Frank St. Leger became its permanent conductor. Robert Simon of the *New Yorker* provided English translations; Deems Taylor, then editor of *Musical America*, also contributed some translations. The ranks widened to include John Gurney, Thelma Votipka, and Charles Kullman, Sophie Braslau, and Helen Oelheim, all of whom later went on to the Met. The sisters Natalie and Bettina Hall, who joined the company at this point, later, together with Charles Hedley, played on Broadway for two years in Schubert's *Three Little Girls*. Bettina eventually married Raymond Rubicam, and they spent their winters in Phoenix, Arizona, where Bettina, as president of the Phoenix Civic Opera Guild, brought Val to direct their musicals in 1958-1959.

One of the most memorable of those from Rochester was George Fleming Houston who was the unforgettable Mephistopheles of that New York opening in the Gallo Theater.

The company was endorsed by Presidents Coolidge and Hoover. In a February 18, 1930, letter to Nicholas Longworth, Hoover stated,

. . . It is a vital movement to establish a national organization for young American singers, composers, and writers. . . . I wish to endorse so fine an effort and to urge all music loving Americans to lend their support in making it a permanent national institution.

Boston acclaimed it as "ushering in the operatic millennium." The *Chicago Tribune* said, "The American Opera has come to teach us what opera should be." Olin Downes of *The New York Times* said, "I would never have believed I could be sitting on the edge of my chair wondering what was going to happen next in a well-known opera like *Faust*."

Margaret Stevenson recalled how, in one of those *Faust* performances, Val suddenly had to replace an ailing tenor. Though he himself had always sung the role in French, he decided to sing it in English rather than violate the artistic principle of "opera in the language of the people." The first act went quite smoothly in spite of the fact that Val was compelled to improvise while singing, and that he got trapped with repeating "Be mine de-delight" a few dozen times in succession. During the intermission, he inscribed cue words on bits of paper and pinned them to scenery or placed them on the floor at various locations where he would be sitting or standing.

Alas, just before the curtain rose, a conscientious stage hand took a last critical look at the set and carefully removed all that clutter from the stage! A serious blow, but Val struggled manfully until he came to the aria, then he relaxed into French. The aria met with such enthusiastic applause that it stopped the show for about ten minutes, after which no one noticed or cared about his difficulties with the English text. But a portion of Robert Simon's translation which read, "She lies there in prison like any common, vile delinquent," especially delighted cast members when it came out, "She lies dere in prison like a b-a-d v-o-m-a-n."

One of the aims of the company was to feature American composers. Charles Wakefield Cadman's *Sunset Trail* had been added to the repertory in 1926 to double-bill with *Pagliacci*; in 1929 the company premiered Clarence Loomis's *Yolanda of Cyprus*.

In centers such as Boston and Chicago, which had a heritage of opera and which up to that point had been exposed to foreign productions, the company encountered its warmest receptions and greatest successes. It played Chicago for three seasons, and the press was outstanding. Even Claudia Cassidy, who could lacerate with brittle rhetoric, showered praise. Rumor had it that Samuel Insull, mogul of the Chicago Opera, wanted to buy out this young rival.

One of the Chicago patrons who helped support the project was Mrs. John Alden Carpenter, then Mrs. Christian Borden. After a public dress rehearsal of *Butterfly*, she spoke to tenor Charles Hedley regarding the scene where Pinkerton and the American Consul drink to each other's health, to the bride, and to America. She said, "You know, my family has subscribed to a box in the Chicago Opera for years. I have seen more performances of *Butterfly* than I can count, and this is the first time I ever knew what that scene was all about."

Val exercised a non-star policy. Names were not stressed in publicity, though they were given full program credit. And it was against the rules ever to take curtain calls until the end of a performance so as not to destroy the dramatic illusion that had evolved. The first act of *Pagliacci* ends, of course, with Canio alone on stage singing "Vesti La Guibba." His heart breaks with the discovery of his wife's betrayal, but he knows the show must go on. It is a great dramatic moment, and traditionally the tenor goes through much melodramatic scenery-chewing to force himself to enter the tent and get ready for the ensuing puppet show. As Val directed it, Canio literally clung to the ropes of the tent where he must assume his make-up and costume. He sees the dagger, dropped during his struggle with Nedda, slowly picks it up, plunges it into his sash, looks vengefully in the direction Nedda's lover has fled, and then — bracing himself — he painfully disappears into the tent. There was always a tremendous ovation following this retrained and sustained climax, but when performed in Chicago, the applause would not stop. It was awing, and certainly gratifying, as the company adhered to its policy of no curtain calls, and the applause literally continued until the curtain rose for Act II. The press said, ". . . The audience filled the intermission with applause."

Despite the unraveling of the country's financial fabric, the American Opera Company was still going great guns. The publicity and acclaim was never greater than that given by Richmond, Virginia, for the season's final engagement in January 1930. Mr. Judson pointed out that, given the country's economic situation, there could be difficulties; however, he presented a cheerful picture. "The Judson booking staff will be out on the road winding up future commitments with all the ability and resources at its command," he said. There was a sardonic smile on the face of Isaac Van Grove, who had succeeded Frank St. Leger. Those near heard him humming the Chopin *Funeral March*.

George Brown, leading salesman of the Judson office, went on his appointed rounds to book for the following season, but he returned in short order. One of his last stops had been Atlanta where people gathered in groups on the street corners, sharing their gloom; no one was interested in promoting a season of opera in 1930.

Seven years of work and a magnificent dream died overnight. Many imitations have materialized since the American Opera Company, but the *Los Angeles Times* critic Albert Goldberg said in 1963, "There has been nothing comparable since." In an article written for *Opera News* by Quaintance Eaton in 1971, she said, "Rosing and his American Opera Company were, it seems, way ahead of their time."

It was Val's personal tragedy that opera would continue for several decades in the same stilted and melodramatic style after a glimpse of what could be. But here and there, seedlings sprang from the fertile soil of his dream to become teachers, conductors, concert artists, and opera stars. Each individual rocked in the cradle of that great inspiration glows when speaking of it, as did Mary Garden when she said, "My enthusiasm is beyond words. . . . I never saw anything like it!"

Chapter 23

Return to London

Val was now a citizen of the blessed country which had given realization to his operatic dream and provided him with a wife and child. What more could he have wanted? But how temporary it had all been. The operatic dream was but a memory. The marriage had not withstood the tragedy and ensuing financial hardship. And after three years of virtual unemployment, Val found himself one bleak day in 1933 with five cents in his pocket. Was he going to accept the paralysis that circumstances seemed to have prescribed? He knew there was purpose for his life. What must he do to find his niche?

That was the day that he received an invitation from BBC to do a broadcast in England! The travel was arranged by BBC, or some divine emissary, and Val was on his way.

London — a breath of hope! There were dear faces that were missing, of course, for it had been ten years, and there were bound to be changes. Val's son, Valerian, now twenty-three, was a radio star and crooner!

The broadcast interview was reviewed by Richard Holt in a monthly brochure, *RECORDS we specially recommend,* under the headline: "Famous Tenor Forgives His Crooning Son." Val was quoted as saying,

> Torch singers, yes . . . they at least are elemental, and express something in the soul of everyone. But crooners! — Well. Most American crooners are so vulgar. It is not only the monotony of their voices, but the cheapness of the mind behind. They sing with

dead eyes. There is nothing there. A voice minimised [sic] and expelled by mechanical means. When I heard my son was going to become a crooner, I was disgusted. But then I heard him! I like his singing — he shows a sensitive personality and background.

It was clarified that both father and son (Valerian later changed his name to Gil Russell) met on the subject of jazz, both agreeing that Duke Ellington's band was rhythm as it ought to be.

The article went on to announce a Wigmore Hall recital scheduled by Val for October 28 and said,

> . . . It is to be hoped that no one will play Rachmaninoff's Prelude in C sharp minor before his first concert on Saturday or they will probably not hear him then. It is the hoodoo of his life.

Ivor Newton resumed his role as accompanist, and concluding groups of English songs by Cyril Scott and Herbert Hughes were accompanied by their composers.

Many old friends had disappeared, but Val's audience was intact. Richard Holt's review stated:

> This incomparable singer has now reached full maturity as an artist. This recital was a triumph, as not only did Rosing reveal all his old gifts of vocal power, interpretative insight and vivid imagination, but his singing showed that time has even deepened his sense of values and psychological portraiture. Equally gratifying was the full hall, which, for a singer who has not (with one exception) sung here for ten years, is a remarkable tribute. . . . Rosing's singing of Moussorgsky is a spiritual experience similar to Chaliapin's Boris.

Readers were urged to attend the next recital on December 12, when Val would "also expound, with illustrations, his novel and even revolutionary principles of operatic interpretation."

One critic, identified only as H.S.G. of the *Daily Chronicle*, wrote, "Rosing's true medium is the cinema. That he could live for ten years in the United States of America without any film director seeing the perfectly obvious fact is surprising." Another critic admitted, "It is not Rosing's singing so much as Rosing himself we go to hear." Still another, identified only as H.E.W., said, "Not even Chaliapin can lay bare the Russian soul in its picaresque moods with surer touch." Some criticized the use of falsetto and distortion of tone for interpretative purposes, but all agreed that his dramatic art was unsurpassable.

Val had lunch with George Bernard Shaw who had just returned from Russia; and he sang, accompanied by Rubenstein, at a Barrymore party where he met Mary Pickford and Douglas Fairbanks. Before long, he was acquiring fascinating new friends — Lord Birkenhead, Lord Snowden, the Somerset Maughams, Prince Paul of Greece. Somerset Maugham's niece, the artist Honor Earle, sketched the portrait of Val which was later used on his printed programs. William Bullitt cabled to announce his appointment as Ambassador to Russia, and Claire Sheridan reported that she was now sculpting a bust of Mussolini. Stalin was making his Great Purge of Russia, and Val lost all contact with his family.

His first production in England was Sheridan's *The Rivals* set to music and presented as a light opera at the Kingsway Theatre, with Queen Mary in attendance. At Albert Hall he gave a recital of Russian songs said by *The Chronicle and Herald* to be "rendered with a depth of feeling and power of interpretation [that] enthralled the large audience." He produced *I Pagliacci* at the Pavilion in Bath, singing the role of Canio himself. *The Chronicle and Herald* had one regret: that it could not have been of longer duration. "Such an attraction," it said, "has been only too rare in recent years." Val made a series of recordings with Parlophone Records, and at Aeolian Hall he produced scenes from operas "to demonstrate the practicability of opera being given in a small concert hall without an elaborate and costly production, thus bringing it within the reach of the general public." He hoped it would serve to introduce a new form of musical drama entertainment, in contrast to the usual type of individual recital.

At Wigmore Hall Studios, Val established an operatic Studio for the Development of British Music Drama and Opera Comique. He stated his objectives: to teach a new technique of operatic acting, to establish a modern standard of operatic productions, and to develop a British Opera Company based on these principles.

Then, in the fall of 1936, he and Albert Coates received backing for a season of opera at the Royal Opera House at Covent Garden. Presented as The British Music Drama Opera Company, its repertoire included *Pickwick*, a new opera by Albert Coates, and *Julia*, a new light opera by Roger Quilter.

On the 13th of November before their opening on the 18th, Val produced the first televised opera in the world. It was presented by BBC and featured the cast of the newly formed company in Coates's *Pickwick*.

Richard Capell of the *London Daily Telegraph* said, "If it had been the regular practice at Covent Garden, to introduce new English operas there during the last fifty years, we might have had an English repertory by now." Ernest Newman devoted two long Sunday *London Times* articles to the same subject.

The following year, 1937, the Covent Garden English Opera Company was organized by Percy Heming with Val as the producing director. They planned to follow the season with a tour of the provinces which would give the singers steady occupation for 30 weeks of the year.

It had been a decade since the American Opera Company had made its sensational debut. The dream had not perished; it had changed nationalities, but it was flourishing. Now that audiences could understand what was going on, they were beginning to see what they had missed, and learned to revel in beautiful vocal and orchestral expertise.

Harold Rosenthal, in his book *Opera at Covent Garden,* said,

> Indeed the first London season and provincial tour were both so successful that plans were made for a longer season and tour in the autumn of 1939, and it was only the outbreak of the war that prevented what promised to be the most successful native operatic enterprise since the days of the B.N.O.C. [of 1922].

The 1937 season opened with *Faust,* and music critic Eric Blom said it was

> distinctly remarkable . . . it was the new and original and thoughtful way in which the opera was staged — really and truly for the first time in one's experience — that made the evening so promising and interesting.

Another critic said, "the Faust conventions of eight decades were replaced last night by intelligence, vitality and beauty."

Albert Coates conducted performances of *Cavalleria Rusticana, I Pagliacci,* Wagner's *The Mastersingers,* and a new opera by British composer George Lloyd, *The Serf.* Eugene Goossens, Robert Ainsworth, Stanford Robinson, and Sidney Beer joined the staff of conductors.

Of *The Mastersingers,* the *Edinburgh Evening News* (Scotland) said, "measured against the highest standards of the past, the performance . . . emerged with complete credit."

On October 5, 1938, Val produced another televised opera, *I Pagliacci,* for BBC.

Val was riding high again. His artistic success was at a peak, and he was teaching and passing along his technique of acting. And yes, he had a new companion. Winifred "Vicki" Campbell had performed as "Lydia" in his 1935 production of *The Rivals.* A spark had ignited between them, so once again Val's life was full.

Vicki's vocal teacher was Georges Cunelli, to whom Val referred many singers, and whose book, *Voice No Mystery,* was published in 1973 with a preface by Paul Robeson. In his book, Cunelli recalled:

> At the end of July 1939 I went for a wonderful holiday in the Alpes
> Maritimes with Rosing and his future wife who were my dear
> friends. . . . We had an enjoyable and exciting time, but we had to
> interrupt it suddenly owing to the widespread rumours of the
> possibility of a second world war. We returned to London on the
> "last train" as everyone called it.

From his office in Covent Garden, Val and his desolate staff watched the
blimps with hanging chains patrolling the skies. Then came the report that the
season at Covent Garden would be canceled. The closing of its doors would
abort any further efforts to establish English opera there for almost a decade.
The American Ambassador advised Val, as well as other Americans, to leave
England immediately.

Val cabled Albert Coates, who had gone to Hollywood, advising him to
remain there. A return cable urged Val to come to Hollywood and organize a
new American opera company. Val married Vicki, and they were the only
couple to get a stateroom for two on a ship where many had to sleep in the pool
area. Aboard the same ship were friends Artur Rubenstein, Paul Robeson,
Alicia Markova, and Leslie Banks. Val had toured with Emma Calvé and
Rubenstein early in his singing career. He had become friends with Paul
Robeson in America — a friendship which continued in Europe.

Prior to his appearance in *Sanders of the River* in 1935, Robeson had
written:

> Dear Vladdy — This is my first letter in years. How I hate to write
> and love to talk. I've been touring around and trying to fight this
> winter. Am almost convinced this is not a Black Man's climate.
>
> Have also been buried with books and gramophone records,
> working upon a thesis which I think may be of value to the African
> Negro in developing his institutions and culture. Will chat with you
> about it sometime.
>
> I feel as you do about the Play. Am hoping I'll find [the right]
> character some day.
>
> The play I have in mind to do is nothing more than a super Edgar
> Wallace — piece is laid in Africa. It's not important, but might get
> me back in the theatre.
>
> How are things going with you? Will certainly try to get to your
> concert and try to come along afterward.
>
> Can't tell you how I enjoyed our talk that day and it started me
> thinking a lot. I'll also talk to you about that when I see you. All

The Covent Garden English Opera Company, Vladimir Rosing, producer, 1938; left to right: Heddle Nash (young Faust), Percy Heming (artistic organizer), Frank Sale (older Faust).

this reminds me of very little boy who always says — Now
"Daddy" — let's have a good talk. Kindest wishes to all at No. 4.
Paul

Val was sympathetic with Paul's desire to elevate the black man's role in the
world, but he advised caution in Paul's enthusiasm for Russia's communist
regime — a regime which might seem to represent coequality, but which, in
reality, simply shifted prejudices.

Paul had visited Russia in 1936. In 1939, just two months prior to the
present crisis, Hitler had made an alliance with Russia's dictator, Stalin. Then
had come the attack on Poland, with Great Britain and France declaring war
two days later. There would be much to talk about on this trip across the ocean.

Chapter 24

From Crisis to Crisis

Val was in high gear. While in London, he had written a letter to the Pope. After soliciting a number of signatures, he had presented it to Joseph Kennedy, the American Ambassador. Kennedy seemed to agree with Hitler's speeches critical of Britain and would later resign his post in 1941. He refused to send the letter. But William Bullitt, who had been transferred from Russia to France in 1936, promised to do his best.

Whatever the scope of the intellectual discussions that may have evolved aboard ship, it was clear to all when they reached America that war was far behind them. The skies were blue and peaceful, and the atmosphere seductive. Val found Hollywood to be enveloped in an apathy for war that was surpassed only by its apathy for opera and live drama. He encountered what he thought was the world's worst kind of aristocracy — an incredible snobbery based on fearful compliance.

The United States was dissected by conflicting thoughts and opinions. Isolationists Charles Lindbergh and Senator Burton Wheeler appeared in the Hollywood Bowl, making what Val called "dreadful speeches."

Val had known what he had to do in 1917, when he had cabled Kerensky to sign a separate peace with Germany in order to preserve the Provisional government and save Russia from communism, and when he had pled with Lloyd George to send an English division to Petrograd to bolster the Kerensky government. Couldn't they see there would be a Bolshevik revolution? And couldn't the United States now see that it *had* to support the war effort?

Did he think he could solve the world's problems? No. What may sometimes have appeared to be presumptuous was a simple, uninhibited clarity of concept that for all the world reminds me of a five-year-old nephew of mine who, on becoming separated from his grandfather in a shopping center, announced to a clerk: "I've lost a grandpa; his name is Emmett." When the clerk questioned, "Are you sure it isn't *you* that is lost?" he looked at her in surprise and answered, "Of course not; I'm right here."

Val knew what he must do. He organized and became chairman of the Federal Union in California. He secured the help of Mrs. Stanley McCormick, Professor Robert Andrew Millikan, George Biddle (brother of the Attorney General), Helen Gahagan Douglas, and many Hollywood directors and stars. Opposing the "America First" isolationists, the German Bund, and its communist allies, he was called a "traitor" and an English spy by his opponents. He unwittingly arranged the initial meeting of the Federal Union in a home inhabited by a Nazi Gestapo agent who chose a unique manner of sabotaging the effort. Every piece of furniture and every fold of drape concealed dog defecation!

Then when Hitler attacked Russia, egg appeared on many faces, and countless opponents hastened to become supporters.

On November 11, 1939, Bernadine Fritz had welcomed Val to "Horrible Hollywood," as the column was titled, in the periodical *Rob Wagner's Script*. "[What a] surprise . . . meeting Vladimir Rosing again after fourteen years." Quoting the late W. T. Parker, she spoke of the effort of Coates and Rosing to "humanize opera" and "bring it out of the dark ages, for," she said, "surely no one can deny that it, of all the arts, has remained static."

Under the Work Project Administration (WPA), Coates and Val established the Southern California Opera Association, and by May 5, 1940, under the management of L. E. Behymer, they were ready for a production of *Faust* in the Philharmonic Auditorium. "Streamlined Opera" they called it, and told their public they had chosen *Faust* because, in such a familiar opera, the public could best observe the modern style of production.

Lawrence Tibbett wrote to Val:

> This is a great opportunity for the operatically ambitious people of Southern California to secure training under you — whom I consider to be among the finest in the world — as well as under the brilliant Albert Coates.

Among the distinguished names on the Board of Directors was Meredith Willson, who would team up with Val in many future productions. Nadine Connor was Marguerite. In little more than a year and a half, she would make her debut at the Metropolitan Opera.

Val Rosing performing Canio in Leoncavallo's *Pagliacci.*

There was a familiar ring to the reviews. The *Pacific Coast Musician* said,

> The first performance by the Southern California Opera Association is convincing disapproval of the stupid notion that opera cannot be satisfactorily sung in English or that American singers are not adequate for operatic roles. . . . The unexpectedly high standard of excellence deserves more detailed comment than can be given here. . . . If Los Angeles fails to give every possible

encouragement and material support to this movement — and that seems unthinkable if we are the cultured city we like to think we are — then opera in Los Angeles will remain the synthetic thing it always has been, produced by foreign companies, and therefore, a forlorn hope except to those who know nothing about opera, are proud of it and attend it merely for what they may think is the social advantage to be gained.

The last paragraph of *Rob Wagner's Script* read: "If this is the beginning of a permanent resident opera company in Los Angeles, it is a good one."

Highlights from *Faust* plus *Pagliacci* were presented in Laguna for the South Coast Music Festival, and the *Town Crier* said, "Such an ovation has never happened before in this city."

The same presentation was repeated at the Embassy Auditorium (with Val singing Canio) and at UCLA's Royce Hall. The chorus was omitted, and the five principals entered from the house rear, utilizing the real audience as chorus villagers while the main stage was simply the stage used by the traveling players. Music critic, Richard D. Saunders of Hollywood's *Citizen-News*, called it

opera as it should be done [with] a higher degree of dramatic intensity than any presentation of the oft-repeated opera previously given here. . . . Opera streamlined and dramatized in such a manner might advantageously be used as entertainment in Army and Navy camps, where it could stimulate musical interest in thousands who know nothing of opera at present.

Exactly what Val would like to do — support the war effort! It had been three months since the Selective Service Bill and the drafting of 16 million young men, but he plugged away at trying to establish an opera company. The Southern California Opera Company had not found adequate financing, so he set up The Hollywood Opera and Drama Studio and presented *La Traviata* at The Assistance League Playhouse in July 1941, with Nadine Connor singing the lead and James Sample conducting. It was repeated at Laguna in August with Val's wife Vicki singing Flora and Annina.

In September came another beginning, this one under the banner of Val's newly organized American Opera Company of Los Angeles, with a performance of *Faust* in the Philharmonic Auditorium, starring Jerome Hines as a brilliant Mephistopheles. In another five years, he would be at the Met. Albert Goldberg reviewed the performance under the headline, "ROSING TURNS *FAUST* INTO CAPITAL 'THEATER.'"

Some 20 years ago, in the original American Opera Company, Vladimir Rosing made what was undoubtedly the most progressive and imaginative gesture toward operatic reform that the American theater had yet witnessed. . . .

Last night in the Philharmonic Auditorium Mr. Rosing again picked up the strands at just about the point he left off a generation ago, and the American Opera Company of Los Angeles came into being with a performance of Gounod's "Faust" that, whatever its musical shortcomings, was stamped with the old Rosing trademark of imagination, vitality and courage.

This was no stereotyped "Faust," an outmoded relic of a dead age, but a briskly theatrical performance that could hold the attention of even tone-deaf customers. Mr. Rosing dares to look traditions in the eye and if they don't measure up to throw them out the window.

Of *Cavalleria Rusticana*, presented in the Embassy Auditorium with the WPA Symphony orchestra, the *Citizen-News* critic Richard D. Saunders said,

The direction by Vladimir Rosing brought out the action exactly as in a stage play. There was no "operatic" semaphoring. Every action was properly motivated and carried the story forward with a definition that "traditional" operatic production never can attain.

Why was it? So much artistic success, but no financial support for it. So many successful embryos, but no births.

And Vicki was homesick for England. She returned, and Val was alone again.

Chapter 25

We're in the Army Now

Because the Nazis were sinking our ships, Congress defused the Neutrality Act in November 1941. Then came December 7, Pearl Harbor's "Day of Infamy."

On January 19, 1942, composer and music critic Deems Taylor wrote to authorities of the United Service Organizations (USO) regarding Val:

> I think you would be highly fortunate to enlist this man's services. . . . I can say without reservation that Mr. Rosing is a brilliant actor, stage director and producer, whose services in connection with any entertainment enterprise would be invaluable.

In 1943, Val was appointed Entertainment Director for the U.S. Army at Camp Roberts in California. Finally he had found his wartime niche. It was also here that he found Mary who would participate in his chorus as a singing actress, act as his assistant director, and become his companion of ten years. Val sometimes presented as many as three shows in an evening, many revues, and seventeen spectacular productions with Hollywood stars. "Leg shows" and revues were prescribed for the GIs, and when Val argued that the GIs's level of appreciation had been underestimated, his immediate downfall was predicted. Of course, he could not give them opera. He couldn't? He did, and they loved it. He even gave them *The Messiah*. The Camp Roberts *Dispatch* maintained: "A salute is thrown in the direction of Mr. Rosing for his

Rosing productions for Camp Roberts: *Girl Crazy* with Red Skelton and Diana Lewis; upper right, *Red Skelton's Scrapbook* with Jan Clayton and Red Skelton.

understanding of what Camp Roberts EM [enlisted men] and Officers want in the way of stage entertainment."

Regarding his "first appearance as director of camp presentations in 1943," the *Dispatch* said,

Mr. Rosing gave G.I. theater-goers their first big opportunity of seeing a first class production.

Just before Christmas of 1943 with an orchestra and all the trimmings, a curtain went up before a jam-packed audience of G.I.s at the Sports Arena . . . all waiting to see "The Merry Widow," an operetta of light songs and gaiety. . . . Camp Roberts had never seen anything like it.

Interspersed with *Rio Rita, Red Mill, Desert Song, Robin Hood, Girl Crazy, Red Skelton's Scrapbook, New Moon, Pinafore, Bill Grady's MGM Revue, Musical Sensations, Rosalie, Naughty Marietta, Hit the Deck*, etc., were — yes, *Carmen, Pagliacci, Cavalleria Rusticana*, and *The Barber of Seville*.

Enlisted men and women comprised 80 percent of the cast, orchestra, and stage hands for each of the productions which were supplemented by stars, among whom were Red Skelton, Turhan Bey, Robert Mitchum, Bing Crosby, Judy Garland, Janis Page, Jan Clayton, and others — all remunerated by Metro Goldwyn Mayer Studios.

Colonel Paul H. Brown, Infantry Commanding Officer, and Captain Maurice M. Wakeman presented Val with a large wood-covered souvenir book containing photos and clippings of the shows. Their enclosed tribute said, "The success of these musical shows has proven them to be a powerful morale factor in entertaining the military personnel of this Camp."

Val left Camp Roberts in November 1945, after the war's end, with the promise to return as a soloist for Thanksgiving services.

Chapter 26

American Opera Company of Los Angeles

In Los Angeles Val joined forces with Hugh Edwards, a former captain in the Army and a professional singer, to organize the American Operatic Laboratory, an opera school for veterans. It started in 1946 with seventeen young singers. Within a year, it had developed into one of the largest and finest schools of its kind in the United States. It became a member of the California Association of Vocational Schools which was affiliated with the National Federation of Private School Associations, and by 1949, it had enrolled over 400 singers.

With Hugh Edwards as general director and Val as artistic director, the Opera Lab eventually acquired a faculty of 112 vocal instructors and coaches, 22 piano instructors, and also offered instruction in the various orchestral instruments, music theory, composition, and conducting. Even piano tuning and maintenance were finally added. The school did not follow the traditional conservatory or university school of music approach. It was interested not in the cultural development standpoint, but in developing professional musicians. In its brochure, it noted that "A survey will quickly disclose the fact that very few professional singers or musicians, or private teachers of music or voice, possess degrees or have been trained in schools offering degrees." In its first three years, the Opera Lab produced 31 grand and light operas and gave close to 200 full operatic performances, all free to the public.

The successful development of the singers led Mr. Edwards and Val to form the American Opera Company of Los Angeles which made its debut in September 1947 at the Philharmonic Theater. *Faust, The Barber of Seville*, and *Tosca* were presented during the same week with guest stars Jerome Hines and Marilyn Cotlow from the Metropolitan, and Anne Jeffreys, film star. Local basso Hines, who had joined the Metropolitan Opera the prior season, was an unrivaled, strutting spirit of the underworld as Mephistopheles in *Faust*. Marilyn Cotlow was the *Barber*'s Rosina, and Anne Jeffreys was Floria Tosca.

In the *Los Angeles Times*, Sunday, September 28, 1947, Albert Goldberg reflected on two styles of opera under the headline, "ORIGINALITY IN OPERA BEING REVIVED HERE":

> [Opera] can be in the grand manner, employing stellar singers, large scenic devices, and adhering closely to accumulated traditions, or it can be individualized and experimental, based on a well knit ensemble rather than stars, and stressing dramatic rather than musical values.
>
> The former is by far the more familiar system to the American public. It is the method employed exclusively nowadays by the two great operatic organizations of the country — the Metropolitan and the San Francisco — and it certainly was the plan followed by the Chicago Opera in the days of its glory. . . . Despite its costliness and unwieldiness it has continued to be apparently the only manner in which the superorganizations can function.

He went on to explain that under this system, called "traditional," a well-prepared singer may walk upon an unfamiliar stage, face an unknown conductor, and with no rehearsal, give an adequate, routine performance. This was because the system was "based on rigidly established formulas." From performance to performance, company to company, the set design, the blocking, and the tempi remained basically the same.

Of the "individualistic method" he said:

> . . . A work was periodically restudied and restaged, old and meaningless traditions discarded, and the opera approached as if it were a first performance with a new and fresh emphasis upon all its points.
>
> America has seen but little of this type of operatic production. A score of years ago a brilliant start was made by Vladimir Rosing's original American Opera Company. Each opera was sung in a good English translation, genuinely gifted young American singers were taught the principles of effective acting, and operas were staged

with a blithe disregard for ancient tradition and a strong accent on the dramatic element. But the public was not ready for so bold a venture and after two seasons the American Opera Company became only a bright page in history.

Now the ghost of that little band seems to have come to life again in the American Opera Company of Los Angeles. Mr. Rosing is once more the artistic director of the group, and the three operas which were recently staged — "Faust," "The Barber of Seville," and "Tosca" — all bore the unmistakable imprint of his audacious, theaterwise imagination.

In a review of *The Barber*, Goldberg noted such innovations as Figaro entering with a pushcart bearing the wigs, tools, and lotions of his trade — yet with "no particular sense of straining for novelty for novelty's sake. There is logic behind each of Mr. Rosing's changes; they invariably make sound dramatic sense."

Reviewing *The Queen of Spades* for the *Los Angeles Herald-Examiner*, Patterson Greene said:

> [Members of the American Opera Company] sang in the language of their everyday speech, which is English. They knew what they were saying which is more than most [young singers] know and more than most of their older and more celebrated colleagues know, when they sing in Italian, French or German. The relationship between speech and song was thus borne in upon them.
>
> Acting, too, profited by their use of their own language. They were restrained from inappropriate, irrelevant gesticulation.
>
> And an English speaking audience had a demonstration (rare in this country) of the fact that opera has sense as well as sound.

The company performed *Marriage of Figaro* for disabled veterans at the Birmingham Veterans Administration Hospital in Van Nuys, California, and received a letter of thanks from W. R. McBrien, Chief of Special Services. He offered an apology:

> You know our hesitation in booking this opera was due to the fact that most musical programs have met with indifference from our patients. However, the excellent programming, the beautiful costumes, the excellent singers, and the good staging made the presentation last Friday night an overwhelming success.
>
> Mr. Rosing is to be especially commended for the professional care he gave to this activity. Patients whose interest in opera was

almost antagonistic came away from the performance with remarks of amazement. This performance was the first indication they had had that opera could be fun, and that operatic singing was beautiful. We really feel that your group was responsible for making a big inroad into opening a new field of interest to the patients of this hospital.

When television had changed the mode of world communication, Val, then in London, had produced the first televised opera. He now originated and directed for KFI-TV, forty-nine weeks of "The Music Theatre" which presented operas in condensed form every Sunday afternoon. It was voted the outstanding musical program of local origin for 1949 by the Southern California Association for Better Radio and Television.

Val was confident that opera in English would finally win the battle. It was only logical that it should be so. "Musical history teaches us," he reasoned, "that when opera becomes part of the cultural life of a country, it has its own national opera. I am all in favor of great international opera companies composed of the best singers in the world, but such companies are only a luxury. The crying need in America," he said, "is for a national opera company based on the artistic principles introduced by American Opera Company. Then it will develop a real market and will provide wide opportunity to our own singers." Regarding poor translations and those that break the melodic line intended by the composer, he said, "That can be rectified; there are already in existence many excellent translations. It may be in some cases that a melodic line is broken, but the general benefit derived by opera in English will easily offset some of the insignificant compromises. I would infinitely rather hear good English than a mutilated original language." He told of hearing a performance of *Carmen* sung in French in an international opera house where the role of Carmen was sung with a Russian accent, Jose with an Italian accent, the Toreador with a Spanish accent, Micaela with a Swedish accent, and Dancaïre with an Armenian accent. "Now that was true murder of the French language."

Val advocated that directors should band together and demand adequate rehearsal time, and that producers should require singers to know the art of acting. "We have entered an era when the audience demands a visual satisfaction as well as an aural one. The time of stupid gestures, of fat prima donnas, of tenors who strut to the footlights for their high notes should vanish. Opera can no longer afford to be pleasant to the ear, offensive to the eye, and insulting to the mind!"

Linda Darnell in *Everybody Does it,* 1949. Operatic sequences directed by Val Rosing. (Photo, ©
1949 Twentieth Century Fox Film Corporation. All rights reserved.)

Chapter 27

Rebound

When Val had returned to London after the demise of the American Opera Company in 1933, he had used his firsthand knowledge of the Russian Revolution to draft a play which he titled *The Crown Changes Hands*. Its action took place on three floors of an apartment building in Petrograd. A general, his family, and servants occupied the top floor; a liberal deputy, his daughter, and his secretary occupied the second floor; and peasant workers lived in the basement. The play divulged the changes in Russia's social structure as the events of the Revolution dramatically affected the life pattern of each character. In the final act, the cellar is a prison, housing the general, and the Bolsheviks have ascended to the top floor.

In 1948, Era Productions offered *The Crown Changes Hands* at the Beaux Arts Theater. It was favorably reviewed in the *Los Angeles Times* under the headline, "Challenging Drama Given."

The following year Twentieth Century Fox called upon Val to direct the operatic sequences of *Everybody Does It* with Linda Darnell. He had just finished when he received a phone call from New York City Opera Company's conductor, Laszlo Halasz. Val's Russian colleague, Theodore Komisarjevsky, whom Val had once engaged to direct his *Opera Intime* project in London, was preparing to direct Prokofiev's *Love for Three Oranges* when he suffered a heart attack. No rehearsals had yet taken place, and Val was asked to come and direct the opera. Said Halasz, "You will have only seventeen days."

Val flew to New York and addressed the company. "Now look," he said, "I know as little as you do, having never heard nor seen the music. We'll start together from scratch."

After reading the script and hearing the music, he realized immediately that it had to be a satire, and that the obvious reason for its prior failure in Chicago had been a disregard of that fact. The Russian designer Dobujinsky was in full accord with Val's conception, and the scenic design and costumes were ready in a few days. The production got rolling and catapulted into a sensational success. *Life* magazine covered it with three full pages of color photos under the headline "A Slaphappy Fairy Tale Makes a Smash-Hit Opera." *Newsweek* called it a "howling success." *The New York Times* gave it two pages of pictures and "wide acclaim," designating it as "an opera and an interpretation which honor the modern theatre." *The New York Mirror* called it "a brilliant novelty that should prove one of the most popular items in the New York City Opera Company's repertory."

William Hawkins of *The New York World Telegram*, headlined his column, "ROSING WANTS SINGERS WHO CAN ACT, TOO." Quoting Val, he said:

> "The conception of the opera [*Three Oranges*] is not to be realistic and hide mechanics, but to show them and laugh at them." . . . Rosing has a most logical explanation for the often weird behavior witnessed on the musical stage.
>
> "The Golden Era of opera," he says, "was the period of Victorian melodrama, when acting styles were broad but finished. There was style, elegance and precision, and body control which was employed in very artificial manner.
>
> "Then through people like Stanislavsky and Reinhardt, and the movies, the stage became realistic. Singers retained the old style with none of the finish, and this ranting is now ludicrous and revolting. . . ."
>
> [Rosing] feels that if critics were harder on the thespian efforts of singers, then managers would only sign actors to sing, and then singers would learn how to act.
>
> "In *Oranges*," he says, "we create style, then make it ridiculous by distorting what is natural. But the distortion itself must have style and line.
>
> "You need form infused with substance. It must both look good to you and touch you."

Headlines multiplied: "Rollicking Curtain-Raiser," "Triumph of Farce," "Zany Fun," "A Big Hit." One paper said it "was so full of excellence that it is hard to single out any one for special praise." Another said it was probably the first performance to be understood in New York, since it was sung in *English*. Its 1921 Chicago performance had been in Russian with a later New York performance in French. Charles Buckley wrote that it "ought to outdraw 'South Pacific.'"

In *Musical America* Quaintance Eaton said it was

> one of those rare and exciting events that justify the term "first night" in all its dazzling connotations. . . . All characterizations developed miraculously as the natural talents of the singing actors were worked, pulled and kneaded by a master of the craft — Mr. Rosing. The company will benefit from his training next year, for he has been re-engaged.

Billy Rose, in his column *Pitching Horseshoes* for the *Glendale News Press*, had been ranting about grand opera through a series of articles the prior year. "Why," he wrote, "doesn't someone coax grand opera into the 20th century?" He suggested a board to run the Metropolitan. Among others, it included Arturo Toscanini for the Music and Vladimir Rosing as Producing Consultant.

Rudolph Bing's excuse for not asking Val to direct at the Metropolitan: "He is old fashioned."

Between trains, on his return to California, Val stopped over in Rochester where he met and dined with Guy Fraser Harrison and ten members of the old American Opera Company. It was his first visit since the company had gone independent 21 years before. He had just produced a great success in New York, and had directed a film in Hollywood that was now packing the Roxy, yet he almost wept with nostalgia when he saw the Eastman Theatre and Kilbourn Hall.

When interviewed by journalist Rose Sold of the Rochester *Times Union*, Val said, "No place in the world has such wonderful facilities, no place is half so beautiful. . . . What a wonderful beginning we had, and how we worked and dreamed." He was "sick at heart" to recall the hopes and dreams he had had for opera in America. "How many times I have jumped over these footlights," he recalled, bounding once again onto the stage. Sold described him as "the greyed and balding artist — the 59-year-old Russian singer who interrupted a rave-evoking concert career in Europe and America to form the Rochester American Opera Company."

The year 1950 was a "stuffed suitcase." In May, Val directed for MGM the operatic sequences in *Grounds for Marriage* with Kathryn Grayson and Van Johnson. Before his July production of *Faust*, which would open the Hollywood Bowl season with Rodzinski conducting and Jerome Hines, Nadine Connor, and Richard Tucker as artists, he would direct for New York City Center Opera Puccini's *Turandot*, Verdi's *Traviata*, Gounod's *Faust,* and a

Van Johnson, Kathryn Grayson, Paula Raymond, Barry Sullivan, and Lewis Stone take part in scenes of *Carmen,* from a dream sequence in Metro-Goldwyn-Mayer's romantic *Grounds for Marriage.* Val Rosing directed the operatic sequences. (MGM photo, courtesy of Turner Entertainment.)

reproduction of *Love for Three Oranges*. *Traviata* was labeled "superlative," and Val's treatment of *Faust*, using two tenors to represent the young and the old Faust, made a great impression. With *Turandot*, City Center Opera had another smash hit on its hands. Critics said it could be a successful broadway extravaganza. Three additional performances were booked and sold out, and Chicago engaged *Turandot* and *Oranges* for November.

Chicago's Claudia Cassidy, whose caustic pen could crucify, acclaimed *Turandot* as "the best performance the company has given here . . . brilliantly staged and lighted by Vladimir Rosing." In her review of *Love for Three Oranges*, she said, "Laszlo Halasz made one of the wiser moves of his vivid career when he engaged Vladimir Rosing."

Back in Los Angeles, Patterson Greene of the *Los Angeles Herald-Examiner* ridiculed Southern California's "discovery" of Val Rosing, prompted by his staging of New York City Center Opera's *Love for Three Oranges*, "the only newsworthy operatic enterprise in Gotham."

He pursued the point:

> Visitors from California congratulated Rosing, and lamented that we could have nothing of the kind back home in Los Angeles. The praise was welcome enough, but it had a wry flavor. For Rosing had gone to New York's City Center after a dozen years of doing the same thing right here in Los Angeles, to the admiration of a discerning few, but without popular reclamé.
>
> In fact, his influence here had preceded his advent as a citizen. As head of the opera school at the Eastman Conservatory in Rochester, N.Y., he had taught George Houston, who in turn founded a group from which our present excellent Guild Opera is descended.
>
> Among the Houston adherents was James A. Doolittle, who "discovered" Rosing years ago, and who, before the City Center furore, had engaged him to direct "Faust" and "The Vagabond King", at the Bowl last summer.
>
> Los Angeles, in matters of talent, often seems to have only distance vision.
>
> Jerome Hines and Nadine Connor will be stars of "Faust" when it opens the Hollywood Bowl season. I wonder how many Angelenos heard them sing exactly the same roles back in 1940 with Rosing's group.

Warren Storey Smith of *The Boston Post* said:

> Mr. Rosing's name is one with which Bostonians used to be

familiar. He came here several years ago as head of the American Opera Company, out of Rochester, N.Y. and anticipated many of the methods for which Boris Goldovsky is now getting so much credit. . . . Opera in English was . . . a part of the game. . . . Nevertheless, the Center sings "Turandot" in Italian. . . . In Stockholm I heard it in Swedish.

An audience of 10,000 enthusiastically greeted the Hollywood Bowl *Faust* in what Goldberg of the *Los Angeles Times* considered

one of the most intelligent approaches to the staging of convention-al opera that has come this way in a long time . . . [giving] the action of the opera a spaciousness of perspective and movement it has perhaps never enjoyed before. . . . Rosing's stage direction seems to be coming in for proper recognition again here and elsewhere after a period of eclipse.

Chapter 28

A Successful Failure

Proper recognition? Well, thought Val, "popularity" might better express this present phase of his career. Proper recognition should, he felt, be associated with the creation of a whole product, such as his American Opera Company had been. Where his magic touch created successes for existing opera companies, each success had to be a "miracle" wrought with inadequate rehearsal time from singers with no knowledge of body coordination. He was filled with self-reproach for what he regarded as prostituting his art. If only he could again have his own organization. But how many times must he rebuild only to see his efforts destroyed again by depressions and wars, as they had been in Rochester, at Covent Garden, and in Los Angeles?

When his opera organizations had been destroyed and his voice on behalf of world freedom had trailed away unobserved, his friend Ed Barber, of Barber Steamship Lines, had called Val a "successful failure." And that was the way he felt even as one success begat another.

The California Story in the Hollywood Bowl, 1950. . . . If he ever created miracles . . . well, even the *Los Angeles Times* called it a "miracle of production," and said, "Rosing had performed a feat of staging which is said never to have been approached in California before." He had demanded a new script, and he had improvised the final act — directing *in costume* and *on stage* — a strategy he would become known for, and which would provide both hilarious and exasperating moments.

Years later, during an under-rehearsed *Prince Igor* at the Chicago Lyric

Opera, my daughter said, "Mother, who is that nut holding onto his hat? Val will be furious!"

"Dee," I said, "do you know WHO that is? It's Val!" Unfortunately, he had to hold onto his hastily donned hat AND his pants, which rendered him helpless to direct.

Soprano Maralin Niska recently reminded me of the prominent tenor who "did not have time" to rehearse *Turandot*, but would devote intermissions of his *Butterfly* performance to "accept" stage instructions for *Turandot*. Val augmented these capsule impartations by acquiring a costume and appearing on stage as one of the crowd at the elbow of the tenor, cleverly moving him from place to place in order to keep his staging intact.

In spite of the tremendous exertion required to pull it together, *The California Story* gave Val the vehicle for portraying the greatness of a nation to its people. The 40-foot flag that rolled onstage during the finale was *Val's* flag! And his was not a flag that smug little boys refused to salute, nor a flag that was flaunted to sell bigoted ideologies. His was a great rippling sea of stars and stripes that waved over his beloved adopted country and flooded the whole of him with love and gratitude. He knew his country's faults, and he watched intellectual snobs lay her bare under their dialecticism; he watched her citizens take advantage of her; he watched politicians distort her virtues and her faults. But he loved her. He loved her for the predominant principled good in her people that has kept her great heroic experiment alive. And *his* flag rippled majestically in the winds of content or discontent. It towered in dignity at a height to which freedom-loving hands had lifted it — far above the rights or wrongs of its people.

This kind of idealism sometimes raised eyebrows, and, indeed, it did not always work in his best interest when signing contracts. He was a genius and a child — a brilliantly gifted child. He never applied for unemployment insurance, and he would be seventy before applying for Social Security. As he took the more-than-expected first payment from its envelope, tears filled his eyes, and he said (thinking of his anticipated *Freedom Story* production), "I want to do something great for the country that has been so wonderful to me." Not exactly an agent's dream. Val was encouraged to think of potential productions as financially profitable ventures.

With *The California Story*, Val had achieved what he considered the greatest production of his career in scope, beauty, and meaning. It would be revived six years later to be presented for three successive seasons in San Diego's *Fiesta del Pacifico*. And from there it would lead to state centennial productions for Oregon, Kansas, and Arizona.

His exciting projects for 1951 were the Hollywood Bowl productions of *Die Fledermaus* in July and the *Air Power Pageant* in August. In the meantime, he had *La Traviata*, *Faust*, and *Love for Three Oranges* to prepare for New York

City Center Opera, three musicals to prepare for Edwin Lester's Los Angeles Civic Light Opera, and another film with MGM — *Strictly Dishonourable*, starring Ezio Pinza.

When the *Merry Widow*, starring Paul Henreid, Jane Pickens, and Robert Rounseville, played in San Francisco, the *San Francisco News* referred to Val as the "world famous stage and opera director."

Soon it was time for *Fledermaus* to open the 30th season of "Symphony Under the Stars." The construction of a series of 30-foot high stage sets began. The sets would be among the most spectacular ever constructed for the Bowl — or for any other stage. The shell was removed so that real trees were part of the setting. Franz Waxman conducted. Miliza Korjus and John Brownlee of the Metropolitan, Yvonne De Carlo, film star, and Marina Koshetz were among the singers. The society pages were filled with pictures of the rich and famous who were hosts and guests, and who filled the box seats. An audience of 7,500 attended the first of five performances. The *Los Angeles Times* had the headline: "*Die Fledermaus Given Spectacular Production in Opening Bowl Season*," and *The Mirror* said, "In casting about for a spectacular work with which to open its thirteenth season, Hollywood Bowl did not go wrong last night in choosing Johann Strauss' comic opera, 'Die Fledermaus.'"

But something did go wrong, for the Hollywood Bowl Association went broke after four performances and had to cancel its season. Thirty years later, one of Val's assistants, Robert Kuyber, who also had the small role of the jail warden in the production that night, wrote an article for the *Calendar* section of the *Los Angeles Times*. He called it "Comic Opera About A Comic Opera," and spoke of Val as

> a brilliant, affable man, afflicted with that type of disorganization that only a genius can afford. Words such as *schedule* and *budget*, were not part of his vocabulary, and perhaps I should have been alerted when I heard "producer" and "Val Rosing" coupled together.

How ironic that it had been less than a month before this production that Edwin Lester of the Civic Light Opera had written to Val stating that he had "never had a Stage Director before who worked with such dispatch and such *complete sense of organization*."

Where did the truth lie? Kuyber implied extravagance in his article, but said the "all star cast" was "selected for the most part by the Opera Association Management," and that "the 'Bowl' had decreed that the addition of a few movie 'names' would really bring in the crowds." Kuyber said that Val wanted him to be an assistant director except that "the management wanted a 'name' director . . . and the 'name' belonged to Sig Arno. . . . But," he continued, "Sigi . . . had only the foggiest notion of what was supposed to happen on stage [and] the Bowl people panicked and reversed themselves." Then, as he told it, he and Val finished the production, Val taking Act II, and Kuyber finishing Acts I and III. Who then was responsible for the fiasco?

Analyzing this many years later, I am curious if this is one of the situations where Val spoke of having mostly male assistants who seemed to enjoy knifing him in the back.

The only explanation of the Bowl closure offered by the *Los Angeles Times* was: "Many things, including cool weather, worked against the success of this elaborate enterprise." Jean Hersholt, president of the Bowl management, stated for the paper:

> The financial situation that has arisen is nothing new. There have been constant losses on many concerts in the past compensated for by certain big popular events, but it has always been a hazardous operation. . . . The unfortunate outcome of the public reception of *Die Fledermaus* happened to precipitate the crisis and that is all. It probably would eventually have happened, but many things combined to lessen the anticipated attendance and we faced the possibility of further losses in subsequent concerts, judging by past experience.

This is not to say there was no fault on Val's part (actually, he was entitled to a failure), but no one seems to have pointed a finger but Kuyber — and that, 30 years after the fact.

One month later back at the Hollywood Bowl, Val directed the *Air Power Pageant* for the Air Force Association, with the cooperation of the motion picture and aviation industries and the U.S. Air Force. An audience of 15,000 filled the Bowl as bombers rumbled and jet fighters wailed overhead. Actor Jimmy Stewart, himself a reserve Air Force colonel, introduced the Hollywood elite, including Bob Hope who took over as Master of Ceremonies. The pageant traced the history of American aviation from the Wright brothers' bicycle shop in 1903, through World War I, to Pearl Harbor and Korea.

Louis B. Mayer, in the *Official Journal of the Air Force Association*, was quoted as saying:

> I just wish the President, the Senate and the Congress had been in Hollywood Bowl. They'd be inspired to feel as I do about the Air Force. If I had all the time at my command I know I wouldn't be capable of doing justice to what I felt when I saw that wonderful spectacle on the history of our Air Force.

Meanwhile, Val was producing his own history of romance. In his American Opera Lab he had met Jean Hillard. Jean was studying opera roles, and she was a talented composer as well. Val and Mary, his companion of ten years and the mother of his son born out-of-wedlock, had parted. Mary met and married someone else, and Val married Jean. Val needed someone at his side, someone whose hand was always there when he reached for it. Not that there was a trace of egocentricity in him — I think I have never known anyone who could love so unselfishly; he gave, and he desired complete devotion, but it had to be in the same geographical area. He wanted the person whose life he shared to be with him daily — in Los Angeles, in New York, in Chicago, in Europe — wherever he had to be.

The year of his marriage to Jean, 1952, he had to be in Los Angeles for the filming of *Twin Titans*, for the Civic Light Opera's *Song of Norway*, for a television and stage workshop at Plummer Park (for which he resigned from the American Operatic Laboratory), and for a new assignment with the Los Angeles City College Opera Workshop.

The following year, he staged the musical numbers for Dennis Day's television shows, and would for the ensuing seven years stage all of his revues at the Riviera and Sahara in Las Vegas and at the Moulin Rouge in Los Angeles.

He also directed the Civic Light Opera's *Great Waltz* with Dorothy Kirsten and John Charles Thomas. And he staged for Los Angeles City College Puccini's *La Rondiné*, Handel's *Julius Caesar*, and Mozart's *Marriage of Figaro*.

Of *La Rondiné*, critic Richard Lipscomb said, "You don't have to wait until next October when the San Francisco Opera comes to town to see a moving and finely staged performance of grand opera."

Of *Julius Caesar*, the *Los Angeles Times's* Albert Goldberg observed, "[One was] not prepared for the dramatic power and fitness that were disclosed in Vladimir Rosing's staging." Patterson Greene of the *Los Angeles Herald-Examiner* called it an "operatic masterpiece [with] credit, in particular, to Vladimir Rosing." After *Marriage of Figaro*, Richard Lipscomb said "Opera Workshop" was a misleading term which at City College "now stands for an almost unremitting string of enjoyable productions."

One reviewer compared the City College Workshop with the city's two university workshops, USC and UCLA.

> The truest workshop performance of the three was the L.A. City College group. The results . . . are little less than fantastic in contrast to [the universities] with their far greater budgets, facilities and administrative interest, . . . the difference between sensible and insensitive stylization and comedy was never better

illustrated than in the difference between Rosing's "Figaro" and Carl Ebert's staging of the "Merry Wives".

Bettina Hall, who had worked under Val's direction on Broadway following his American Opera Company days, was now married to Raymond Rubicam and resided in Phoenix, Arizona, where she was president of the Phoenix Opera Guild. The Phoenix Civic Light Opera was floundering, so Bettina got on the phone and did what columnist Bobbie Johnston of *The Phoenix Gazette* called "the impossible." She got Val to come from Hollywood and direct *Brigadoon*. ". . . He forgot about money, flew to Phoenix and whipped *Brigadoon* into shape." He became their permanent director, and after the following year's *Kiss Me Kate* (1954), the same columnist wrote:

> Rosing has taught them where to move and when to move. They know what to do with their hands and their faces when they are not using them. The chorus sounds professional, the leads and supporting players are at ease, and the dancers have found new life.

Meanwhile the Metropolitan Opera had presented *Carmen* and *Bohême*. Bettina Rubicam came across *The Christian Science Monitor's* review by Jules Wolffers protesting a complete lack of credibility — "efficient and competent" by musical standards, but wholly "unbelievable by theatrical standards. The American public is not satisfied" he said, "with stock, wooden characters moving through directed pacings and waving their arms . . . in a wild sweeping gesture for intense emotion, [with] a feeble flutter of hands for more pathetic situations."

Then Wolffers switched pens:

> An exception to the evening's trend must be taken for Jean Fenn, who served as an object lesson for the "new look". Vivacious, pert, and comely Miss Fenn sang and acted with conviction and high artistry. Her Musetta was appealing and vital with singing to match.

Bettina wrote to Mr. Wolffers:

> Twenty-five years ago, Val Rosing, the artistic director of the American Opera Company was the voice crying in the wilderness. He was teaching the public — and those of us fortunate enough to be in that well remembered experiment [the A.O.C.] that credibility and opera were not antagonistic. It was most interesting to me that you should have singled out Jean Fenn to "serve as an

object lesson for the New Look." Miss Fenn is coaching her roles with Mr. Rosing.

You may remember that Mr. Rosing was the man picked by Billy Rose (in that controversial letter he wrote to *Fortune* about what he could do with the Met) to be the artistic director of the Met! Maybe Mr. Bing is missing something. You have recognized what it is.

Jean Fenn herself had written to Val: "Never can I thank you enough for all you have done for me. My God, if I had faced this without your guidance and the thorough grounding you gave me!"

His staging of *Faust* for New York City Opera that fall was described in the New York *Post*: "the entire performance had the vigor of a Breughel painting, no small compliment."

One of his exciting productions for the year was *The Elk Story*. Conceived and directed by Val, it was written by Franklin Lacey, with Nadine Connor and Joseph Gaudio as stars.

In 1955, Val surpassed himself. He staged the operatic sequences for MGM's *Interrupted Melody*, the life story of opera singer Marjorie Lawrence, starring Glenn Ford and Eleanor Parker; he gave New York City Opera its greatest hit of the season with Nicolai's *The Merry Wives of Windsor*; he captivated Phoenix, Arizona, with *Song of Norway*; he re-created the *Pilgrimage Play* — outdoor spectacular of the life of Christ; and he and Jean produced a son — Richard.

Interrupted Melody was an inspirational drama which recounted Marjorie Lawrence's affliction with polio at the height of her singing career, her terrific struggle, and her final ability to sing again in public by drawing on the strength of her devoted husband's love and support. *Variety* gave "Great credit [to] Vladimir Rosing for his staging," and the *Los Angeles Times* called it "spellbinding." Harper MacKay, in an April 1992 issue of *Opera News*, judged it to be the "best film of the operatic-biography genre."

The *New Yorker* awarded laurels to New York City Opera for its production of *Merry Wives* and noted that "Vladimir Rosing skillfully maintained the Elizabethan horseplay on a highly entertaining level."

The *Pilgrimage Play*, opening in the elegant outdoor setting across from the Hollywood Bowl, was produced by John Arnold Ford who said, "If Val Rosing hadn't been available, I would not have attempted to present the *Pilgrimage Play*." It had been four years since the last presentation of the play, and Val stated that it had been formerly pre-supposed that everyone in the audience was familiar with the Gospels. He gave it a new treatment by providing narrators who, representing Matthew, Mark, Luke and John, read their respective versions of the gospel. There were tableaux on the stage and on the hillside: of the Angel of Annunciation appearing in a flash of light, the

Eleanor Parker in the 1955 film, *Interrupted Melody,* the life story of soprano Marjorie Lawrence, who was born in 1909. (MGM photo, courtesy of Turner Entertainment.)

Holy family on its pilgrimage to Jerusalem, the Child Jesus astounding the wise men in the Temple, and the carpentry shop of Joseph. With the beginning of Christ's teachings and miracles, the players took over. Val vowed "there will be no elocution, no heavy dramatics. The points of this story are too powerful to need emphasis: religion is too great to need selling."

Richard Rosing, Val's son, born in 1955.

And RICHARD — a bundle of joy, already looking and acting like his Promethean father, took over the Rosing household. Richard would emerge as a poet and lavishly talented composer. At the early age of eighteen, he was commissioned by the American Guild of Organists to write a work for its annual service at St. Paul's Cathedral in Los Angeles. At twenty-four he was directing the choir of Mt. Hollywood's Congregational Church in Hollywood, and had already composed more than fifty works for solo voice, orchestra, brass, organ, guitar, and chorus. By age twenty-eight, he had won two national awards: the 1982 Grand Prize for *Song Search,* and the 1983 Grand Prize for the *American Song Festival.*

Early on, Richard exhibited his inborn identity with rhythm and motion. He was seven when he arrived to spend his summer vacation with us in Wichita, Kansas, where we were presenting *The Kansas Story* for the state's centennial celebration. Lost in his world of toy soldiers, Richard directed their positions and movements about him on the living room floor as his father talked with a visitor. Val was relating a former experience, and his voice became quite animated. Simultaneously, the soldiers stepped up their action, and Richard became an orchestra pouring forth frenzied music to accompany his father's voice. It was our laughter that broke Richard's concentrated absorption.

Val and Jean, Richard's mother, had purchased a home in Hollywood, and when Richard was born, she became totally absorbed with parenting. When he was two or three, she wanted to find employment and help solidify the family's future. She was very practical minded and wanted to establish roots. Eventually, she returned to teaching as she had done earlier and stayed with it until she retired. Val had lost his traveling companion.

However, he kept hitting all the baskets with his productions. A double bill at New York City Opera featured Liebermann's *School for Wives* and Mozart's *The Impresario*. Val directed the latter, and in various papers headlines read: "Comes to the Rescue at City Center," "Saves City Opera Bill," "Hit of the Evening."

But this wasn't enough for him. To be traveling and developing projects by himself was not his idea of the way life was supposed to be. His disappointment was like Richard's tearful assessment of Wichita when he appeared in our bedroom at dawn on the first day of his visit: "There are no birds singing on your street, like at home."

Val's creative impulse was never spurred by the desire for money and fame. His creative energy was expressed with an artistic passion. He did not know how to give less than all of himself, and he wanted to share life, love, everything in the same manner. How could he enjoy artistic fulfillment unless he shared it? He thrived in compatible company, beamed and bubbled, was lavish with his affections, and flourished when loved. His hungry eyes began to seek out companionship. He demonstrated infidelity and was characterized as a womanizer.

Chapter 29

Stepping Stones

Val did not tiptoe through life. When I met him at Universal Studios in 1956, he stated, on the evening of my first rehearsal with him, "I have been waiting for you all my life." Well, he was not one to suppress cardinal issues. Nevertheless, he had not been inactive while waiting. Later, he told me he had gone that same evening to free the girl with whom he had been having an affair.

He came to the church where I served as soloist to hear me sing. He drove to my home to give me a private coaching lesson. In order to direct him, I met him at a designated corner marked by a shopping center overlooking an embankment. He stood waiting, and when I drove up on the street below, he enthusiastically waved from above and fell down the embankment. Fortunately, there were no broken bones; he knew how to fall.

When his early proposals of love met with resistance, he accepted the decision with knitted brows and wilted body. "If you don't want to spend your life with me, then at least let me be a stepping stone for you to a better life," he responded.

I thought I had a pretty good life — complete with a husband and daughter — but there was no doubt about my being irresistibly drawn to Val's artistry, and here I sensed expanding horizons. How I longed to reach for them if it could be accomplished on a professional basis.

Val could be very "Ellis Island" in appearance, but as an individual and as an artist, he commanded the utmost from himself whether it involved the interpretation of a song, absorption with an *affair de l'amour*, or the preparation of a beef stroganoff. To give less than all of himself was unthinkable. He even seemed to have the ability to give other people their own unrecognized entities. There was much to be learned from him.

Val had a rich appetite for life. It was epicurean, eager, unrepressed, never arrogant, and never vulgar. Jealous? Yes! If he felt he was being betrayed in a love relationship, his eyes would narrow to slits, and his features would become those of Mephisto's. When working with him as an assistant director in Phoenix, Arizona, he ripped the telephone out of the wall of the guesthouse I was renting because, while rejecting his advances, he erroneously suspected that I was interested in someone else.

One morning in Los Angeles, I waited for a coaching lesson at Plummer Park where Val had a workshop. He never appeared, and I finally returned home. My phone rang, and it was Val calling me from his hospital bed. He had undergone emergency surgery for a urinary tract obstruction. There was a tumor to be removed, but Val said he didn't have time for an operation. He was due in San Diego shortly to begin rehearsals on *The California Story*, and then he had Dennis Day's shows to direct in Las Vegas. It was a delicate physical situation, but the doctor agreed to equip him with a temporary drain on the outside of his body which he somehow utilized for a number of months before submitting to the surgical procedure for removal of the benign tumor.

His immediate need, however, was for an assistant who could cover for him in San Diego while he was in the hospital. At the New York City Opera, Val had met a stage manager, Chris Mahan, who had once filled in as a stunt man on stilts, advertising the Cafe Momus in a production of *Bohème*. During a rehearsal, he had fallen nine feet onto a cement floor, but had dusted himself off, said he was okay, and gone ahead with an afternoon rehearsal of *Trovatore*. Having difficulty moving chairs around, he kicked them into place. By seven o'clock he knew something was wrong, but the director of that evening's *Troilus* came running in with the news that he was short one Trojun priest. "Find me a costume, and I will fill in," said Chris. At least he could stand still. When the performance was over, he was taken to a hospital where it was discovered he had broken alternate arms and wrists. With both arms in casts, he managed *Trovatore* and *Carmen* performances, as he described it: "rushing around — an armless idiot, kicking chairs with my feet, turning pages with my tongue."

Val had been greatly impressed and decided to call him. "I never saw anybody work like this. I want you to come to California for a big production."

"Val, I hate California," Chris responded.

"No, but this is a big, outdoor spectacular."

"I hate pageants!"

From the hospital, Val called *California* producer Wayne Dailard, and said,

"You must call Chris Mahan in New York and urge him to fly to San Diego immediately. He can handle things until I get out of the hospital."

Chris caught a Saturday plane, and when he reached San Diego, Dailard said, "Your first assignment will be to speak to a group of thirteen hundred people on Monday."

In partial paralysis, Chris asked, "What about?"

"To tell them all about this vast production and their part in it."

So Chris flew to Los Angeles to get an overnight indoctrination. Val tried to keep his hospital equipment carefully concealed, but there was a red glove hanging on the bedside, and a sudden movement of his hand spilled its contents over the floor.

"Oh, my God!" he exclaimed, as Chris began to mop it up with towels. Hating his helplessness, Val begged, "No, no, no — you mustn't do that."

"Nonsense," said Chris. "You just do the directing, and let me manage the stage."

When Val managed to escape from his imprisonment, and before leaving for San Diego, he attended one of our evening rehearsals at Universal Studios. During a break, many of the group went for coffee while others stayed to chat. Val made his exit a solitary one and then, despite his knowledge of lighting effects, he stood outside one of the glass partitions by the door, to make use of the light coming through, and in full view of all those who had remained inside, he raised his trouser leg to inspect the level of "fullfillment." Conductor Weiskopf turned immediately to the piano and tried to recapture everyone's attention.

Following Chris's overnight briefing, he faced the mob of people at their first rehearsal, and he held the tremendous jigsaw puzzle together until Val arrived. Then he became production stage manager with twenty-eight assistant stage managers, all equipped with earphones. He admitted that it was "The kind of thing that makes a breakthrough in your chosen profession. Learned more that year than in ten previous years. Easy to handle the little old Met switchboard after that." Chris later became the executive stage manager for the Metropolitan Opera.

A group of deaf people wished to participate as extras. Val said, "Yes, yes, yes — we need bodies." But when it came to lip reading his instructions, there was a problem. The previous year, Val had paralyzed a facial muscle by exposing it to sudden cold shock after treating it with excessive heat. This, plus his Russianized English, made lip reading awkward. Chris covered for Val, without his awareness, by asking assistant David Sell to stand behind Val and "mouth" his words.

Chris said of the deaf group, "Even getting it second hand, they were galvanized."

As with the 1950 Hollywood Bowl production, Meredith Willson con-

From left to right: Val Rosing, director; Lloyd Mitchell, producer; Meredith Willson, composer and conductor for *The California Story*, Hollywood Bowl, 1950. (Rothschild photo)

Ruth Scates, soloist and actress, in rehearsal for *The California Story.* (Photo, San Diego Historical Society, *Union-Tribune* Collection)

ducted his own music. Franklin Lacey revised the former Ainsworth and Moffitt script, Lotte Goslar choreographed, Norman Nesbitt was the commentator, and Clark Dewse was choral director. It all came together in the huge Balboa Stadium where, during two weeks of performances, it was viewed by 162,000 people. An enormous main stage, supplemented by

Grand finale of "Fiesta del Pacifico" production of *The California Story*, directed by Val Rosing, 1956, 1957, 1958.

numerous smaller stages, provided a continuous unfolding of scenes accompanied by a 70-piece orchestra, a 160-voice chorus, dancers, professional actors and soloists, hundreds of local volunteers, covered wagons, tanks, cannons, early autos, and a patriotic finale with hundreds of military personnel, and a 40-foot roll-on flag.

Enormous headlines declared it "A SMASH HIT," and an editorial elaborated:

> It was too gigantic, thrilling and beautiful to grasp at one performance. . . . Take all the superlative adjectives you can think of, or can find in any dictionary or thesaurus. Put them in a hat and draw any one out: it's a description of "The California Story."

It was a once-in-a-lifetime thrill for me the following year when I witnessed this production as one of the soloists. Val had asked me to audition with Meredith Willson. Though I had appeared in recitals and opera productions, and with symphony orchestras, I was never one gifted with an abundance of self-confidence, so I was astounded to hear Meredith say, "If you have *her,* why do you need anybody else?" I did not take it seriously. Anyway, other soloists had been engaged, and I joined them. I shall never forget the anticipation of an evening's performance with dusk settling over the arena. Areas were blocked off around the outskirts for vehicles, props, sound booths, dressing rooms, and animals. Horses eyed us with their penetratingly omniscient eyes, Chris's white tennis shoes appeared and disappeared in the darkness — flying across the ground as though self-motivated — and Val would make the rounds with last-minute inspections and instructions in staging, lighting, sound, and direction.

The principals, the visual acting cast, star soloists, sound cast, principal dancers, corps de ballet, and vehicle drivers were all professional members of Actors' Equity or guilds under whose jurisdiction they qualified. Choral groups, folk dancers, supers, and extras were also approved by various guilds and unions, and would rehearse for several months with a small directorial staff. All of the visual cast except the vocalists worked in pantomime while a dual sound cast located in a glass booth originated all of the voices. The technique of synchronization was one of the wonders of the production. As *The San Diego Union* stated, it was "an indefinitely complex job — the blending of drama, music, costumes, settings, lighting effects, dancing and sound into an absorbing cavalcade of California history — [and] the world's largest outdoor pageant."

Arthur Godfrey and Art Linkletter were guest stars in 1957 and 1958. Claudia Guzman was the set designer, Anna Sokolow became the choreographer, and Pat McGeehan the dialogue director with Thomas Henry as narrator.

The 1958 production moved to its new location at Westgate Park. There twenty-one crosses and bell towers were placed at various levels on the hill that rimmed Westgate Park to signify the California missions. Lighted one by one, it was a memorable scene. Ninety floodlights and four "super-trooper" beams were used on top of the stadium to augment the music and drama and to highlight the scenery.

One columnist said:

> Though Rosing is no longer a young man, he's still an amazingly agile one. He covered the field Friday night with the speed of a Padre rookie trying out for the first team. Nothing escaped his eye. A spear carrier whose lance was canted at a little less than the right angle found Rosing at his side correcting him. The fiesta dancers found him in their midst urging more tempo and spirit. The "49ers" wagon train saw him racing from one end of the procession to another offering suggestions.

Val's great talent lay in his ability to look at the sapling and see the towering oak; to look at a page of musical notes and see the barren steppes of Russia or the cold interior of a peasant's hut; to look at a script and see an ox-drawn train of prairie schooners attended by 500 pioneers spreading out onto the massive stage of an outdoor stadium, or a Father Serra limping alone across a 100-foot proscenium; to look at an amateur and see an actor. When the vision was captured, no effort was spared to achieve the perfect result.

In June 1957, Val had presented me with a contract confirming that I would be an assistant to him at New York City Opera, Chicago Lyric, and Montreal for the fall and winter season. It included terms for collaboration on a book regarding his system of body control. I was to act as his assistant director in the Greater Los Angeles Opera Association (which never got off the ground) and as his assistant in the master classes at the Sutro School. He was to have the option of re-engaging me for the spring season at New York City Center and for the production of *The California Story* in the summer of 1958.

At the Sutro School, Val gave a series of master classes in body control and operatic repertoire. Then he auditioned singers and prepared performances of *La Tosca* and *Madame Butterfly*.

Val's unique instruction lit up the night sky for me! All that I had studied had been so abstract: "establish emotional values, pace yourself, create empathy, generate emotional power!" Why hadn't anyone taught us some craft? Artists, authors, dancers . . . they all have to begin with emotional power, but they are all given rules for externalizing it. An artist studies form and color; an author learns grammar, characterization, dialogue; a vocalist learns correct use of the vocal cords and how to read music; but a singing actor is told to EMOTE!

Val began his lecture:

> After certain basic precepts, the path of the singing actor and that of the straight, dramatic actor quickly diverge. While the non-singing actor is subject only to the written word and the instructions of his director, the singer has a definite pattern or mold into which he must fit. He must circumscribe his acting to whole notes, quarter notes, and rests. He must move in quarter time, waltz time, or whatever other rhythm might have inspired the composer. His style of acting must change for staccato, legato, rubato, etc., and when he has accepted all the do's and don'ts laid down by the composer, the singer may suddenly find that his own interpretation and tempi must be discarded for that of the conductor. He must, furthermore, adjust his action so that he can maintain constant contact with the conductor's baton.
>
> The singer must indeed be somewhat of a juggler to give his attention to the many exterior demands made upon him in addition to his all-important task of performing upon a delicate vocal instrument with skill, color, and beauty.
>
> To give the perfect performance, the musical score, vocal technique, and acting technique must be thoroughly ingrained into the singer's subconscious. To be truthful, there are few examples in operatic history of perfect performances. There have been singers with such phenomenal voices that other faults have been overlooked; these are few and far between. However, when the beautiful voice is combined with an acting skill that knows how to coordinate itself with musical composition, the effect is ELECTRIC.
>
> This type of performance might have occurred more often had the science of acting for singers had more exponents. It has remained largely an unexplored field. Directors are usually concerned with when and where one enters, exits, sits, stands, etc. This type of director is a glorified stage manager.
>
> How few operatic singers know that there are rules for the use of gestures; that there is a definite time, place, and reason for the beginning of a gesture and a definite time to retrieve it; and that ALL gestures MUST BE RETRIEVED! Indeed, many singers do not even realize the necessity of any planned procedure.
>
> Operatic workshops fall short of their mission if they have no answer for the young student singers who say, "But what shall I do with my hands?" or "How shall I maneuver my feet?" Usually the

answer comes back, "Emote — feel what you are singing, and if you are sincere, it will find expression." This is wicked waste of a student's hard-earned money, youth, and ambition.

After Val covered visualization and analysis of the poet's words and absorption and translation of the music into corresponding vocal color and life — then he approached the subject of the body sculpture that would reflect meaning, mood, style, and character of the music. By body sculpture, he was not yet referring to motion or movement. He was referring to the concert stage. It will be remembered that his great success there lay in his ability to portray, both physically and vocally, the interpretation of a song.

> When it comes to action, as on the operatic stage, you project with the body in a series of MOVE and HOLD . . . MOVE and HOLD . . . as though a series of still shots is being photographed. Every unnecessary movement must be eliminated so that clarity greets the eye.
>
> Body coordination depends upon thirteen joints. When the actor has mastered the rules for the independent action of these parts of the body, and has then learned to coordinate them, he will at any given moment be able to sculpture his body into the picture he wants.

The thirteen joints are the wrists, elbows, shoulders, ankles, knees, hips, and head. He taught the movement of each of these joints, together with the HOW, the WHEN, and the WHY.

This was over thirty years ago; yet for the most part, opera seems still to be draped in its "hallowed traditions."

With the conclusion of the master classes, we were off to New York City Opera. Julius Rudel had taken over the musical and artistic directorship that year and would develop it into a first-rate company. In its contemporary repertoire, it would surpass the Met.

Val revived *Turandot* for the opening. His other operas were *Faust* and *Madame Butterfly.* How thrilling it was to observe the development of these productions, to become acquainted with the artist and familiar with backstage operations.

Frances Yeend, as the icy Turandot, took the cruel tessitura in stride. Her offstage personality was the complete antithesis. She was friendly, warm, and humorous. Guiseppi Gismondo, a young tenor, made a stunning debut as Calaf and then faded away into Italy. One rehearsal not to be forgotten was with Adele Addison, the most effective Liu I have ever seen. As the slave girl, who secretly loved Prince Calaf and watched him flirt with death by trying to answer Turandot's riddles, Adele sang "Signore ascolta" with such restrained anguish that tears filled her eyes and rolled down her face. Her voice was momentarily silenced, and those of us who were present felt the depths of Liu's agony. Adele apologized.

I have previously mentioned the perfectly choreographed approach that made the Ping, Pang, Pong sequence such a highlight. All of the papers, plus the *New Yorker*, covered the production with glowing reviews.

Norman Triegle's agile and stylized Mephistopheles in *Faust* was spine-tingling. He literally spiralled through the air like an electric current.

While in New York, Met baritone Robert Merrill, Val, and I accompanied basso Jerome Hines to the Salvation Army where Jerry and Robert Merrill sang. We all sat on the platform surrounded by instrumentalists, chorus, and Salvation Army personnel. Men of all sizes, shapes, and colors continued to shuffle in off the street until the room was packed. A hymn was announced, and we all stood and sang. Between hymns, I heard a hissing sound behind me and turned my head. A Salvation Army woman officer apologized. "I'm just spraying some cologne. Someone out there has smelly feet, and it would be difficult to locate the offender."

Chicago's Lyric Opera was next. There Val directed *Cavalleria Rusticana* and *Pagliacci*. I watched him work with that wonderful artist Tito Gobbi in the role of Tonio. They communicated and understood each other, and Gobbi was receptive and cooperative. Mario Del Monico, who sang the role of Canio, sat with his wife in the auditorium watching the two work. Del Monico's wife nodded toward Val and whispered, "Listen to him . . . do what he says."

Lyric Opera, of course, was Italian influenced, and the artist for the most part represented the rather inflexible "hallowed traditions." But, to its credit, here one heard the great voices of the world: Eileen Farrell, Renata Tebaldi, Eleanor Steber, Birgit Nilsson, Anita Cerquetti, Guilietta Simionata, Jussi Bjoerling, Richard Tucker, and the list goes on. It was a rich experience indeed.

There were treasured associations with General Manager Carol Fox, her then Executive Secretary Ardis Krainik, who would later move up to head the company, Assistant Manager Byron Belt, who has remained a special friend through the years, the conductors, Chorus Master Michael Lepore, and Choreographer Ruth Page.

Anna Moffo made her debut with the company that season. An American singer, she had studied in Italy, had just returned from LaScala and Vienna, and would go on to the Met the following year. Under Val's direction, she sang Lucia in *Lucia di Lammermoor*. The voice was beautiful, but there was no communication on the acting level. I was astonished to hear her reply to Val's direction. "But Maestro, I must have an inner motive for what I do." She had no understanding of what was available to her. Consequently, the "mad scene" came across with a flavor of intoxication rather than madness.

These were things Val did not understand. "In Russia," he spoke euphemistically, "we sought out our masters and learned at their feet."

One of the singers imported from Italy for the season found himself musically unprepared for one of the roles he was engaged to sing. Searching out Carol Fox, he made an attempt to transfer the blame and save his own prestige. "It is impossible for me to sing two major roles within the period of time that you have scheduled them," he said. "The second opera will have to be canceled."

The general manager was not so easily placed on the defensive. "But," Fox said, "you received a contract stating the dates of the performances."

"The figures were so small that I neglected to read them," he said accusingly.

"Then tell me," Fox quickly countered, "why did you not neglect to read the amount of your fee, the figures of which were in the same size print?"

Between the two Chicago productions we went to Montreal where Val was to direct *Falstaff* the following January for the Montreal Opera Guild. Madame Pauline Donalda, its founder, was a prima donna of the Golden Age of opera who had shared the stage with Caruso and Scotti. Her right-hand secretary-treasurer, Sara Berne, was gracious and charming, sturdy and staunch. She has remained a friend for many years.

Mme. Donalda invited the press to her home to meet the new director. Covering the interview in *The Montreal Star*, Eric McLean quoted Val on the subject of opera singers:

> Rosing said he preferred working with Americans for whom the repertoire was fresh, and uncluttered with traditional ideas of staging and movement. Of the European singers, only a few of the great ones are receptive to changes in staging; most of them fall into their own stubborn patterns after they have performed a role a few times, and become unreceptive to new ideas.

* * * * *

Then finally, home for the holidays. My eight-year-old daughter, my husband, and my home were precious to me, but this further adventure into the musical world with its prolonged separations was no small test for a marriage which was already treading on thin ice. My Christmas gift was a set of luggage.

Val had presented me with another contract designating my duties as associate producer, co-writer, and assistant director in all of his productions through May 4, 1958, and in January, we were to go to Europe for a minimum of five weeks for the purpose of projecting a television program, "Showhouse of the World."

First, we returned to Montreal for *Falstaff*. When I met the conductor, Emil Cooper, I saw demonstrated what Val had said about the Russian attitude toward their masters. He spoke with reverence and respect. "When I was starting out in Russia," Val said, "Cooper was the god of the Russian Imperial Opera. I consider it a great honor to be given this opportunity to work with him."

Maestro Cooper handed out sheets of music to members of the orchestra, and with his Russian accent said politely, "Please take these home and overlook them."

He was a calming influence. When the female heads of the organization, Mme. Donalda, her sister Mae Lightstone, and Sara Berne would enter into animated discussion, he would sit quietly until it reached white heat, then he would utter a few words of quiet wisdom, and complete calm would return.

Falstaff was a gem. Thomas Archer of *The Gazette* headlined it as "The Great Falstaff." In the Guild's 16 years, he said, no performance had ever equalled this one. ". . . everything tells me that I will never see a better *Falstaff* than this. . . . Certainly I have never seen a better operatic production anywhere at any time."

Robert Savoie, who sang the title role, was receptive and flexible. Every motion blended with the musical rhythm. Val was able to heighten characterizations and enliven the stage to the point that the audience rippled with laughter throughout the performance. The same opera seen later in Chicago was hardly recognizable.

By now Val was possessed with the inspiration of visiting European capitals to explore the possibility of filming highlights of entertainment typical of each country and presenting them as televised shows in the U.S. under the title, "Showhouse of the World."

We left for Europe after the Montreal production. The Secretary for Public Affairs at the Department of State had provided Val with introductions to the cultural attachées of England, Belgium, Germany, Switzerland, Austria, Italy, and France.

In London we met Marie, Val's first wife (whom I would later refer to affectionately as "our wife") and her son Billy. We had appointments with conductor Sir Adrian Boult, and with Covent Garden's general administrator, David Webster. We also attended Benjamin Britten's *Peter Grimes* at Covent Garden. I was astounded to observe so much stage technique, particularly with chorus and extras, that seemed to bear Val's touch. But when I mentioned it, he immediately "shushed" me. Thirty-six-year-old Geraint Evans was in the cast and would appear in the U.S. the following year. Certainly, he had the distinction of being a real singing actor. Christopher West was the resident producer. He would eventually come to New York City to direct, and he would become Val's assistant director for the Kansas Centennial where we had productions going in two cities, Topeka and Wichita.

In Europe, we were in Val's world. Doors opened to him, warm hands were extended, and I was privileged to share the experience. His enthusiasm carried us from one spectacular place or performance to another as he created his format of entertainment in each country. From street musicians, medieval horsemanship, marionettes, and cabarets to opera houses, cathedrals, and palaces, we absorbed the beauty and wonder of it all.

We went from London to Belgium, Paris, and then Switzerland. There was electricity, suspense, and awe in the hushed expectancy with which we approached Montreux. Before the train stopped, Val hastily seized all the luggage, resisting any help. When the train jerked to a halt, of course, he dropped it all. But it was quickly recaptured, for he could not wait to step on the soil, breathe the air, and bless the mountains and the lake of his beloved childhood home. His joy bubbled up and spilled over as he proudly portrayed and shared all of its spectacular qualities with me.

Lake Geneva was a blue-green mirror of unbelievable clarity. Mont du Midi, with its snow-clad peaks, rose above it all, leaving me to wonder if we had ascended to another dimension. When dusk arrived, each hillside formed its own galaxy of lights.

After Munich and Vienna and Venice, we met Tito Gobbi in Rome. With him as our guide, we visited the Baths of Carcalle and other historical places which totally altered my perspective of history, previously cradled in the *Mayflower*. Another jolt to my equilibrium was to hear Gobbi say, "You know, Val, Mussolini did some good things for us. He improved our country with much reconstruction and restoration." In America, we'd have looked at the author of such a statement as a traitor. An "evil man" was not supposed to have any redeeming features.

Five days of ocean-crossing on the *Sylvania* was a time to digest all the wonders of the world we had seen, to anticipate *The Ballad of Baby Doe* at New York City Opera, and to contemplate the future.

Douglas Moore's *The Ballad of Baby Doe* raised the curtain on the first opera season in history devoted exclusively to all-American opera. It triggered headlines in all the newspapers, musical magazines, *Saturday Review*, etc. Beverly Sills sang the title role, with Walter Cassel and Martha Lipton in co-starring roles. Emerson Buckley conducted. *Variety* said that Val's staging "maintains an almost unbelievable speeded tempo for opera." Other reviews congratulated Rosing's "brisk" and "stylized" direction — "so fetching that it drew applause again and again at the very rise of the curtain."

During a *Baby Doe* rehearsal, Beverly Sills chatted with me about the stepchildren acquired with her recent marriage. She did not yet have her own two, who would bring a great measure of love, and also a great element of tragedy with them. I was filled with the anticipation of seeing my own daughter after a long separation, but that joy would be linked to the pain of ending my marriage.

The latter was accomplished in Las Vegas, Nevada, where my mother was living, and where I extracted enough from the slot machines to repair the damage inflicted on my car by the babysitter during my absence. Also during this time, a rigid diet had relieved me of the excess pounds Val had procured for me in Europe with his repeated eyebrow-raising impeachments: "But when will you again have the opportunity to sample such delicacies?"

When the six-week ordeal was over, I flew to Phoenix where I was to be Val's Assistant Director with the Phoenix Light Opera, and where rehearsals were already in progress. With the help of Bettina Rubicam, Val had located a guesthouse for me. His idea was to share it since there was an extra room and bath separated from the rest of the house by a long hall. Even though my daughter would be with me, I knew it would be taken for granted that we were living together, and I was prejudiced against this modern mode of habitation. He soon found another cottage for himself, but evoked my sympathy by claiming to have found a scorpion in it. Eventually, Dee and I moved to a charming adobe cottage, one of a number clustered on a former date-palm orchard, and Val took an apartment adjacent to the Civic Opera office.

What an experience it was to watch the man work untiringly with young artists who were willing to learn. Whey they used their hands for "swimming" across stage, he would threaten to handcuff them. "Return your hands to base after a movement! Keep your body stationary when you pivot your head — like a small dog when he reacts to a sound." The newspaper critic observed, after working with Rosing, performers learned "what to do with their hands and their faces when they are not using them."

In the meantime, Val had composed his "Showhouse" television formats for Munich, Bavaria, London, Vienna, Italy, Paris, Brussels, etc. — thirteen in all. He had secured the cooperation of each country and had established a network of correspondence to support it. In France, the Minister of Culture, Roger Seydoux, appointed a coordinator and committee to work with Val, and the Grand Opera and Comedie Francaise, among others, had expressed the desire to cooperate. In England, the project was represented by P. Filmer-Sankey, a film producer and former executive of the Rank organization. Germany was represented by film producer Kurt von Molo; Vienna by Joseph Sills, the former general director of the American-Austrian radio; and Italy, by Tito Gobbi.

To Val's great disappointment, he came up against strong resistance in the United States. Advertisers were very skeptical that they would be able to sell such a show unless they could display two or three pilot films. To do this Val would have to form his own syndicate. As he plunged into *The California Story* rehearsals, he wrote to P. Filmer-Sankey: "Too bad that television powers here seem to have no imagination; the whole mentality surrounds Elvis Presley, quiz shows, and mystery junk."

Val had also hoped to take the American opera, *The Ballad of Baby Doe*, to the Brussels International Exhibition where the Russians were sending their top-notch artists and artistic attractions, and where the United States was represented by a few major artists and a college glee club. In addition to the opera, he proposed a "Gala Hollywood Stars Evening" with famous film personalities appearing in their various acts.

Jean Dalyrymple, who was the coordinator for the U.S. Performing Arts Program in Brussels, wrote to Val:

> I agree with your two fine ideas. . . . Of course, it is understood that our program has NO budget to undertake the financing of such projects, but if these evenings could be worked out by you without cost to us except, perhaps, for orchestra rehearsals and per diems, we will be most grateful to you. . . .

Val was not a money broker; he was a Van Gogh expressing the poetry of life.

The California Story in San Diego would keep us busy from July till mid-September. Then we were due back at New York City Center for a repeat of *Turandot* and *Baby Doe*.

In Chicago, also, Val would direct *Turandot*. Tullio Serafin, a quiet, calm, and patient man, was the conductor; and Guiseppi Di Stefano, as Calaf, matched the brilliant, soaring tones of Birgit Nilsson's Turandot. *Musical America*'s Howard Talley wrote: "Tullio Serafin's conducting was masterly; equally so was the stage direction by Vladimir Rosing, particularly his part in training the large chorus not to move in phalanxes but to act as individuals."

Moussorgsky's *Boris Godounov* (Rimsky-Korsakov's version) was Val's next assignment, with Boris Christoff in the title role. Conductor Artur Rodzinski was the pet of Chicago's red-headed critic Claudia Cassidy, who, every season, bathed the opera house anew in verbal acid. He was returning, ten years after his abrupt dismissal as conductor of the Chicago Symphony, to conduct *Tristan und Isolde* and *Boris Godounov*. There was a one-week interval between the two productions, and Val made an appointment with Rodzinski to discuss *Boris*. Val's return from the meeting was insulated with silence. When I questioned him, he looked at me with incredulity: "He said he couldn't *think* about *Boris* while he was still working on *Tristan*!" The truth was that Rodzinski had told his wife he would have to cancel *Boris*, but she, feeling he was exaggerating his physical condition, continued to postpone the decision. Even when the doctor advised him that *Boris* was out of the question, no action was taken. After his final performance of *Tristan*, Rodzinski suffered a heart attack. To conceal the fact, he refused to be taken to a hospital, saying they could take him out in a coffin, but not an ambulance. It was then that he sent a message to Carol Fox that he had the flu and could not conduct *Boris*. He even went through with an interview for *Time* magazine and refused a wheelchair at the airport when leaving Chicago, so as to shroud his condition in secrecy. Nine days after leaving Chicago, he died in a Boston hospital.

Carol Fox had been able to secure a last-minute replacement in Georges Sebastian who was conducting *Aida* on alternate nights. He conducted with dignity, vitality, and an ability to bring the best out of the score.

Boris was greeted with this headline in the Chicago *Daily News*: "LYRIC'S 'BORIS' CROWNS SEASON." And Don Henahan fairly floated in space with his review.

> If you make it a practice never to read rave reviews, then pursue this one no further. There is no other way to discuss Lyric Opera's production of Modeste Mussorgsky's "Boris Godounov," presented Monday night in the opera house. . . .
>
> Staging by Vladimir Rosing was of a quality Lyric has been in need of. . . .

Val was interviewed by George Murray for Chicago's *American*. The article was titled: "ROSING: OPERA NEEDS ACTORS."

> Vladimir Rosing, out of a lifetime of experience in grand opera, threw me off-balance . . . when he echoed the man in the street:
>
> "Opera is often horrible. The acting can be atrocious. Singers can get up there and wave their hands and arms without rhyme or reason."
>
> Rosing . . . called such nonsense a hangover from the Victorian era. . . .
>
> Rosing wants singers who are trained to act. He wants actors who are trained to act. He wants actors who can perform with thought, with emotion, with trained body control. He scoffs at a Victorian critic who said the three most important ingredients of opera are voice, voice — and again — voice. . . .
>
> . . . Rosing said [of his American Opera Company]: "We hoped that American singers, using English translations, might make opera as popular as films. It was a noble experiment."

Murray continued to quote Val regarding the time and money invested in a

Deletta (Dee) Scates makes her debut in *Boris,* as the daughter of Boris Godounov, at the Lyric Opera of Chicago. (Photo, by Nancy Sorensen)

musical while an opera must be prepared in three weeks.

Concurrently, Rudolph Bing of the New York Metropolitan Opera was the subject of an article by another critic, Roger Dettmer. Dettmer stated that "This year, like clockwork [Bing] sniffed disdainfully at opera in English . . . and also opera produced elsewhere in the United States."

Someone who made a debut in *Boris* without getting her name in the paper was my nine-year-old daughter, Dee. Val gave her a walk-on role as Boris's daughter Xenia in the coronation scene. A couple of years later, the costume department took her on as an errand girl. She would deliver costumes to the dressing rooms of artists, pick up emergency supplies, etc. When I had to be at the opera house early, she would breakfast alone at the cafeteria across from the hotel, and then walk to the opera house a few blocks away. One morning, a woman, surprised to see a child eating alone, questioned her about her activities. Dee answered with great pride and dignity, "I work for the costume department of the Chicago Lyric Opera."

We returned to Phoenix for a highly successful production of Rogers and Hammerstein's *Carousel*. Then in January 1959, Val staged Verdi's *Macbeth* for Montreal while I rehearsed *Plain and Fancy* in Phoenix.

Thomas Archer of *The Gazette* called the Montreal production *"A Great 'Macbeth.'"*

> [It] is the most stirring all-around production this enterprizing institution has given since it was founded by Pauline Donalda in 1942. . . . It is hard to imagine a performance that could more rightly be called a model one. Emil Cooper as conductor and Vladimir Rosing as stage director are masters of the business of producing a great work like this in the right way and with the right emphasis on its noble style, its intense dramatic accent and its wonderful flow of Verdian music. . . .
>
> What [Mr. Rosing] did was a triumph of imagination and foresight. . . . [He] somehow managed to keep our eyes as well as our ears absorbed. How he did it is his secret. . . .

Margaret Tynes, Bill Chapman, Chester Watson, and Andre Turp were all highly praised for their performances.

In Phoenix, Maggie Savoy interviewed me for her column *Savoy Fare*. Under the title, *"Her Dream Did Come True,"* she covered my musical career, my work with Val, my daughter's backstage and onstage activities, and then added, "There's another member of the family, too: 'Pico,' a little dog they found huddled and shivering in a [restaurant] doorway. . . ."

During *The California Story* rehearsals in San Diego, we had gone to a trolley car restaurant in an outlying woodsy area, and the little Boston Terrier was sitting on the doorstep, trembling with an unremitting perseverance. Val and Dee were consumed with sympathy, especially when the restaurant owner said he had been there for three days and would have to be gotten rid of. The dog shook harder and looked at me. Dee and Val looked at me. How could I be so insensitive? We named him for General Pico in *The California Story*. He traveled all over the country with us and was a great source of entertainment and companionship. We were all broken-hearted when we eventually lost him.

Annie Get Your Gun was coming up. Also, on March 15, Val would produce a 90-minute, governor-supported telecast in advance recognition of Arizona's territorial centennial and 50 years of statehood, which would take place in 1962.

But something had been brewing which I had to discuss with Val. My former husband had visited Dee and me during the prior Christmas holidays; tender memories had ignited, and we wished to try a reunion. When I broached the subject with Val, the atmosphere became oppressive and stormy, but the discussion concluded with a request from him that I wait until he could negotiate with a girl he had met at the Globe Theater in San Diego, to see if she could come to Phoenix and help him. Before I even knew she had arrived, my car passed Val's one day on Camelback Road, and she was sitting beside him. She had moved in and was sharing his apartment.

I sublet the cottage, packed the car, and Dee and I drove to Los Angeles. I arrived in a state of exhaustion, which was a poor stage setting for new beginnings. But it was evident that the reunion was based more on memories than on possibilities for the future. What was I to do?

Within a few weeks, producer Dailard telephoned that Oregon was going to hold a centennial celebration and wondered if I would be interested in working as an associate director and script editor. I jumped at the chance, agreeing to be in Portland in May.

At about the same time, I learned from former Phoenix neighbors that the couple to whom I had sublet had absconded. It was necessary to return and put things in order. I shall never forget the sense of peace that pervaded me as I sat in my Phoenix home watching the sunset bathe Camelback Mountain in its afterglow. I must have made a right decision.

Both newspapers carried headlines on Val's telecast. *"TV's 'Arizona Story' Termed Big Success"* and *"Arizona Spectacular Of Network Quality."* Everything he touched seemed to be a success — artistically, at least.

I attended his Civic Opera production, after which Val proposed that I drive us to Portland in my car. Later, he suggested we take his friend as far as Ashland, Oregon, where she wanted to join the Shakespeare Festival.

The Oregon Story would open September 3 and run through September 17 in Portland's Centennial Exposition Arena. This meant we would be in Portland for four months. Dee flew up to join me and performed in the Spectacular.

Val put me to work on the script, writing to the existing format. "Field General" Chris Mahan was there early on. So was Arliss Kirschmer, assistant to producer Dailard. We were a compatible group, and those to arrive later included Stephen Papich with his Hollywood Bowl dancers; Thomas B. Henry, narrator; Pat McGeehan, Red Skelton's "straight man" and Art

Linkletter's announcer, as sound cast director; and, of course, Meredith Willson along with conductor Frank Allen Hubbell. These were all congenial and jovial people, but when set designer Claudio Guzman came on scene, he really kept things bubbling with his carbonated sense of humor.

On one memorable occasion, we all met at a restaurant to let off some steam after a late rehearsal. Papich and Guzman told one hilarious story after another. We were in hysterics. Then Chris began what seemed a rather droll yarn, and I thought, "How can he be so drab after all this delirium?" It was something about a man inflicted with a tapeworm. He was seeking medical help, and, according to Chris, "The doctor offered a very unorthodox remedy: peel six hard-boiled eggs and insert them in the posterior region while in a kneeling position. Do this for ten days." I felt the atmosphere deflating, but Chris was unperturbed. "Each time, follow this with the insertion of a piece of lemon meringue pie." Chris, who always spoke with great composure, continued, "After ten days, there was no improvement, so the patient returned, consumed with indignation. But the doctor said, 'Just relax; some things take time. You are now ready for the final treatment.' Unbelieving and tense, the patient, nevertheless, submitted to one last treatment. But nothing happened. The doctor, however, reassured him, 'Don't worry and don't move.' Ten minutes passed without incident. Then, suddenly, a small head appeared and demanded [in a high nasal register] 'Where is my lemon meringue pie?!' Instantly, the doctor grabbed a mallet and demolished the vile offender!"

The surprise ending demolished *us*. Chris had demonstrated theatre at its epitome — contrast and unanticipated denouement. Whenever and wherever we met across the country after that, Chris had to render an encore of that story, and it always brought on hysteria.

In August, Val and I flew to Los Angeles where Val would direct "An Evening with the 'Music Man' in Person" for the Hollywood Bowl. The evening of our arrival, the Bolshoi dancers were slated for the Bowl, and our anticipation was in high gear. We had to fly at night, after our own late rehearsal, and by the time we had made our contacts and secured hotel rooms, there was no time for sleep before the performance. I worried that our exhaustion might cause this great show to receive less than our total attention. That was an idle concern. We were totally absorbed, with adrenalin levels running high. Afterwards, Val asked the director how long they rehearsed for such a show. The director looked him coldly in the eye and answered, "We rehearse as long as is necessary, and we spend as much as is needed, while you Americans spend and rehearse as little as possible to make as much as possible."

Rehearsals began for the "Meredith Willson Night" which would feature selections from *The Music Man* and a scene from *The California Story*.

Meredith conducted, while his wife Rini sang and played a comedy role. The King Sisters and Earl Wrightson also participated; there were 76 trombones, a massed choir of 300, a Chinese drum and bugle corps, pompon girls, and representatives from the Salvation Army, American Red Cross, and U.S. Armed Forces.

Strange to say, the *Los Angeles Herald-Examiner* greeted "Meredith Willson Night" as "*Rosing Program A Triumph.*" Herbert Donaldson followed up his adulatory headline with:

> How Vladimir Rosing . . . overcame the limitations of stage space in devising movements and positions for a cast of 500 is a mystery to me but a credit to him. . . . You would not think it possible for such a cast to perform as a unit. Yet they did this . . . thanks to a stage director with skill and imagination and a large number of intelligent persons capable of learning quickly and following directions.

After that, we returned to Oregon where Val was interviewed by the *Oregonian*. After the reporter had covered the type of spectacular *The Oregon Story* was to be, plus the history of Val's singing career and operatic ventures, his musical recordings and directorial assignments, he asked Val what had been the most exciting thing in his long career. Without delay, Val replied, "Women!"

At the time of the American Opera Company in Rochester, bass-baritone George Fleming Houston had warned Val to stay clear of having an affair, lest it become known. Later on, when Val had returned from an American tour, he found the whole school agog over a scandal concerning Houston. An adage evolved with the company, "When George Houston and Val Rosing are around, lock up the Virgin Mary."

Mark Hatfield, governor of Oregon, gave *The Oregon Story* a great send-off. Val and I had a very cordial relationship with Thomas Vaughan, Director of the Oregon Historical Society, and his wife Sherry. They resurrected Oregon history, entertained, picnicked, and warmed our Oregon experience with their friendship. Janet Baumhover was a Portland actress, labor official, and member of the Centennial Commission, who played Queen Elizabeth and later came to join the cast of *The Kansas Story*. Her friendship has been treasured over the years. She is now ninety, still poses for television commercials, took part in a 1987 James Garner movie, and is active in Portland theatre.

Various reviewers described *The Oregon Story* as a "dazzling extravaganza," "brilliant production," "skillfully and thrillingly told," "best entertainment and the best dramatization of history that this state has been privileged to see," "never a dull moment." And what was to Val the greatest compliment was written by Frank Jenkins of the *Herald News* in Klamath Falls: "The Oregon Story sent those 3700 Oregonians home BELIEVING IN THEIR STATE and with a new faith in its destiny."

Ruth and Val honeymooning at the Fairmont Hotel in San Francisco where Val was directing the Dennis Day show, October 1959.

Chapter 30

New Rules of Grammar

I did not know the extent of my love for Val until that autumn of 1959. When I concentrated on the age difference between us, and on Val's four previous marriages, I wanted to run; but by the final performance of *The Oregon Story*, I recognized that viewpoint to be peripheral. I became aware that the future would loom gray and drab upon any horizon that did not know the all-encompassing warmth and dynamic vitality of a Val Rosing. That face, full of beauty and sweetness, which lit up whenever I entered the room — what could there be in a future darkened by its absence? I felt emotionally released from my former marriage now, and I was free to love this man unreservedly.

We were married that October and spent our honeymoon at the Fairmont Hotel in San Francisco where Val was directing Dennis Day's revue at the Riviera. He had directed Dennis's revues since 1953. I wanted our ceremony to be in a church, not a courthouse, so we canvassed the city until we found an available minister.

That night Val told me that his love for me was not as overwhelming as it had once been. The tears were secretly absorbed in my pillow. I think Val wanted to punish me somewhat for my long-delayed decision. And I think I probably deserved what I was getting, for I must have caused him much pain. But there had been much pain in my own life as well, and to this day I don't know how I could have done things differently.

A short time later, Val completely reversed his statement. And a few months later, when I had to leave him in Riverside, California, and return to Phoenix

Clockwise from left: Ruth Rosing, David and Sylvia Ziskind, unknown, Dennis Day, Armand Tokatyan, Val Rosing, unknown, unknown, Lauritz Melchior, and Mrs. Melchior at the Moulin Rouge, 1960. (Photo, B. C. Mittleman)

to start my daughter in school, he wrote (there was never punctuation except for dashes — and sometimes important words were capitalized):

> My dearest dearest Love — its only four days since you left and it seems like an endless time I miss you so veryveryverymuch and life without you is just an empty space — its specialy bad being in a lovely place which could be so enjoyable if you were here. . . .

Then he told me of talking with Meredith Willson who demanded that he read James Michener's *Hawaii* with a view to making a pageant of it, and then interrupted with,

> Oh I am so lonely without you I hope we wont have to be separated like this again.

He then described the cast for *Rigoletto*, the costumes and the rehearsals, and broke in again with,

> I will be so happy when its over — and we will be back together without you it feels as if I am only half alive.

He continued the letter the following morning:

> This morning beloved I seem to miss you even more — today the committee [Kansas Centennial Committee] is meeting in Kansas to decide — I pray they definitely accept — but if they dont I wont worry — I know we will succeed in our own production company — *I KNOW WE WILL* I love you beloved Love you so much Give a hug to Dee — and all the kisses and love to you my adored wife your Husband Val.

This, and another letter received from him the only other time we were ever apart, are my treasures. They were indicative of the way he always expressed himself. Val was offended when I would refer to *his* productions. Crestfallen, he insisted they were *ours*. I was separating us! Another thing he taught me never to say was, "I love you, too." To him, this was a ditto remark that did not come from the heart.

When he moved into my rented cottage in Phoenix, he came minus all of the material accoutrements and manifestations of his long, colorful, and successful career. Trunks of mementos, programs, reviews, correspondence with the world's political leaders and renowned artistic personalities, etc., had been stored in basements of hotels which had changed hands while he was crossing oceans. His personal possessions were left in divorce courts. He was shocked at the activity on that squalid level of thinking and walked away from it.

So, he collected himself and moved in with a suitcase of clothing and two paintings. He said the suitcase had to be returned, but he could keep the paintings which he had purchased at auction for a dollar each. One was a pastel of Paris rain in the gloaming; the other was someone's version of Switzerland's Chateau de Chillon which was so integrated with his childhood memories. But he brought a great wealth of experience, friendships, and artistic greatness.

Of course, I was very well off, having sold my Steinway grand for $2,000. But I am heartbeats ahead of my story.

Val had agreed with Carol Fox of Chicago Lyric Opera to work with Leontyne Price while we were in San Francisco. Leontyne would be doing the title role in Massenet's *Thaïs*, which Val would be directing for Lyric Opera in November. Leontyne is one of the loveliest individuals I have ever met. She is warm, outgoing, and possesses a marvelous sense of humor. Of course, her voice was, and is, ravishingly beautiful.

She would be making her debut at Lyric as Liu in *Turandot* which preceded *Thaïs*. As in the prior season, Nilsson and Di Stefano were again featured, and again drew praise from the critics. Claudia Cassidy called it "stunning" and "even finer than last year." She described Price's voice as "One of the loveliest of our time."

Byron Belt, after leaving Lyric Opera in 1959, became a critic-at-large on art, music, and dance for the *Newhouse News Service*. In 1979, he reminisced for *Opera News* on the "Lyric's Silver Celebration." He spoke of the "superlative production [of *Turandot*] by Vladimir Rosing, the great Russian tenor-turned-director who was responsible for many fine productions. . . . Audiences went wild."

Then came *Thaïs*. For this French opera, Fox imported two artists from France, conductor Georges Prêtre and baritone Michel Roux. It was Prêtre's debut in this country; he would, of course, become internationally famous. In 1962, when Val and I first met with him in Paris, he said his career was taking off so fast that it made his head swim.

We became a foursome because of Val's fluency with the French language, which no one else spoke in an "Italian" opera house. We referred to them as "the boys." They were fun to be with, for they were both endowed with a great sense of humor. Prêtre was incredibly handsome with a spellbinding smile. Sitting beside Leontyne in a rehearsal, I once whispered, "How do you like your conductor?"

Leontyne rolled her eyes and murmured, "He is a doll! And every time he gives me a cue, I miss it!"

At the dress rehearsal, Leontyne appeared in costume. It had yards and yards of flowing green chiffon which, in addition to being draped over one shoulder, had panels clipped to bracelets at the wrist. Suddenly, the simple, sculptured movements she had been studying disappeared — to be replaced by layers of green chiffon billowing in rhythm to the music.

Byron Belt, in his 1979 *Opera News* article, maintained:

> The Price voice, as none other, was *made* for Thaïs. Had the soprano taken advantage of Val Rosing's willingness to work extensively with her the summer before the November premiere, it could have been her greatest triumph. Even if dramatically awkward, Thaïs was glowingly sung by the soprano with tenor Simoneau, debut baritone Michel Roux and a new, passionately intense conductor, Georges Prêtre.

Val seemed to be able to mentally encompass half a dozen projects simultaneously. I had to have my facts on paper; he carried them all in his mind. I felt like a cricket jumping from one spot to the next, while he hovered like a hawk, surveying the entire area. During the Chicago season he was negotiating the Kansas Centennial production, planning *Carmen* for Montreal, *Can-Can* for the Phoenix Light Opera, *Rigoletto* for Riverside, California, and putting together a production for Richard Charlton's Sombrero Playhouse in Phoenix.

He secured Kathryn Grayson to star in Sombrero's *Tonight at the Opera*, and we flew to Los Angeles to make arrangements with other artists, choose costumes, etc. Then we flew to Montreal for *Carmen*. It would be our last opera with conductor Emil Cooper, who had been the soul of the company for a quarter of a century. He died the following November.

While Val was rehearsing the production, he was interviewed by Jon Anderson of *The Gazette* (Montreal). The subsequent article was entitled: *"Foe Of Operatic Pomposity Wipes Egg Off Singers' Faces."* He quoted Val:

> The heyday of opera was during the Victorian era and many of their ridiculous gestures have become part of the operatic tradition. I've been trying for years to bring opera acting and production up to the standards of the theatre.

Anderson introduced Val as "one of the world's great opera directors" and quoted his views on the state of opera today.

> On acting: "There is a fundamental difference between acting in opera and in theatre. Singing is four times slower than speaking. . . . We must have movement on stage to fill . . . bridges and

sustain interest. Movement means interest, but it must be rhythmical. If the singer finishes his movement before he completes his
line, he stands there with egg on his face until his next action."

On translations: "Opera in England and America has suffered
tremendously because it hasn't been translated. . . . Of course,
some snobs say they just adore opera in Italian and German — but
when it's over they usually haven't understood a bit of what was
going on."

On subsidies: "Governments give money to museums for dead
things. Why shouldn't they support the living arts?"

The opera, featuring Margaret Tynes as Carmen and Jon Craig (substituting
for Brian Sullivan) as Don Jose, was sold out for both performances.

The Gazette and *The Montreal Star* did not rave about the production, but
were complimentary. What amused me was the unvarnished deportment of the
French paper *La Presse* which termed it "*'Carmen' un grand succès!*" and
then did a special article by Claude Gingras titled, "*Une 'Carmen' vivante et
colorée*" (lively and colored). After stating that it was prepared with much
care and one must truly see it, that all was not perfect, but that quality was
predominant, it stated: "*Tout d'abord, la Carmen est excellente. Une Carmen
nègre, et qui n'est pas Carmen Jones, cela est gênant, je l'admets.*" (Firstly,
Carmen is excellent. A black Carmen, and who is not Carmen Jones, that is
disturbing, I admit.)

The English-speaking paper would not mention Tynes's color; the French
paper had no inhibitions regarding it.

Tonight at the Opera was due to go on at the Sombrero on March 8 and run
for a week. The Sombrero was one of America's top regional theatres, the
most adorable and fashionable in the West. It seated 500 and had a season of
ten weeks, during which great stars of film and theatre appeared — Katherine
Cornell, Walter Pidgeon, Linda Darnell, Sarah Churchill, Helen Hayes, and
others.

Kathryn Grayson had a clause in her contract that permitted her to withdraw
by February 1, which would give Val three weeks for reshuffling. She did not
withdraw; instead, she decided to change the opera from *Bohême* to *Traviata*.
Since the opera was, of course, to be done in English, this meant a recopying
of all parts. Henry Reese provided the translations and was engaged as
conductor. David Poleri was to sing the role of Alfredo, and others, including
Val's son Gil would come from Los Angeles to join the cast.

But wait — Kathryn did not know all of *Traviata*. Now what were we to do?
Val shuffled things around ingeniously. First, he presented "Operatic
Masques," which began with Pagliacci singing the "Prologue." He was
interrupted by Basilio, Musetta, and the Duke coming down the aisles to

introduce the evening's highlights. Following this was Act I of *La Traviata*. After intermission, the complete story of *Faust* was given in four scenes. Another intermission and then, Act I of *Bohême*. The audience, whose first evening included Mamie Eisenhower, and the press loved it. The *Hollywood Reporter* said, "Opera lovers normally must sit through two hours of grand opera before one of the famous numbers is sung. Here they get the leading, familiar arias . . . in one glittering package. . . ."

Cobina Wright flew to Phoenix for the performance and reviewed it in the *Los Angeles Herald-Express*. She, too, commended the unique manner of the introduction and the filtering of the "best from various operas" with added "theatrical touches which provoked audience attention and gave great interest to the performance."

Kathryn Grayson demonstrated a voice of beauty and quality. She quickly won the affection and admiration of everyone with her lovely disposition, understanding, and patience. David Poleri was a good performer with a lovely voice, but one never knew when he would erupt like a volcano.

Val "rested" during his preparation of *Can-Can*, due March 31, for the Phoenix Musical Theatre. He wrote to Sombrero's associate producer Ruth Burch in L.A.: "Things are so quiet here! — comparatively speaking, that is. With CAN CAN, I have gone on a sit-down strike. It has been so long since I have had the 'at-home' feeling, that I want to experience it fully." We would have an added week after the March 31 *Can-Can* before we were due at Lake Tahoe for Dennis Day's revue.

Val and I had been married for five months, and we were, for the duration of these two Phoenix productions, actually living in our own home. He taught me to make beef stroganoff. I typed his business correspondence and became his chauffeur — for he terrified me when he was driving. I had the feeling he was off somewhere on a stage, performing or directing.

He walked Jepito, the Chihuahua he had bought for Dee while in Oregon. He rented a horse at the stables so Dee could always ride the same one and feel it was hers. He requested that I not press her father for child support.

This was the man I married, and when I allow myself to open the memory bank of those days, I am slapped with the aching absence of the loving warmth and security with which he surrounded me. He gave of himself so freely, so fully, and not only to me, but to all. He spoke always with energy and inflection, eyes alight, leaning toward the person with whom he was speaking.

Artistically, he drew on creative power and used it lavishly. He was a failure in tests of shrewdness and calculated profiteering.

He was completely uninhibited. Oblivious of bystanders, he would clasp his hands behind his neck, pull his head forward, and bend backward over any available chair or railing, popping the vertebrae of his back. He would trace the figure 8 horizontally in the air as he mentally performed his brain exercises.

He did not relinquish his Russian superstitions. A coin found was carefully preserved for the good fortune it would bring, and salt was never passed from his hand to another's for the bad luck it could incur.

He sometimes looked very "Ellis Island." He had a built-in resistance to spending money on himself. Indicative of this was the way in which he would cringe when we passed a mens wear shop, for fear I would draw him inside. Subconsciously, he would quicken his step and pick up the tempo of his conversation to divert my attention. But he loved to gift *me* with articles of clothing and jewelry.

When we went to Lake Tahoe for Dennis Day's opening at Harrah's Club, I jotted down the following conversation (unbelievable, but factual) on a piece of hotel stationery after getting Val off to the show.

A TYPICAL EVENING OF DRESSING VAL 4-11-60

V: You'll be proud of me tonight in my new black suit.

R: Black? Your new suit is brown!

V: Really? I thought it was black.

R: Here are brown socks and a clean shirt. Don't forget your cuff links.

V: This shirt doesn't have the right kind of cuffs for cuff links.

R: Yes it has — that's why I laid it out.

V: Well, look!

R: Val! You haven't put on the one I laid out. You have the same one on that you've worn for two days in the car.

V: Oh! I guess you're right. (He changes.)

R: Don't forget your tie clasp.

V: (Puts it in place.) There!

R: Val! You haven't shaved!

V: I shaved last night.

R: You shaved 24 hours ago.

V: Yeah, I guess I do need a shave. (Undresses and shaves, then replaces shirt.)

R: Val, don't you need a clean undershirt?

V: Yes, guess I do. (Takes off shirt again and puts on undershirt.)

R: Now, let me shine your shoes. Wear the dark tie and don't forget your cuff links and tie clasp.

V: Alright, I'm ready to go.

R: Do you have a handkerchief?

V: No.

R: Here's one.

V: (Folds it and places it in his pocket.) I'm ready.

R: Don't forget your glasses and the key. (He never forgot to reward me with a warm embrace.)

The following September, when Val went to Montreal without me for a week, I carefully coordinated and packed a separate set of clothes for each day so he wouldn't goof-up or goof-off. *He* went to Montreal; the suitcase went to Mexico, and what I got back from Montreal was a husband and a once-white Van Heusen shirt which he had purchased, and which never did come clean.

Val was frequently the subject of laughter for his malapropisms, his Russian-English, or simply his uninhibited actions. He participated in, and enjoyed, the laughter as much as anyone else. Well — no one could have enjoyed as much as I the time he went to the liquor store to buy bourbon for me — "Blackbird Bourbon." The puzzled salesman figured out that he must mean "Old Crow."

That fall, Val received a letter from G. F. Stegmann of the University of Stellenbosch, South Africa. The country would be celebrating its fiftieth anniversary on May 31, 1960, and Stegmann wished to broadcast a program of Val's recordings. He wrote:

> The more we listen to your records, the more real inner enjoyment we derive from them. They have truly set a standard for the future! Because I believe that such singing as yours is never heard these days, I am preparing a new series of programmes on "Singers of Yesteryear".

He asked Val to select five or six recordings and asked for a short personal message for the listeners. Val listed his preferred selections, congratulated the Union of South Africa on its anniversary, and said, "I am deeply moved that through the medium of recordings we are able to meet and commune in the universal language of art." A second program was broadcast in 1962.

Jack Gurney, the Metropolitan bass who had been a member of Val's American Opera Company, had interceded with Val to come to Riverside, California, and direct *Rigoletto*, which James K. Guthrie would conduct, and in which Jack would sing the role of Sparafucile. Meeting Jack and his lovely wife, Roma, renewed for Val, and began for me, a beautiful, long-lasting friendship. The Gurneys opened their home to us, a home that radiated elegance, warmth, and cordiality.

We would return to Riverside in November, for a production of *Butterfly*. Maralin Niska, who sang the title role, recalled the first staging rehearsal. She said the accompanist was late, while everyone who had to drive long distances was early. She described Val as a bit annoyed, but said he very kindly asked, "Have you ever played *Butterfly* before?"

The pianist answered, "No, but I am an excellent sight reader."

Val said, "I'm sure you are, but we will work without you tonight. It is not possible for *any* pianist to sight-read *Butterfly*."

The respected critic Charles D. Perlee of San Bernardino's *The Sun Telegram* praised the performance as

> one of the finest . . . I have ever heard.
>
> It was not only a beautifully staged production, backed by an orchestra that was almost out of this world, but it was dramatically intimate. The tragic story of Cio-Cio-San came more alive for me than at any other time. . . .
>
> Maralin Niska's Cio-Cio-San was sung and acted in such a manner as to keep this reviewer on the edge of his chair whenever she was on the stage.

He praised the other performers and then concluded his article with: "And as a postscript, I must say that Miss Niska's 'One Fine Day' was so realistic that it was not an aria."

Maralin continued to work with Val, driving from San Pedro to Los Angeles when we were situated there during the coming summer and fall months. She recalled one of his stage techniques which she called the "wheel" principle. The theory was that when moving from a stationary position, the movement should be preceded by a reverse movement — "rolling back a bit and then forward, thus avoiding a stiffness and simulating what happens on the wheel of a wagon."

Maralin cited a famous tenor who credited Val for all he knew dramatically, but she said that Val was reluctant to accept the compliment, "since two arm gestures simply didn't reflect his directorial abilities."

When Val felt Maralin was sufficiently prepared, he arranged an audition for her at Chicago Lyric Opera. For this big event in her life, Maralin arrived to find a rehearsal in progress on the stage. Everyone involved was asked to stop momentarily while she sang her audition. As one of her arias, she sang "Un bel di" from *Butterfly*. After this rather unorthodox and stressful hearing, the general manager said, "You are not ready to sing in such a large house, and you will never sing *Butterfly* in this auditorium. However, if you would go to Italy and study with the wife of our artistic director for six months, you would then be prepared to sing small roles, such as Musetta, with the company."

Maralin recalled that Val was indignant and said to her in private, "You do not need to go to Italy to study. You will be singing on this stage within two years." And she did. She sang *Butterfly* with the Metropolitan's National Company and in the second row was the general manager, who invited Maralin to dinner after the performance and plied her with questions concerning her unexpected growth and progress.

Some years later, on 36 hours' notice, Maralin went to substitute as Violetta in Chicago Lyric's *La Traviata*, receiving the best review of any Violetta in the preceding ten years.

During the previous Riverside production of *Rigoletto*, in the spring of 1960, it was necessary for me to return to Phoenix, but I rejoined Val for the performance. By this time, Kansas had come through with the go-ahead on the Centennial spectacular, which would be staged at the Mid-America Fairgrounds in Topeka for two weeks starting June 30, 1961, and then for two weeks in Wichita.

Within a week, we made the return flight to Phoenix and boarded a train for Kansas, where we would visit thirteen cities gathering historical data, giving newspaper and television interviews, and meeting fascinating Midwesterners who were proud of their historical heritage. Val had been digesting Kansas history while in California, and he found Kansans to be his cup of tea. They were sincere, patriotic, enthusiastic, hospitable, and each city wanted to be sure it was well represented in the historical celebration.

In Topeka, we met Nyle Miller, Secretary of the Kansas Historical Society, who became a wonderful friend. He was impressed with Val's knowledge of the state's history, displayed to us the state's thirty-four-star flag, and enriched our historical awareness.

We were amazed to realize that the Santa Fe Trail had impregnated its story so deeply into the soil of Kansas that the pattern was still there. We were escorted to pastures outside of Fort Larned to view the deep ruts still imprinted in the earth. As we left the parked automobile and climbed over the fence, Val exerted some special charm which drew the cattle to him. I said, "Sing to them, Val." He did, and they gave him their full attention, then walked away. "Best audience I ever had," declared Val.

Lee Rich of the Junction City *Daily Union* gave quality to our visit in more ways than one. We wrote back to him: "There would seem to be no place in the script for one of the things which most impressed us in Junction City — pecan pie."

In Newton, Bethel College supplied us with information regarding the immigration of the Mennonites who brought Red Turkey wheat grains with them from Russia, and made Kansas the greatest wheat-producing state in the Union.

Of course, the most dramatic thing about Kansas history was the fact that free and slave states were equally divided before her entry into the Union. She had the responsibility for deciding the fate of the nation, and she became "bloody Kansas" in the process.

On visiting Dwight Eisenhower's childhood home in Abilene, I was "awarded" one of the buttons from his underclothing.

We visited libraries, museums, and historical sights. In Dodge City, a committee consisting of the County Attorney, the City Marshal, and a member of the Chamber of Commerce showed us about the city. Then they presented Val with a cowboy hat.

We wrote back to them that

> the strange combination of Val's Russian accent and THE HAT caused us to be apprehended on our return trip. Officers were sure he was trying to conceal his true identity. We referred the authorities to the Marshal of Dodge City, but they said Dodge City was outside the United States, and if we had been there, we would be in possession of a visa. Some "tall talk" later, we are here in Hollywood where Val wears THE HAT to his rehearsals in the Hollywood Bowl, and it draws great admiration. Of course, you can get by with anything in Hollywood!

We settled in at the Fireside Manor, not far from the Bowl, to launch the scriptwriting and prepare two Bowl productions: a repeat of *Meredith Willson Night* and *Madame Butterfly* with Dorothy Kirsten.

Thirty-thousand people thronged the Bowl for Meredith's *Family Night*. Critic Albert Goldberg said "spectacular" was a mild descriptive term for the show.

The association with Meredith and Rini was always anticipated. They radiated a simple warmth and a strong love for one another.

Kirsten's *Butterfly* was in semi-concert form with a fine cast, and was well described as "superb" and "rewarding." Of course, Kirsten's voice was the main attraction, and the pattern of things was really in her control, so Val felt he should restrict himself reasonably to that mold. It was interesting to note that the critics felt the semi-concert form was an excellent way to present this particular opera because of its "static plot" which was an "affront to the logical senses." Yet, three months later when Val staged the same opera in Riverside, the critic "sat on the edge of his chair" and said it was "dramatically startling."

It was a happy time — those months of Kansas scriptwriting. The history was rich and dramatic, and our time together was happy and creative. First, we shaped and clarified, and then I wrote. As I typed away, Val would sing softly, walk the Chihuahua, prepare a gourmet dish. But when the keys were silently waiting for inspiration, he would pace the floor, suffering through what he interpreted as a period of stagnation.

When it was finished, Val glowed and embraced me. "This will really be *our* production," he said. But first, "we" had Gounod's *Romeo and Juliet* to direct in Montreal, an *Aida* in Riverside, and three productions for the

Sombrero Playhouse in Phoenix.

In Montreal, Wilfrid Pelletier picked up Maestro Cooper's baton, and Thomas Archer of *The Gazette* called the production "a triumph." He said the opera "got a performance . . . which, in style and spirit, could hardly have been surpassed anywhere."

Riverside's *Aida* made the editorial page. The editor, under the heading *"Meaningful Success,"* ended his article with "We hope the *Aida* production is not a high point of success, but rather a beginning of a new series of successes." The opening night crowd was the largest in history, and critic Charles Perlee praised everything about the opera, including Walter Du- cloux's English translation. He expressed gratitude to Val for three welcome innovations: bringing the High Priestess on stage in Act One, instead of hiding her behind the scenery; bringing the "Trial Scene" into view of the audience; and bringing the chorus on stage for the "Death Scene."

Val brought Maralin Niska, Sylvia Stitch, John Guarnieri, his own son Gilbert Russell, Ned Romero, and Joseph Fair to Phoenix for the Sombrero production of *Butterfly*. *The Arizona Republic* announced in headlines: *"It's Opera Time at Sombrero.* It's full scale grand opera — not excerpts . . . ," it explained. This was a first for the Sombrero, and it was the only regional theatre of its size producing professional full-length opera.

Butterfly would be followed by Moussorgsky's *Boris Godounov* with Met basso Jerome Hines. Val and the Sombrero's producer Richard Charlton met Jerry at the airport. Each of them was shoulder-height to the towering six-foot- six-and-a-half-inch bass. They gave a three-sided interview to *The Phoenix Gazette's* reporter, to whom Jerry said, "I'm a champion of opera in English, and presentation of the story through acting. Doing opera in a foreign language marks us as cultural barbarians."

Each opera would be augmented by local artists and orchestra (Joseph Esile conducting), would be presented in English, and would run for three consecu- tive performances.

One of the two Phoenix papers headlined *Butterfly* as a *"Glorious Produc- tion;"* the other — *"Delights Audience."* As usual, Val's name was syn- onymous with success. After *Boris*, *The Arizona Republic* said it "was a noble and artistic effort . . . a musical and visual miracle." And *The Phoenix Gazette* — oops — what? The title on an unsigned review was *"Opera Here Harmed by Brevity."* Val read, seethed, grabbed his pen, and responded. The paper printed his letter.

There will always be people who proclaim themselves great devotees of opera while they simultaneously choke every effort to bring it to the people.

The critic said that the small stage, small chorus and chamber orchestra created a "mockery" of the great opera. A number of years ago, George Bernard Shaw and I had many discussions on the deplorable state of opera. With the advent of star conductors and of composers like Wagner and Strauss there came a demand for large orchestras and choruses. Opera could no longer exist without government grants or — as was the case in England and America — without subsidies from wealthy patrons. The operatic stage was, and is, a spectacle of exhibitionism with hefty sopranos and stoical tenors, irrational arm waving and excessive musical padding.

TOGETHER, Mr. Shaw and I formulated a plan to reduce vast dimensions and give intimate opera productions in small theaters, with every singer and actor looking and acting his part. We formed an orchestra of 13 (two less than we used at the Sombrero) and engaged an unknown conductor, Adrian Boult — now Sir Adrian Boult. Our Intimate Opera Festival was acclaimed a great success by both public and press.

Producers must diminish the costs of immense operatic productions if the American people are to have operatic fare in more than three or four of their largest cities. Your critic found our stage "ridiculously small." Glyndebourne, which has become a great, international opera company, began its life in a barn seating 300 people, with a stage 20 feet wide, and a small orchestra. The critic dismissed our sets with a brief, "As usual, the scenery, costuming and lighting greatly enhanced the production's effectiveness." He had the opportunity to write praise of outstanding sets that were a masterpiece of Russian style, color and mood —- contrived with beauty and ingenuity, and constructed for quick changes between scenes. He dismissed all these outstanding values in a few words as though afraid to give due praise.

THE ORCHESTRA, he complains, was "stuck off to one side." Does he mind if we say it was "placed" to one side, and that the audience benefited by having complete vision of the stage? Jerome Hines has performed Boris where the orchestra shared the stage because there was no orchestra pit.

The critic credits us with setting a record for brevity. He apparently does not know that when Boris is given in the small theaters of Russia, the prologue is often completely cut, and the Kromy scene is rarely done.

Richard Charlton has attempted to bring opera to Phoenix, and his effort to do something fine and artistic has been greeted in this criticism with an attitude of, "If the people can't have the whole cake, they shouldn't have any." This attitude is inaccurate, ungrateful, and prudishly misleading to the public; and this "harms opera" more than the brevity of any production could harm it.

VAL ROSING,
Director, Sombrero Playhouse

Twenty-four years later, July 9, 1984, an article written for *Newsweek* by Annalyn Swan at Glyndebourne said, "The only problem with Glyndebourne is that it's apt to spoil an opera lover for life. . . it's striking how different opera is when it's small-scale, intimate and polished to perfection."

Jerry had worked with Val over a period of years. He was a dedicated Christian, often seen carrying his Bible under his arm. He had written an operatic trilogy on the life of Christ, called "I Am The Way." It would have its first production the following week in Wilmington, Delaware, and Val worked with him on the staging of it while they were together in Phoenix. A couple of months later, Val wrote to him that there was a possibility of staging it in the new Convention Hall Auditorium in Las Vegas. Was he interested? "You see," Val wrote, "even if I'm not one of your converts, I want to help you convert the rest of the world."

The week after *Boris*, Val made a considerable switch in style and directed Frank Loesser's *The Most Happy Fella* with Robert Weede and Lucile Norman. One reviewer said, ". . . it may become [Sombrero's] best remembered offering this year." But Ray Walter of *The Arizona Republic* declared, ". . . *Madame Butterfly* . . . and *Boris Godounov* . . . were without doubt, Producer Charlton's outstanding accomplishments this past season."

From left to right: Ruth Rosing; Nyle H. Miller, Secretary of Kansas State Historical Society; and Val Rosing, Wichita, Kansas, 1961.

Chapter 31

A Russian Creates American History

Val was really in full gear when creating a patriotic production. Heart, soul, and body were involved. He seemed to be fulfilling that tearful promise he had made with great Russian simplicity, upon receiving his first Social Security check — "To do something great for the country that has been so good to me!"

The scenes of our *Kansas Story* were woven together by narration. It was a most dramatic effect, for the narrator's voice was embraced by the darkness which preceded and blended together the scenes appearing on many stages.

In our script we moved to the dawn of Kansas history with the Spanish cry of *"Conquest!"* and the lust for *gold*. The golden kingdom dissolved as a gigantic myth, and eventually the Louisiana Purchase forced the Indians to exchange the Spanish flag for the Stars and Stripes. New territories became an invitation to the malignant inheritance of slavery. Kansas fought long and bitterly for her right to cross the threshold of the Union. Judges were replaced at gunpoint; ballot boxes were stuffed; six Territorial governors were expelled; and men were tarred, feathered, and massacred. Then, when she finally acquired statehood, Lincoln's election triggered the secession of the Southern states and brought on the Civil War. There were grasshoppers, cyclones, blizzards, another "war to end all wars," the "Roaring Twenties," and the Crash! And finally, Kansas, the heart of the nation, had woven her story into the story of the nation. What a plot to work with!

For the finale, Val would have the ballet, under the direction of Ruth Page, interpret the "Roaring Twenties," the Crash, and the period of recovery. Then the dancers would run screaming across the field and out as Nazi motorcycles entered the arena — half of them with fixed bayonets and half with American flags. Tanks and military equipment would circle the field, and on the hillside, tanks and machine guns would open fire while motorcycles retreated and rockets lit up the sky. Then to represent victory, the Statue of Liberty and the Iwo Jima statue would roll onto right and left stages as a tremendous American flag rolled onto the main stage. A procession of all of the flags of the United Nations would enter from all sides of the field, and the Kansas flag, seal, and other state symbols would occupy center field while chorus and soloists sang "America."

But the "bloody years of Kansas" had to survive some bloody politics that were imported from California.

After Val had presented the televised version of "The Arizona Story" in Phoenix in 1958, he had sold Governor Fannin on the idea of a spectacular to celebrate Arizona's 50 years of statehood and her Territorial Centennial, which occurred in 1962 and 1963 respectively. He then influenced the governor to appoint a Centennial Commission. At this point he received a telephone call from Wayne Dailard in California, asking to be allowed to come in on the negotiations. With what would eventually prove to be ill-placed loyalty, Val introduced Dailard to the Commission, with the proviso that he not bring MCA into the picture which could inflate the budget (he later did that in spite of his promise).

Dailard had negotiated with me to take the introductory trip to Kansas alone. I couldn't figure that one out. I may have given it the "dignity" he wanted, but what was the crust of the pie without the filling? I had no desire to go alone, and it would only have been a humiliation to Val. Naturally, Val's involvement evoked a great love affair between Kansas and himself.

Dailard had always refused to negotiate with Val's agent. He also induced us to waive our authors' rights under the assertion that each State Centennial Commission demanded full script rights. Val gave him some static over our Kansas contract. Apparently, since we were now married, we were supposed to be two for the price of one.

It began to be obvious that Dailard wanted to divorce this, and any future productions, from the past, and acquire for them a new identity as "Dailard Productions." It appeared that he resented Val's friendship and negotiations with Arizona officials, and he wanted it forgotten that Val had masterminded the original production.

Since that first production, Val had been almost completely responsible for staff and talent. Indeed, for the first revival of *The California Story* in 1956, his contract even held him responsible for the budget and the format. So when, regarding Kansas, Dailard stipulated that Val should have an assistant director to stay with the Topeka production after we moved on to Wichita, Val named his choice. But Dailard said, "No, I have already hired one." It was Christopher West who was well known to us, an opera director from Covent Garden who was now directing at New York City Center — a full-fledged director.

On his eight-page fact sheet prepared for the press about *The Oregon Story,* Dailard took credit for the original Hollywood Bowl production of *The California Story.* Then, in a full-page, color edition of *The Kansas City Star*, he broke boldly in print with the statement that he and Willson were the "creators" of this musical spectacle.

> When we first took on the staging of this spectacle, we studied all the records of pageantry we could find and adopted ideas we felt would be of use. I talked with the producers of big outdoor spectacles all over the world for ideas.

He even claimed to have developed the idea of numerous stages and the dual sound system. He quoted paragraphs from our script, giving us no authorship credits. Then he somehow related the dramatic effect of the spectacle to the Old Vic players of England, the result being the importation of West from that country! Far-fetched, but he was making his point. In fact, he had attempted to omit Val altogether from that article, but a photographer stopped by Val's rehearsal to ask where he could find the director. Val introduced himself, but the photographer showed him a slip of paper with the name of Christopher West on it. Val collected West and went with them so that Wayne was forced to include him in the photograph. All I can see in that photo is the wounded expression on Val's face.

The next day Dailard explained to Val, "It isn't a question of who created the show; it's who owns it — and I do." He continued, "Val, to succeed in our business, one has to be ruthless. The difference between us is that you are soft, and I am hard."

What a difficult and depressing atmosphere in which "to do something great for the country that has been so good to me."

Val did not understand this kind of activity. It was his nature to be open, generous, uncalculating. As Zula "Peggy of the Flint Hills" Greene of *The Topeka Daily Capital* observed, "If Val Rosing is getting paid for directing 'The Kansas Story,' it's that much extra. I'm sure he is having enough fun to balance the account." On the occasion she is referring to, he had broken up the rehearsal by joining in the ballet steps.

Dailard's former secretary, Arliss Kirschmer, was not available for Kansas.

So he hired a new girl who in three weeks had her fill, and returned to California. She said Dailard had advised her to avoid Val; this was the last production he would do with the man he called the "monster."

Val would, of course, give nothing less than his best to his work. Fortunately, we had already established a warm relationship with Kansas officials and personnel, and that gave us beautiful inspiration and support. The only vengeance I ever knew Val to take was something I discovered many years later. When Dailard had the scripts copied, the title page read: "THE KANSAS STORY, Conceived and Planned by Wayne Dailard." Val had scratched through his name, and beside it had written "Liar."

Chris Mahan was again our production stage manager; Tom Henry, our narrator; and Pat McGeehan, our sound cast director. Val brought Lucille Norman, Maralin Niska, and Stephen Kamalyan to be our soloists. He secured Ruth Page from Chicago as choreographer, and Paul Coze, Arizona artist, French Consul, and dear friend, as the scenic designer. Meredith Willson, of course, was the "Music Man," assisted by Frank Hubbell.

Among the Kansans on our staff, we were especially drawn to Dale Easton, a Topeka theatre director whose friendship is still treasured. Likewise endeared to us was Marie McKinney who was the assistant to Maurice Fager, chairman of the Centennial Commission.

We sublet a house for the four months we would be in Topeka and enrolled Dee in school. Kansans were warm and friendly, and Kansas was home. It didn't take long to realize we were in the Bible Belt. If you went to a restaurant on Sunday, mobs of people crowded in at 12:30 p.m., just as church let out.

Alf Landon frequented the "Chocolate Shop" and invited Val and me there to lunch. It was a simple, homey place, obviously crowded with political personalities and close associates. We sat in wooden booths with narrow carved arms which reminded me of my grandmother's rocking chair. In it, little squares of wood which had joined the arm and leg had become recessed where, as a child, my mother had picked at them with a pin while being rocked to sleep. Suddenly I cringed inwardly as I saw Alf Landon put out his cigarette in the same patterned arm of the wooden booth where we were seated.

The elegant Landon home sat back on a grassy slope, looking much like Mount Vernon. There we were beautifully entertained, and I have always loved to tell that Alf Landon picked the cherries for the cherry pie we had for dinner.

It was dress rehearsal weekend at Mid-America Fairgrounds, and *The Topeka State Journal* featured a full page of photos capturing chorus, ballet, dramatic scenes, backstage preparations, soloists, and, as the writer stated, "Val Rosing [who] dashed and skipped back and forth across the 115,000 square foot of stage shouting directions."

The *State Journal* interviewed some of the performers. One said, "This is the biggest show I've ever seen. I get the greatest charge out of director Rosing. He energizes everybody all the while he's eating raisins." Another said, "I've learned more about Kansas history from this than I ever learned in school books."

The same paper, in a full page of photos, showed Val crumpled on the stage as he "[threw] himself into his work by violently demonstrating how to fall, Western style. His thrashing drew applause from the members of the cast who [then rehearsed] with extra enthusiasm."

As the show, with its 1,000-member cast, full orchestra, and chorus, began its dress rehearsal, Val said to a reporter: "All shows have to have a night of fault-finding before opening night. . . . We have to find faults so we can made repairs. If it happens perfect the first time, it is only by accident."

For the first two nights we were rained out. But the third night was a charm, and *The Topeka State Journal* headline was, " 'Kansas Story' Rises to Stars After Rain Clouds Disappear." The reporter waxed poetic:

> ["The Kansas Story"] rose to the stars . . . in bright blazing glory. Strung upon a golden bracelet of pageantry, drama, dance and music were a multitude of scenes . . . each a particular gem-studded charm in its own right. . . . "The Kansas Story". . . is told with an impact that left [the] audience filled with near-tearful gratitude that the heritage has been spelled out in such masterful strokes.

The *Topeka Daily Capital's* headline was " 'The Kansas Story' Is Truly Colossal." Its writer, Zula Greene, said, "Whatever stupendous or colossal adjectives a person thinks of can be applied. . . ."

In the editorial column of the same paper, under the headline " 'Kansas Story' Expertly Told," was this statement: "When the Centennial Commission scouted for a show to mark the dramatic high point of the state's birthday observance, it wanted the best. . . . It is evident the commission got it. . . . 'The Kansas Story' is a smash hit."

The *Daily Capital* showed a series of shots headlined, "Val Had A Big Night Backstage and — Oops, Onstage, TOO!" He was racing from group to group, giving last-minute instructions, and then as he joked with the cast, an Indian maiden decorated him with her headdress.

> Equal to the occasion, Rosing launched into a short war dance, much to the merriment of the Kansas actors gathered around. But moments later, much to the astonishment of the actors onstage, there was another actor in their midst — Rosing himself . . . Rosing had donned a Jesuit priest's hat, had pulled his cape around

Val and Ruth Rosing and Ruth's daughter, Dee Scates, with their Chihuahua Jepito in Topeka, Kansas, for *The Kansas Story.* (Photo, *Topeka State Journal,* 1961)

his suit, and . . . moved slowly [among them] . . . voicing instructions. . . .

Nyle Miller, Secretary of the Historical Society, wrote to us:

I feel I could talk non-stop for days about the wonders of the production. . . . The show came alive and the audience became an "eye witness to the history of Kansas." . . . You come away from this show stunned that all the rave notices about it were REALLY NO EXAGGERATION!

Val was compensated. What more could he have wanted?

We moved on to Wichita, sublet a house, and were joined by Val's seven-year-old son, Richard. Dee was rehearsing and performing, and Richie wanted "to get some acting experience," too. He got it, but he had a small argument with the director. He didn't understand why there was no spotlight on him.

The home we were occupying was one of those which had been lived in for so many years that it was stockpiled with extraneous commodities. One day a rat crawled into a crowded corner of the garage and died. The summer heat having descended, the odor was intolerable. Val tried to uncover it by poking around with the kitchen mop, but his talents were not adaptable to this type of drama. After getting hit in the face by the mop several times, I closed the door on the affair and urged Val to go to his rehearsal. When he was gone I began to clear out the shovels, hoes, boxes, and debris until I discovered the rat. I delivered him to the incinerator, swept the garage, packed things back in the corner, had a shower, and was decent by the time Val returned. He was horrified that I had dealt with such contamination!

We returned to Topeka's weekend performances, accompanied by the two children and the Chihuahua. I paid Dee a dollar and a half to keep peace with Richie while we were absent, only to have Richie tell me later that his father had paid him secretly for the same purpose. We snuck Jepito in and out of the hotel under a coat, and a good time was had by all. Well — there *was* one mishap. Val ripped the inner seam of his pants from crotch to knee. He had it sewed up backstage, ripped it out again the next morning, sent them with the valet to be mended in our single half hour of free time, and received them back at the end of the half hour with a "Sorry, Sir, the seamstress wasn't in today." He walked knock-kneed while we had coffee at the Landon home and lunch with Nyle Miller.

There were ten performances in Topeka, nine in Wichita. Wichita's opening at Veteran's Field triggered additional heady reviews. *The Wichita Eagle*, in an editorial, proclaimed, "'The Kansas Story' — Delightful Experience."

The show has the luster of a professional stage production; the broad scope and sweep of the Kansas prairies, making the movies' vaunted "Cinemascope" seem puny by comparison; the sparkle of a Broadway revue, and the authenticity of a history book. . . . The

According to the *Topeka Daily Capital*, 1961, Val had a big night backstage before opening of *The Kansas Story,* delivering a "peptalk" to the actors and giving last-minute instructions. (Photo, *Topeka Daily Capital*)

show . . . is history, entertainment and art, wrapped in a package that will cause any viewer to go away from the stadium exclaiming and singing of his state.

The *Eagle*'s front-page headline was, "Kansans Applaud Opening of

Val backstage in Topeka, decorated with a cast member's headdress. (Photo, *Topeka Daily Capital*)

'Story.'" "Kansans," it said, "felt a little bigger and better about Kansas" after opening night. And the *Augusta Daily Gazette* noted that "the audience applauded so long and vigorously that the lights had to be turned on again and again as the . . . performers . . . took five 'curtain calls.'"

We moved into a hotel the weekend prior to our departure, and suddenly the

Val onstage at *The Kansas Story* opening, much to the surprise of the cast. (Photo, *Topeka Daily Capital*)

television newscasts came up with tornado warnings. I was in bed. Val was pacing the floor. Anxiously and impatiently, he insisted that I get up and prepare for this terrible thing. Finally I got out of bed, took inventory of the closet, reappeared in my black lace nightgown and announced, "Okay, I'm ready."

The tornado centered on a small neighboring town, but the elements whipped through our stadium, carrying scenery, lights, tents, etc. We canceled a full house to make repairs so we could reopen the following night.

Back in March, when we had left Arizona, Val had preceded me. A few days after he had left, the Arizona Legislature adjourned, having tabled the appropriation bill for *The Arizona Story*. Chairman Frank Brophy and I then met with Governor Fannin to explore the remaining possibilities. The governor said he was going to call a special session of the legislature in July, and he would try to bring up the matter again, if I would leave some speech material relative to the production. I did so and left the next day.

Charles Garland of the State Fair had told us that if the legislature failed to pass the appropriations, he would be interested in doing *The Arizona Story* through the State Fair. Before long, he told us that Dailard's MCA agent was "pestering" him, but he was remaining noncommittal.

We invited him to Kansas to see the production, and he said, "I will come in June and bring some commissioners with me. Will call and let you know the date." When he reached Kansas City and phoned for Val or Ruth Rosing, we were in Wichita preparing for the July 4 opening. Wayne Dailard said we were "not there," but did not divulge our whereabouts. His wife picked them up, and Dailard obtained seats for the performance and entertained them afterwards. He presumably spent the evening telling them how he had originated this show, owned the copyright, and no one else could use the format.

"Well," said Garland, "my negotiations have always been with Rosing."

Surely by this time, we were concerned about the negotiations and the problem of continuing to try to work with him. Val said, "As soon as our contractual obligations are completed, we will go on our own. I am not, and never have been, married artistically to Wayne Dailard."

The warm friendships we had developed proved to be Val's survival kit. He knew he could never go through such a thing again. "We will do our own productions," he said. And he began to dream of a television series to cover the histories of the fifty states, a "Civil War Story" — and then, he literally glowed as the inspiration consumed him. "We will do *The Freedom Story!*" He took my hands, "This will be my greatest artistic contribution to America and to the cause of freedom in the world. And it will not be for the purpose of filling my own, or anyone else's coffers! We will base it on the history of freedom in the world, with the United States playing the role of the first nation in which freedom became a birthright!"

We returned to Phoenix where Garland was waiting to discuss plans and budget. He said, however, there were some legal matters to be cleared up first.

Val thought when we left Kansas that we were out of Dailard's embrace. But the man who had grown so much in "wisdom and stature" since his first production with Val, when he had made Val responsible for budget, format, staff, and talent, now was making "threats" regarding his "copyrighted" material.

With the assistance of the attorney general of Arizona, William Morris Agency, and the counselor for the American Federation of Television and Radio Artists (AFTRA), it was not difficult to prove the fallacy of such contentions, but it was painful, offensive, and time-consuming. And the legislative council postponed its postponements until Arizona's birthday party was getting squeezed off of the calendar. Eventually, Val proposed that the Semi-Centennial of Statehood be combined with the Territorial Centennial due in 1963.

While the legislature played with this new idea, Val went to Montreal to make preparations for the coming *Traviata* which Julius Rudel would conduct in January. He returned to direct Scottsdale's *Miracle of the Roses* pageant which was annually produced by Paul Coze in cooperation with the Scottsdale Chamber of Commerce. Guests of honor included the secretary of state, the Mexican consul, and the mayor.

On our way back to Montreal in January, we stopped overnight at the Toronto Hotel in Toronto. We were ushered to our reserved room which was lavish far beyond our expectations. An enormous portrait of the Royal Couple hung on the wall. "This is the Royal Suite," Val informed me in a hushed voice. He was nervous over being assigned to such expensive accommodations. "Maybe it's because they know who I am," he said. But he decided he had better go to the desk and find out. He quickly came back with the answer. "It was the only thing they had left."

While in Montreal, we received a phone call one Friday from Phoenix saying that the Fair had swung support to our *Arizona Story* project because it had become aware of the excellence of our proposed plan and budget. We drank sparkling burgundy and celebrated. On Monday we heard that the head of our Semi-Centennial Commission had been labeled a "John Birch" board member by a Phoenix paper. We cried in our beer. The atmosphere had an uneasy calm like that prior to an earthquake.

To his agent at the William Morris Agency, Val said, "I'm getting a baptism of blood in politics and will be ready to run for the legislature next year."

The Arizona project continued to struggle over desks, into files, through strange hands, and into committees. It would not receive its birthright until January 1963.

Sandwiched between Montreal, Canada, and Riverside, California, was a Dennis Day Revue in Las Vegas and a Statehood Day observance in Phoenix, for which Val directed the performance of about 500 singers, musicians, and dancers, and for which I wrote the governor's "Historical Narration." Participating in this Admission Day Ceremony on February 14, 1962, was Senator Carl Hayden who had begun his still active career in 1912 with the admission of Arizona into the Union.

Any available time was devoted to incorporating Rosing Productions and writing formats for *The Freedom Story*, *The Civil War Centennial*, and other historical spectaculars.

En route to New York City for a repeat performance of *Baby Doe* in March, we stopped over in Kansas to visit with Alf Landon, Maurice Fager of Mid-America Fair, and Nyle Miller of the Historical Society who were lending their support to *The Freedom Story*, which the State Department was interested in sending abroad.

From New York we would be going to Italy, where Carol Fox wanted Val to negotiate costumes and scenery for Alexander Borodin's *Prince Igor*, which Val would be directing for Chicago Lyric in the fall. Igor Gorin would be singing the role of "Igor," so while in New York, we met and dined with him and his wife Mary. Igor wanted us to share his favorite kind of food at his favorite Armenian restaurant. He was obviously enjoying himself, and with his Russian accent and fragile English, he ecstatically exclaimed, "This just warms my cockles." There was a moment of silence, but when Mary's and my eyes met, the room exploded with our laughter.

At a reception in a private home, we met Zinka Milanov. I had always idealized this Metropolitan soprano, and expressed this to her with extended hand which caused her to drop the glass of champagne she was holding. Well, it was obviously time to leave the country.

But prior to our departure, we spent a day and a half on Capitol Hill where we gained a number of endorsements for our prospective *Civil War Story*. Among those lending their support were Representative Garner E. Shriver of Kansas, Senator Wayne Morse of Oregon, and Representative Fred Schwengel of Iowa. When we walked into Representative Schwengel's office, he turned to me and sang Schumann's "Wie bist du eine Blume," a most unexpected reception from a politician. He was a man of statesmanlike qualities whose conversation consisted primarily of quotations from poetry and excerpts from Lincoln's speeches. Sometimes you felt you were turning the pages for him.

While waiting in Senator Morse's small reception area, Adlai Stevenson walked in and sat down beside me. After a moment of silence, I stood and said, "I feel I should stand in the presence of a great man." He rose, shook hands, and explained that he was trying, without an appointment, to get in to see Senator Morse. Val insisted on giving him our appointment.

I wrote of this to Nyle Miller, saying:

> I think a great deal of Val's admiration for the man stems from those worn-out soles on his shoes. Of course, you wouldn't understand this unless you knew Val's abhorrence for shoe shops, menswear shops and barber shops. Only once was the veil of terror lifted from

Guest dancer Rudolf Nureyev in the Polovstian Dance sequence from the Lyric Opera of Chicago's 1962 season opening production of Borodin's *Prince Igor*, which also starred guest ballerina Sonia Arova, Boris Christoff, Igor Gorin, Consuelo Rubio, Carol Smith, David Poleri, and Jeanne Diamond. Val Rosing staged the opera while Oskar Danon conducted. New settings and costumes were designed by Nicola Benois. (Photo, by Nancy Sorensen)

the latter. I had forced him into a Topeka barber shop; the barber, recognizing him, had run for a photographer, the shoe-shine boy begged to be included in the picture, and Val emerged like a boy who had been to a circus.

There is one other outstanding memory of Washington, DC. It was late afternoon, and as we walked along the tree-lined street, there was a massive chorus of chirping, chattering, and warbling as the birds welcomed dusk by nesting among the branches of the trees — a sound I had not heard since my childhood, as this does not happen in the West.

After breakfast with Representative Schwengel at the House of Representatives, we took the plane for London where we met with Rudolph Nureyev who, refusing to return to Russia, would make his American debut in *Prince Igor* for Chicago Lyric Opera's 1962 season under Val's direction.

After visiting with "our wife" Marie and her son Billy, we flew to Milan and met Nicola Benois, costume and set designer at La Scala. Not as fluent as he would like to be with the Italian language, Val apologetically asked, "*Peut-être, le Francais?*" Benois, cooperatively, if not enthusiastically, agreed. So they began speaking French, which was a concession to me as well. Very soon, Val seemed to detect something. He hesitated, and then asked, "*Peut-être, le Russe?*"

Not a word was said. The two men silently embraced each other. Then the Russian flowed. Val had not known that Nicola Benois was the nephew of Alexandre Benois — the famous Russian artist. I wish Val could know that I now have in my home paintings by Alexandre Benois made for Stravinsky's ballet, *Petrouchka*, and for Francis Coppola's film, *Napoleon*.

Our European assignment had come so unexpectedly and suddenly that there had been little time for making necessary arrangements. We first planned to take Dee with us, but it meant putting the ocean between her and her father, so we acceded to her father's wishes that she spend the time with him. When she later observed that she had been canceled from our passport with a big black X penciled through her photo, she was furious. After arriving in Italy we surrendered our cottage in Phoenix, requesting that our furniture be removed to storage. We had spent so much time and effort on the Arizona Semi-Centennial, which had seemed such a certainty, that we now needed to economize wherever possible.

We found a beautiful piazza in the little village of Moltrasio on Lake Como. Ours was a room that had been occupied for two weeks by Winston Churchill back in 1952. We were about an hour from Milan, so we could imbibe the beauty of the country and still commute to Milan. This was the least likely and most wonderful thing that could have happened to Val after the beating he had taken for the last year. We had an ecstatic preview of spring. Then a few days later, I opened the shutters in the morning to see everything from the lake on up to the tips of the mountains covered with a quiet velvet snow that had drifted down during the night. After that it rained for five days, and then spring returned.

In our "Shangri-La" we developed presentations for *The Civil War Story* and *The Freedom Story*, and supported them with an enormous amount of correspondence.

Val wanted to celebrate the centennial of the Civil War for its role in the construction of a strong and unified nation, rather than to reopen old wounds of a bloody conflict. He would portray a nation performing its own painful surgery and healing its own wounds, standing as a tower of strength against the ever-present danger of mankind's enslavement. He would lace the facts of history together into an ultimate and harmonious fabric of strength and endurance. Each child and adult must be imbued with pride in his state and nation — not embittered by a revival of wrongs that were still being righted.

He felt that history so portrayed should have a tremendous educational impact. When he had first presented *The California Story*, it was J. Edgar Hoover who had stated to the press that every child in America should see the production.

Rosing Productions had become an entity, and the William Morris Agency had fallen for *The Freedom Story* and agreed to start booking it in the fall for the 1963-1964 season. Meredith Willson would write music for it, and the State Department had given us introductions to the Cultural Attachés in Europe.

The Civil War Centennial Commission held its national convention while we were in Europe, and the William Morris Agency represented us there. We had already met and interested several Advisory Board members, and the agency reported to us that it felt it had made an effective presentation and would now wait for the delegates to meet with their local committees.

The Centennial Committee in Prescott, Arizona, wrote asking for information regarding a potential spectacular in its own city.

A letter from Senator Wayne Morse addressed *The Freedom Story* as "an interesting subject, and I am glad to note your proposal is receiving sympathetic attention in the Bureau of Educational and Cultural Affairs in the Department of State."

Frosting on the cake — we were invited to spend a week with Stevie (Margaret Stevenson from Rochester's American Opera Company) and her husband Bill Herrmann in their charming Hotel Seehof on Der Bodensee in Langenargen, Germany. That week was a piece of heaven — a chunk out of Paradise. Little did we know that it was pre-compensation for the nightmares that lay ahead. There was beauty and wonder to be absorbed from visiting nearby sites: the Castle of Montfort which extended out over the lake, Lindau with its ancient lighthouse, the ancient pile dwellings of Unteruhldingen, the breathtakingly beautiful cathedral at Birnau. There was humor and pathos as Stevie and Val relived American Opera days. There was the growth of a permanent and treasured friendship.

Stevie was much amused by a western bolo, given Val in Kansas, which, I claimed, he wore because he disliked wasting time putting on a tie. It won considerable respect for him in Italy since, in answer to inquiries of "*Che cos'è quello?*" — he explained that it was a gift from the Indian Nation!

After visiting Paris, Florence, Venice, Naples, and Pompeii, we returned to London and sailed for New York. There we learned of the serious illness of my mother, who was with my sister in Las Vegas. After touching base in Los Angeles, we flew to be with her and remained for several weeks. There I observed a Val who, though removed from his artistic background and activities, tirelessly furnished companionship and entertainment to my mother, playing cards with her, creating topics of conversation, bringing warmth and amusement into the atmosphere.

We soon received a letter from a member of the North Carolina Confederate Centennial Commission:

> I do not consider the Civil War Centennial observance in any way a "celebration" and I regret that anyone considers it in that light. If our Commission has $55,000 to spend, or any other amount, I would oppose spending it on any type of pageant.

From Tennessee:

> Our Commission is operating on a very modest budget which does not permit any expenditures for activities of this scope. . . .

From Vermont:

> . . . Our Committee, owing to our small budget, has voted not to indulge in this kind of endeavor.

Then came a letter from Montreal saying the Canadian government had decided not to give any financial support to the Opera Guild unless it used all Canadian talent.

Val wrote back to Montreal:

> I was indeed sorry to hear of the narrow point of view your Council has taken. It is a kind of false nationalism that does not make for better understanding or improve friendly relations between na-

tions. In America we have and are welcoming Canadian singers. We value them for what they are and what they give.

In his Rochester days, Val had given scholarships to five Canadians, and three of them helped to create the sensational production of *Faust* which he presented in Montreal and Toronto. He wrote:

> How ironical that this opera should be the one chosen by your Guild to discriminate against the director who used it to revolutionize the style of opera. It was the one opera that I always wanted to do for you.

Montreal's music critic, Tom Archer, remembered that *Faust* of many years ago and wrote to Val:

> I shall miss our January rendez-vous immensely. . . . But you may count on it that the name of Rosing will play its part. It will be thirty-three years in November since I reviewed [your] *Faust*, and this will be a key time to bring it up and bang it on the right peg.

On September 1, Val directed *Student Prince* for the Hollywood Bowl. The *Los Angeles Times* said:

> The 41st Hollywood Bowl season could not have had a happier end than Val Rosing's production Saturday night of "Student Prince" by Romberg.

The *Citizen-News* said:

> The most brilliant achievement in connection with "The Student Prince" was Val Rosing's staging done with simplicity and ingenuity. He had realized the Bowl's limitations and put this to his advantage.

Igor Gorin was Dr. Engel in this production and also sang the title role in *Prince Igor* for the Chicago Lyric Opera the following month. With Boris Christoff taking the roles of Galitsky and Kontchak, and Rudolph Nureyev and Sonia Arova leading the Polovetsian dancers, the opera had four sold-out performances. In her *Daly Diary* column of Chicago's *American*, Maggie Daly wrote:

> Vladimir Rosing donned a Russian Cossack costume at the Lyric

theater Friday night and, bypassing orchestra pit and wings, mingled with the cast and directed "Prince Igor" on stage. Most of the audience didn't know.

Shortly after, Val received this telegram from Leningrad: "I SANG FOR YOU AT BOLSHOI AND KIROV BIG SUCCESS LOVE — JERRY HINES." Val was deeply moved. He sat quietly with the telegram in his hand. Finally, he spoke, "How I wish he had asked me to go with him."

Val had written to Arthur Schlesinger, Special Assistant to President Kennedy, regarding *The Freedom Story*:

> With the advent of this Administration, which has so strengthened the American picture, we have hoped for a comparable strengthening of our American cultural contributions to the world. It is unfortunate that culture must be looked upon as a weapon; but since Russia is so effectively following Lenin's policy of "art as a means of cultural battle" against capitalism, the free world must counter it.
>
> Our purpose is to create a vehicle of entertainment which will glorify freedom, inspire a unity among the peoples of free countries, create a resistance to enslaving ideologies, and at the same time uplift American artistic prestige.
>
> Artistic endeavors are frequently blocked by narrow channels through which they must pass — whether financial or political. So we would like to plant a seed of interest as close to the heart of the Administration as possible lest a vehicle which we feel can be greatly useful to the nation, might find it impossible to clear all the hurdles in its path.

Was this, perhaps, a ridiculous undertaking for an ex-Russian? On the other hand, who could more appreciate this country, the first in the world to make freedom a birthright?

The William Morris Agency was finding that there was a rather slim chance of securing substantial guarantees from arenas for the size of the production that Val was anticipating. This lessened the agency's optimism, and it was proposing a postponement to the season of 1964-1965.

We prolonged our stay in Chicago, following *Prince Igor*, to pursue *The Freedom Story*. Val had gained the interest of the John H. Krafts and Luis Kutner. Kutner was a prominent lawyer and the author (nominated for the Pulitzer Prize) of the book *World Habeas Corpus*. He worked with Val to set up a non-profit organization for *The Freedom Story* and had brochures printed for the State Fair Convention which was meeting in Chicago.

Our Advisory Council soon acquired many prestigious names: The Honorable Alf Landon, The Honorable Harry S. Truman, Luis Kutner, Paul Horgan, Mrs. John Alden Carpenter, Nyle H. Miller, Richard Tucker, Jerome Hines, Igor Gorin, Dennis Day, Linda Darnell, Art Linkletter, Mr. and Mrs. Raymond Rubicam, and others.

With the purpose of inspiring financial backing, Mrs. John Kraft of the cheese empire arranged for us to meet H. L. Hunt of the oil empire. So on our return to Los Angeles, we stopped in Dallas, Texas. It was Hunt's attorney who met with us. We listened in disbelief to suggestions that this wonderful man, Hunt, should himself be the subject matter of such a spectacular. As Val and I left the building, there was silence between us. Finally, I said, "I need a straight shot of something."

Val said, "I need to vomit." That seemed to sum it up. I don't remember ever discussing the interview again.

In Arizona, the governor's office was always cooperative and encouraging, but it finally admitted that it seemed a waste of time to try to obtain a state appropriation for *The Arizona Story*. The owner of an insurance company who was bitten by show business, and whose wife was musically inclined, offered to act as fund raiser for our corporation. His name was Si DeBardas. Val named him associate producer, and I soon named him Sly-Si. Norman MacDonald was once again our narrator; Pat McGeehan, our dialogue director; the musical score was by a local composer, Joseph Perley Lewis; Paul Coze was the art director, and Claire and Glenda Folk were choreographers.

Maggie Savoy interviewed Val and me for *The Arizona Republic*. She quoted us as we joshed together with each other:

> In his words, "We work well together — because we fight all the way." In hers, "He stands over my head — which is over the kitchen table — and tells me that he must have this scene in a few minutes. Hurry up!"
>
> He has the impatience of the doer; she the patience of the researcher. She spent days locked in the Arizona room of the Public Library ("when I dialed 72 they'd come in and unlock me").

She ended by quoting Val regarding *The Freedom Story*:

> "We are as great as our history. The biggest challenge of my career has been to capsule the greatness of history into pageantry. All the rest has been good to look back on, but is only background for this — to show the greatness of our country in a living, vital, dramatic way to all."

The *Arizona Days And Ways Magazine* published two full pages of photos introduced by my opening lines to *The Arizona Story* — the lines that would be narrated with orchestral accompaniment to precede the opening scene.

Spun of beauty and woven with dreams
Through flowering sands and sparkling streams . . .
With brilliant nights and burning days
Of mad splashed color and warm, languid rays,
Of emerald lakes and ermine hooded peaks . . .
Sculptured with monumental grandeur that speaks
From the brink of beauty where words die young,
And a song fades away unsung —
Change not one grain of sifted sand;
This is my Arizona land!!

In eight weeks we managed to achieve a great artistic success. The mayor admitted, "This is without question the most spectacular production I have ever seen." The *Gazette's* headline: "'Arizona Story' Worthy of Name." The *Republic*: "Arizona Story Gets Enthusiastic Reception."

But it was not a financial success. Cold weather and rain combined their forces to outdo us — and did. Could public apathy be legitimately blamed? A letter published in *The Arizona Republic* under "The People Speak" stated:

I had the pleasure of seeing the Arizona Story and consider it one of the most memorable experiences of my lifetime. . . . [It] portrayed in pageant form the sweat, blood, tears and lives sacrificed in delivering our present Arizona as we now see and enjoy it today. . . . The magnificent production was not done justice by attendance which, of course, falls in the lap of ticket sales, publicity and enthusiasm in general.

We were not remunerated for our efforts. In fact, we made a personal loan to help settle the financial indebtedness.

Val had not been well for weeks. He had even wanted, at one point, to give up the production. Doctors had not been able to diagnose the cause of a daily temperature. I didn't know whether Val had developed a low-grade infection, or whether it was "Sly-Si-itis." This would be a new one for the medics, but I was tempted to diagnose it as a slow, battle-fatigue disintegration resulting from continuous encounters with a partner who switched his pitch hourly and filibustered his way to all decisions.

Of course, Si took a financial beating, and that could call for sympathy, too. But when Si hit bottom, he lashed out at everything and everybody until he discovered a new pitch which converted our loss into a "contribution to the community." At this point, he noted that he had begun to call me "Dear" again. It had fallen short of my attention!

When the Senate Appropriations Committee approached Val on reviving the production in the autumn, Si recovered to the point of taking a Las Vegas vacation.

New York City Opera wanted Val to come and direct *Love for Three Oranges*, but he could not capture the physical strength to do so and had to decline.

Val's female counterpart to Jerry Hines was opera star Frances McCann. About this time, she was shot and killed in a hotel in Italy. He had poured into her all of his dramatic technique, and she had matured into a tremendous artist. He was so grief-stricken at her death, it was as though he died a little with her. What a waste of both her glorious talent and his consecrated artistry.

Chapter 32

Return the Greener Blade

Under Val's patient, assuring guidance, I had written the scripts for three centennial productions. With the Arizona script, each scene, as it came from the typewriter, played without changes. He took my hands in his and said proudly, "You've won your wings!"

But Val was ill. He had fought too hard for *The Arizona Story*. It was one of his most beautiful productions, but the elements and intrigues that seemed to defy him to pull it off broke his spirit as well as his bank account. Great men and great ideas come under heavy fire, but in his simplicity and sincerity, Val seemed not to understand this. Responsibilities fell heavily upon my shoulders as I tried to protect him from little people and big underhandedness. One thing was uppermost in his mind: "I cannot fail!" And he pushed ahead in spite of persistent chills and fever. Doctors were still not able to identify a cause.

June 1, 1963, we returned to the West Coast. Jack Gurney (bass from the American Opera Company and, subsequently, the Metropolitan) and his lovely wife Roma graciously opened their Riverside home to us. We hoped and prayed that a period of rest would restore Val's health. Eventually, however, he was hospitalized, and after weeks of testing, a strep blood infection was identified. While in the hospital, he dictated correspondence and tried to dispose of the Arizona scenery and props that had been left in storage. He wrote to Mrs. John Alden Carpenter (wife of the composer, and mother-in-law of Adlai Stevenson): "This is the Golden Anniversary of my artistic life, and I hope to crown it with 'The Freedom Story.'"

In September, Val returned home to a cozy cottage I had located and rented a few blocks from the UCLA hospital where he was being treated. He had his first haircut in four months. It was, I said to him, cheaper than buying a violin.

We loved our little home. I can remember him sitting on the sofa in our living room, singing *"Mon Coeur, Ce Bats, Ce Bats"* (My Heart, It Beats) from *Pique Dame*. The pianissimi hung on the air like silk threads. "What is this?" he said. "My health is gone — and my voice improves!" So often in those days, he would look at me with moist blue eyes and say, "How I love you."

Charles Hedley, tenor from the American Opera Company of Rochester days, lived in Los Angeles with his wife Mary. Charles realized Val's physical and financial plight and motivated a recognition of his Golden Anniversary in the theatre (1913-1963) from his American Opera associates. I was mortified when I realized what was happening. Letters were flowing in — letters rich with expressions of appreciation and embellished with *financial gifts*. There was only one thing to do — remove myself from the setting and let Val receive the expressions of love and appreciation that were pouring in. And what loving warmth they conveyed!

One that was worded with particular sensitivity came from composer Nicolas Slonimsky who has authored books on music, musical dictionaries, and musical encyclopedias.

> I never forgot that you brought me to America, and so played a decisive role in the shaping of my life. . . . I have a strange recollection — forty years ago, when I just arrived in Rochester, you somehow arranged for me to get $250 from the school at once, even before I had occasion to earn it. Now that you are temporarily out of action, I have an idea that this money may come in handy for you. So I am enclosing a check for the same amount, so as to pay an overdue debt of gratitude to you. At that time it was to me an inconceivably large amount.

Val's improvement was short-lived, and on that terrible day, November 22, 1963, I called for an ambulance, and made two requests of the driver and attendant — no sirens and no mention of President Kennedy's assassination! Val's final curtain was going to coincide, as had his previous life crises, with a national tragedy.

That night he faded in and out of consciousness, casting and directing what he had visualized would be his final masterpiece — *The Freedom Story*. He asked if I was going with him to the "readings," if the soloists had arrived, and whether the "selections" had been made. His great soaring spirit would not give in to a body that could not keep up. At 7:25 in the morning, in the throes of rehearsing a great pageant, his hand grew cold in mine.

* * * * *

On November 27 the sunlight was overly brilliant, strident voices ballooned, and the scenery seemed as false as a movie set with the camera pinning down for a close-up. The limousine arrived, and the driver had to fill the radiator from our garden hose. Surely, with this absurd incident, the nightmare could end and all things fall into proper focus.

But it continued. Meredith Willson's warm, Iowa-bred voice was delivering a eulogy. "You had to love Val Rosing the first time you met him. . . . His only problem was that his heart was too big for the world he lived in. . . . But he was always a gentle man; a thoughtful, kind, articulate, overly generous, selfless, gentle man."

How could all of that man be confined to a small plot of real estate jigsawed into the rolling green hills of Los Angeles? It was an outrageous thought that I alone was responsible for the filing away of this quietly resting genius!

I sat alone at the writing table in my bedroom. An insensitive sun dropped to the horizon while rooftops caught at the afterglow and relinquished it slowly. A gentle ocean breeze at the window affirmed that the day was at an end, and loneliness leapt from the walls to engulf me in a nightmare whose reality was deepening.

All the magic that was Val was gone! There would never again be the breathless excitement of watching his genius bring to life great artistic creations while he penetrated the atmosphere with his powerful voice, molded stage pictures, and pantomimed with limitless energy. There would never again be that silent communion between us on nerve-shattering "opening nights," the shared glory of his successes, participation in his disappointments. Above all, there would no longer be the strength, the vibrancy, the selfless gentleness of Val's presence — the minute-by-minute thoughtfulness that had held me in the embrace of his all-encompassing warmth and love. Out of this void I wrote:

> Grief yawns her chasms at my frenzied turnings,
>> floods her restless river with defiant churnings,
>> plows jagged furrows into trenched retreat
>> and bans deliverance to beleaguered feet.
> Come, craving earth, begrudge some measure of relief
>> and host my moldy afternoon of grief.
> Where countless wired and woven wreaths now rest
>> let sorrow penetrate your hardened breast
>> until, embraced in cool recesses of your musty loam,
>> my anguish sinks to an eternal home.

There from my tears return the greener blade
    that used to spring beneath his feet;
    quench thirst of bloom and bud
    that lift their head no more
    to see my sweet Valodya . . . my Val.

* * * * *

Hundreds of notes, telegrams, and letters had arrived. Many had not yet been opened, and I turned to them now. There was a repeated theme that ran through so many that they might well have been authored by the same pen. They read:

His inspiration has given me a goal in life.

He was to us a poet of inspiration.

He has left with us a light for the theatre that will never go out.

People like Val are only loaned to us earthlings. He managed to give us wings.

His great gift to my life was his recognition of the artist in me. I probably join a large group of little souled people who never took the time to let him know their gratitude for the gifts he gave so freely.

He was the turning point in my life.

I knew that Val was not halo potential. What a waste that would be; he would be as unmindful of it as of his menu-patterned ties, unmatched socks, and lived-in clothes. In fact, I am sure he would never be entrusted with one, for he would be sure to misplace it! I can remember when in one day he managed to lose a new hat, a new pair of glasses, and his car keys. But he never lost his kindliness, his warmth, and that unique talent for developing the best in others. The grass was greener where he walked, and the earth less parched. Indeed, the "return of the greener blade that used to spring beneath his feet" was making itself evident in these messages that came by wire and by handwritten note from all parts of the globe.

I reached for another.

You'll be picking up the threads of your life again, trying to weave a firm fabric. Certainly there will be bright colors, sparkling gems, and the strong, tough fibers of a wonderful companionship to use. And the love that you and Val shared will be the loom on which you'll weave. Nothing . . . no circumstance can deprive you of that.

The magic that was Val began to stir. It was a part of me! This great and beautiful heritage — could I, in reality, have thought of burying it and living in a spiritual wasteland?

Someone had said to me, "If he'd had a really good agent, he would have achieved more recognition." But what does it matter that all of his greatness was not splashed across the headlines? Much of it had settled down into the crevices and furrows of human need. His genius scaled many heights and experienced many avalanches, but the real monument to his greatness was the gift of himself which flowers and bears fruit in the lives of others.

And that was my Val!

Vladimir

No silent stars will blink bereavement on your burial plot,
No blossoms bend on mournful stems to prompt
The nodding heads that turn
For verified remembrance in an earth-held urn.
I have not buried you, my Love.

And I defy the falsity of fingered time
To lay her wreaths of forged forgetfulness
Upon a plate of brass which yellows blades of grass
Beneath the graven name of "Vladimir."

A twisted trunk, their straining eyes will not perceive;
My branches blossom heavy with your leaves.
Your throated songs pervade the vacant night;
Your laughter spills in silvered flight.
They dare not bury you, my Love.

Sweet grief will carve no tragic heroine
To mourn with breasted head where last was seen
Your image, nested there upon the green;
The universe still holds our dream.
I have not buried you, my Love.

Ruth Glean Rosing

Sources

Sir Adrian Boult, *My Own Trumpet* (London: H. Hamilton, 1973)

Neville Cardus, *NEVILLE CARDUS Autobiography* (Ontario: Harper Collins Publishers, 1947; 1955)

Georges Cunelli, *Voice No Mystery* (London: Stainer & Bell Ltd.; New York: Galaxy Music Corp., 1973)

David Ewen, *Living Musicians* (New York: H. S. Wilson Co., 1940)

Eugene Goossens, *Overture and Beginners: A Music Autobiography* (London: Methuen & Co., Ltd., 1951)

Paul Horgan, *Encounters with Stravinsky* (New York: Farrar, Strauss and Giroux, Inc., 1972)

_____, *The Fault of Angels* (New York: Harper and Brothers, 1933)

Ivor Newton, *At The Piano* (London: H. Hamilton, 1962)

H. F. Parker, *EIGHTH NOTES: Voices and Figures of Music and the Dance* (New York: Dodd, Mead and Co., 1922)

Harold Rosenthal, *Opera at Covent Garden* (London: Gollancz, 1967)

R. Murray Schafer, ed., *Ezra Pound and Music* (New York: New Directions Publishing Corp., 1977)

George Bernard Shaw, *The Perfect Wagnerite*, 4th ed. (London: Constable & Co., 1923)

Permissions to Quote

Discography

THE RECORDINGS OF VLADIMIR ROSING

Fourteen Songs of Mussorgsky — Decca DL 9577 (1951) with Myers Foggin, Piano

"Yeremoushka's Cradle Song"
"Gopak"
"The Star"
"To the Dnieper"
"Reverie of the Young Peasant"
"The Orphan"
"Mushrooms"
"Trepak"
"Cradle Song" or "Death's Lullaby"
"Death Serenade"
"Field-Marshal Death"
"The Goat"
"Ballade"
"Savishna"

Vladimir's Cavatina — from Prince Igor (Borodin) — Twenty Great Russian Singers of the 20th Century, Tap Records, T320
Danse Macabre (Saint Saens) — Decca 25468A with Ivor Newton, Piano

Lullaby (Gretchaninov) — Decca 25468A

My Father Has Some Very Fine Sheep (Hughes) — Decca 25468B

Romance (Cui) — Decca 25468B

Black Eyes and *Haida Troika* (Russian Gypsy Songs) — Decca 25370A with Olga Alexeeva, Soprano

The Old Vaise and *Two Guitars* (Russian Gypsy Songs) — Decca 25370B

If You Ever Knew from *Pique Dame* (Tchaikovsky) — His Master's Voice DB266

Forgive Me, Oh Divinity from *Pique Dame* (Tchaikovsky) — His Master's Voice DB266

The Song of the Volga Boatmen (Traditional) — Parlophone E11240, XE6335

The Song of the Flea from *Faust* (Mussorgsky) — Parlophone XE6334

Do Not Depart (Rachmaninoff) Op.4 #1 — Parlophone E11251, XE6415 with Ivor Newton, Piano

Hunger (Cui) Op.4 #1 — Parlophone E11251, XE6415 with Ivor Newton, Piano

Vesti La Giubba from *Pagliacci* (Leoncavallo) — KFI Broadcast

Cavaradossi's Aria from *Tosca* (Puccini) — KFI

Je Crois Entendre Encore from "The Pearl Fishers" (Bizet) — KFI

Le Reve from *Manon* (Massenet) — KFI

Songs of Famous Russian Composers — Decca Album #9 (1940) with Hans Gellhorn, Piano

> "O, Do Not Sing Again" (Rachmaninoff) Op.4 #4 — 29050A CXE8382
>
> "The Island" (Rachmaninoff) Op.15 #2 — 29050A CXE8382
>
> "In the Silent Night" (Rachmaninoff) Op.4 #3 — 29050B CXE8381
>
> "Spring Waters" (Rachmaninoff) Op.14 #11 — 29050B CXE8381
>
> "Do Not Speak Beloved" (Tchaikovsky) Op.6 #2 — 29048A CXE8380
>
> "Why?" (Tchaikovsky) Op.6 #5 — 29048A CXE8380
>
> "At the Ball" (Tchaikovsky) Op.83 #3 — 29048B CXE8372
>
> "Again As Before" (Tchaikovsky) Op.73 #6 — 29048B CXE8372
>
> "The Sea" (Borodine) — 29047A CXE8448
>
> "The Rose and the Nightingale" (Rimsky-Korsakov) — 29047B CXE8374
>
> "Southern Night" (Rimsky-Korsakov) — 29047B CXE8374
>
> "Song of the Poor Wanderer" (Nevstrueff) — 29046B CXE8449
>
> "The Drunken Miller" (Dargomuizjsky) — 29046B CXE8449
>
> "Northern Star" (Glinka) — 29046A CXE8373

"Virtus Antiqua" or "Crusader's Song" (Glinka) — 29046A
   CXE8373
"The Mournful Steppe" (Gretchaninoff) Op.5 #1 — 29049B
   CXE8537
"Snowflakes" (Gretchaninoff) Op.47 #1 — 29049B CXE8537
"Rain" (Gretchaninoff) Op.66 #2 — 29049B CXE8537
"Lullaby" from "Dream on the Volga" (Arensky) — 29049A
   CXE8383
"Autumn" (Arensky) Op.27 #2 — 29049A CXE8383

Glinka—The Journey — VOC B. 3114
Frank Bridge—Isobel — Decca Records G20364

Gramaphone Co. records listed in John R. Bennett, *The Russian Catalogues
. . . 1899-1915* ("Voices of the Past," Vol. II, 1977):

Massenet — Pourquoi me reveiller? (from *Werther*)
Puccini — E lucevan le stelle (from *Tosca*)
Rechkunov — Spanish Serenade
Tchaikovsky — We Sat Together (Op. 73 No. 1)
Grechaninov — Cradle Song
Glinka — Romance
Bagrinovsky — Give Me This Night
Grechaninov — I Wish I Were With You
Rimsky-Korsakoff — Levko's Song (from *May Night*)
Tcherepnin — Autumn
Jakobson — Nature Morte
Glinka — Hebrew Song
Leoncavalla — Mattinata
Tchaikovsky — Forgive Me, Bright Celestial Visions (from *Pique
   Dame*)
Tchaikovsky — If You Ever Knew (from *Pique Dame*)

Index

by Lori Daniel